Handbook of
PASTORAL STUDIES

New Library of Pastoral Care

Handbook of
PASTORAL STUDIES

LEARNING AND PRACTISING
CHRISTIAN MINISTRY

Wesley Carr

First published in Great Britain in 1997
Society for Promoting Christian Knowledge
Holy Trinity Church
Marylebone Road
London NW1 4DU

Second impression 2002

British Library Cataloguing-in-Publication Data

A catalogue record for this book is available
from the British Library

ISBN 0-281-04977-7

Typeset by Pioneer Associates, Perthshire
Printed in Great Britain by
Antony Rowe, Chippenham, Wiltshire

Contents

such learning is applied in the specific ministering of a specific church, constraints emerge. Many of these, for instance, concern who is the agent of pastoral care. Pastoralia has long been a topic in the training syllabus for the churches' professional ministers. Pastoral studies have largely replaced and amplified it. At the same time there has been a growing recognition that pastoral action is not the prerogative of ordained ministers. The distinctive contribution of the laity to the pastoral care offered by the church has been widely recognized, although as yet more powerfully within the churches than by those outside who may be seeking some pastoring. And the function of the congregation as a whole, especially when social or political action is called for, has attracted interest (Lambourne 1963; Selby 1991).

Further enlarging and enriching the field are such influences as class, ethnicity and gender. The work of the churches in urban priority areas has historically been a prominent dimension. The Anglican report *Faith in the City* (1985) is just one of the more recent studies of the task of the Church in socially deprived areas. Both the black churches and groups within the mainline churches have drawn attention to the specific needs of ethnic groups within churches and society. Gender arises through the now well-established feminist contribution to theology. The impact of authorizing women through ordination has yet to be fully absorbed and evaluated. The first books on feminist pastoral care are beginning to appear (Graham and Halsey 1993). There are also major questions before all churches of how to address varied forms of sexuality, of which homosexual relations are the most obvious. It is impossible to handle all of the issues separately. What can be done, however, is to establish a model of working with which the churches and their ministers can at least engage with some of these issues as they present themselves.

Most students, whether as ordinands or those on church-based courses for congregations, undertake a course in pastoral studies. The main problems seem to be twofold: first, where is the limit to what is to be studied? Courses of pastoral studies seem to be a classic example of Terence's dictum: *homo sum; humani nil a me alienum puto* [I am human; I count nothing human as irrelevant to me]. When we add the range of theological enterprise to the study of humanity, the task is daunting. The second concerns the Church, its ordering and ministries. When we consider the place of the Church in society there are many variables: the presumed ecclesiology of the Church, the type of authorizations that follow, the shape of its ministries, the structure of the prevailing society in general, the specific expectations of a local community, and so on. Putting these two points together, however, generates the basic stance in this book. First, that pastoral work in every church, whatever its distinctive ecclesiology, is not solely concerned with the congregation or believers. It always involves those who are not its members. Obviously churches will differ according to what has historically and traditionally been their role. In England, for example, the Church of England as the established church has customarily offered such a ministry. But there are areas where, for example, the assumptions about the 'establishment' are focused more in the Roman Catholic Church than the Anglican. Elsewhere the Methodist Church may perform this role. Second, however much the structure of any church may seem to be created and maintained internally, all churches only exist in interaction with their environment; they are not isolated. Whether this is acknowledged or not, the shape of any church exists as a consequence of this interaction (Reed 1978; Carr 1985).

No single text can cover all these issues. But they can be noted and acknowledged. In this book I have tried to offer the student, whether lay or ordained, of whatever church and whether ordinand or experienced minister, information about the knowledge that has to be acquired, a method of learning and working, and an exploration of the work of ministry through the task of the Church and the roles of the ministers. The first chapter introduces many of the themes surrounding the word 'pastoral'. Part One, the following four chapters, introduces the tools for pastoral studies – psychology, sociology, dynamic theories and theology. Part Two consists of two chapters in which the mode of theological reflection is discussed at length. These are not easy chapters, but they are important. 'Theological reflection' is now almost universally the proposed mode for pastoral studies, whether in college teaching or in church courses for congregations or groups of lay people. It has many strengths. But one persistent weakness has been not only how to define what we mean by theological reflection but how to escape the trap of anecdote. Chapter Six, therefore, explores some of these issues in what I have called 'the standard mode' of theological reflection. Chapter Seven argues that the holding topic of 'role' is essential for any minister, lay or ordained, or congregation, who attempts theological reflection.

Obviously, however it is done, pastoral theology is a distinctive activity of the churches.[1] Part Three, therefore, examines how understandings of the local church and models of ministry correlate. The final two chapters of this Part, and of the book, explore two specific aspects of the ministry that has been discussed in principle in the previous chapters. The first is common religion, which is a social phenomenon. The second is the distinction between ministry and therapy, which draws more attention to the way in which the pastor and the individual relate to one another. Finally three appendices are added. In them I try to amplify three themes that have been discussed in the text. The first is specifically addressed to students who have to do a placement as part of their training. It shows how this experience, which is central to pastoral training, can be a way of learning the basic stance of ministry. The other two examine two major themes: what we mean by 'experience' and how religion and irrationality are related.

There are many gaps. But I hope that this book will be sufficiently wide-ranging to stimulate further study yet focused enough to offer a way of thinking coherently about pastoral theology and practice. There is an extensive bibliography of works mentioned in the text.

Behind this text lie some years of studying, lecturing and writing. Ideas, therefore, will have been taken at different times from many sources. I have tried to acknowledge all of these. But it is inevitable that some may not receive due recognition. If so, I apologize. I have also used my own writings to some extent, especially *The Pastor as Theologian*, which is essential further reading to Chapter 5, and *Brief Encounters*, which underlies Chapter 10. From time to time people have been kind enough to enquire whether I was intending to produce a new edition of *The Priestlike Task*. I hope that much of this book may illuminate further some of the ideas that were initially published there.

Language remains a problem, not least in pastoral studies. It is essential sometimes to refer to individuals in the singular. Where that happens 'she' may always be construed as 'he' and vice versa. A similar convention applies to 'minister', 'pastor' or 'clergy'. Although most people think of these as ordained people, in this text – apart from when it is obviously a reference to an ordained person – these words may be construed to refer to the lay Christian and sometimes to the congregation as a whole. I hope that the glossary of names may be of some help to those unfamiliar with some of the key figures referred to. The names are indicated by the sign (†).

It remains only to thank many colleagues and critics over the years for advice, comment and even sometimes the request that I take things further. The reader for SPCK offered many challenges and insights, all of which have stimulated improvement. I am grateful to all.

Wesley Carr
Bristol

CHAPTER ONE

Pastoral Theology

Pastoral work expressed in care for others has been central to the Church's life from its earliest days. The first Christians took much of their practice directly from their Jewish origins. For example the lists of duties and responsibilities (*Haustafeln*) – Col. 3.18–4.1; Eph. 5.22–6.9; 1 Pet. 2.13ff; Titus 2.1-10; 1 Tim. 2.8ff, 6.1ff; *Didache* 4.9-11; *Barnabas* 19.5, 7; *1 Clement* 1.3, 21.6-9 – are derived from Jewish and pagan prototypes. There seems to have been no difficulty in Christianizing existing wisdom (Lohse 1971, 154ff). The core theme that evolved was the belief that to love God was also to love our neighbour. This was encapsulated in much of Jesus' reported teaching. The notable affirmation of the two commandments (Mk. 12.28-34/Matt. 22.34-41) is expounded when the parable of the Good Samaritan is offered as an answer to 'Who is my neighbour?' (Lk. 10.25-28). The linked themes of God's love for us and ours for others is elaborated by St Paul. It finds classic expression in Jas. 2 and 1 John 4.19-21. This concern for the neighbour arose from and led to reflection on the nature of God and what he might demand. Pastoral activity always required theological thinking. Its recent evolution into a distinctive discipline called 'pastoral theology' took time. But at no period of the Christian era has the Church considered pastoral theology merely an option. The simplest expression of Christian belief shown in care for a neighbour is a theologically laden act.

Like other theological disciplines pastoral theology has changed over time. Once, for example, it focused on the role and function of the priest. As this was professionalized the corresponding notion of professional skills emerged. These were learned through instruction in pastoral studies (Russell

1984). More recently this assumption has in turn been questioned as the formal definition of pastoral theology has been questioned (Schuster 1969). But such changes are not peculiar to this discipline. The study of the Bible, for example, once meant knowing the text and being able to bring allegorical parallels to bear. Critical study, however, has permanently altered what we mean by biblical studies. We can look back to the older style, often with affection. We might even envy those who could do it. But we cannot escape what is now demanded of us. The same is true of all theological disciplines, including what we now call pastoral theology. It has inevitably become more specialized, and in so doing seems to be more complex. So we need to be especially clear about the terms we use.

This chapter offers an overview of some of the themes and their historical origins. Many ideas mentioned here are examined in more detail in subsequent chapters.

THE TERM 'PASTORAL'

In 1978 the cardinals of the Roman Catholic Church elected a new pope, John Paul I. They reportedly chose him because of his pastoral gifts. He was soon known as 'the smiling pope'. One month later he died. Peter Hebblethwaite describes what happened:

> There was a remarkable unanimity – the effect more of spontaneously working together than of any conspiracy – which led them [the cardinals in October 1978] to redefine the concept of 'pastoral'. True, in August they had sought for and found a 'pastoral' man, and in the August scheme of things 'pastoral' clearly meant 'coming from a diocese'. But then, in October, they tumbled over each other in their anxiety to explain that this was too narrow a definition.

John Paul's death provoked second thoughts about everything. Work in the marriage tribunals, dealing with canon law, and the Curia's bureaucratic activity was redefined as 'pastoral'.

> It was left to Cardinal Gantin to broaden the scope of the term even more widely. 'All the cardinals,' he chivalrously

explained in the week before the conclave, 'are in some sense pastoral men, and many of them have administered dioceses – including myself.' And even those whose experience had been entirely confined to diplomacy or administration had carried out their work 'in a pastoral way'. Pope Pius XII, it was recalled, had never been the bishop of a diocese, but that had not prevented him from being a 'pastoral' pope. Thus 'pastoral' became a broken-backed word. If it applied to all 111 cardinals indiscriminately, then it was useless as a criterion for determining what they might do this time. (Hebblethwaite 1978, 134)

This is an extreme instance of an attitude that may be found in all churches. 'Pastoral' is a word against which little can be said. So it can be invoked to stop serious debate or as a defence against critical scrutiny of a church's activity. It used to be said of the clergy of the Church of England, for example, that you can tell them that they are not good preachers and they will, with regret, agree. Tell them that they are poor administrators and they will probably chuckle and take it as a compliment. But tell them that they are pastorally naive or incompetent and they are offended and become resentful and defensive. The same is probably true of ministers in other churches, too. 'Pastoral' – that 'broken-backed word' – should always sound warning bells when it is encountered. When it is indiscriminately applied it often obfuscates and may be used to avoid hard decisions or to escape the charge of unclarity.

PASTORAL CARE

This phrase describes ministry, whether by ordained or lay people, which is concerned with the well-being of communities or of individuals. Today it is as, if not more, widely used outside the Church as within. Pastoral care is offered as a selling point by schools which appoint pastoral counsellors. It is a routine notion in various social agencies. The phrase, however, is rooted within the Jewish/Christian tradition, deriving from the image of the shepherd and the way he cares for the flock. Today this picture is sometimes resisted on the grounds that it diminishes the autonomy of believers.

Who, it is asked, are the sheep? But the theme of the shepherd is not chiefly about how care (or, as we shall see, authority) is exercised. It prevails because of the way it permeates so much Jewish and Christian imagery of God. Even when the theme of the shepherd/pastor has been abandoned, pastoral care remains grounded in the Jewish/Christian faith.

Historically, such care was primarily offered through spiritual direction. In the early centuries of the Christian era, for instance, it focused on confession and penance. The exact details are tantalizingly sketchy, particularly for the earliest period. But between New Testament times and the sixth century, preparing people for penance was a major pastoral activity. Subsequently this ministry declined, until it was revived in the twelfth century by Peter Lombard† and endorsed by Thomas Aquinas†. Elaborate systems of confession, absolution and penance were established in order to pastor people from the cradle to the grave. There were many consequences for social behaviour and moral implications. But these were founded on the way in which authorized ministers, priests, offered the faithful reconciliation with God and guidance with spiritual sustenance throughout this life.

Life today is more fragmented and moments of ministry are more fleeting. Because of social changes the old idea of spiritual direction has also altered. We might, therefore, sum up the primary aim of contemporary pastoral care in a more general way. The undergirding theme of pastoral care is characterized by the Hebrew word *shalom*. This is usually translated 'peace', but that is inadequate. Greek ideas dominate western thought. As a result 'peace' has come largely to mean 'the absence of war', a state which produces prosperity and well-being. But the Hebrew is more positive.

1 God gives *shalom*: it is always something greater than human beings can conceive or achieve.
2 It weaves the individual and the community inseparably together: individual sins and social injustice can both destroy it.
3 *Shalom* is mainly discovered through relationships.

Shalom has little to do with our contemporary preoccupation with the individual's inner peace. Jesus himself was reported (Matt. 5.9) as having said 'Blessed are the peacemakers', people who generate *shalom*. Such people do not just prevent conflict or resolve disputes. By their lives they actively encourage the sort of relationship that removes (or at least diminishes) the causes of such struggles. To do this, however, the individual needs his or her own sense of support. Thus the concept of inner peace, which arises from God's sustaining, correspondingly increases. The point is made by St Paul in Phil. 4.7: 'And the peace of God, which passes all understanding, will keep your hearts and minds.' The gift is greater than anything that we can devise ourselves.

Shalom is the foundation of the Christian ideal of pastoral care. The first recipients of this peace were fellow Christians. The felt tension between Israel and the nations is often expressed in the Old Testament. A similar feeling re-emerged as Christians began to explore the world that they inhabited. As a result they began to try to define who was in and who was out of fellowship. Much of the New Testament shows how they vacillated. The Fourth Gospel, for instance, is notable for the way in which it runs the theme of God's universal love alongside the critical nature of the individual's decision for or against Christ. But the universal dimension of *shalom* always lurked. Christians found that the definition of 'neighbour' could rarely, if ever, be restricted to their fellow believers alone.

Two stories from the New Testament illuminate this process of change. In Acts 10 Luke tells of Peter's dream and his subsequent meeting with the Roman soldier, Cornelius. Could the latter become a Christian and be welcomed (offered *shalom*)? The answer in the text is unequivocal: 'Then to the Gentiles also God has granted repentance unto life' (Acts 11.18). The idea of neighbour is extended in a way that was previously inconceivable. The second story is the parable of the Last Judgement (Matt. 25.31–46). This is a pastoral story, based on shepherding and the shepherd's selections. Some scholars have argued that 'the least of these my brethren' (Matt. 25.40) refers to needy Christians. This is possible, although there is no consensus and the words could refer to the needy in general (Jeremias 1963, 206; Schweizer 1975, 479). The phrase soon acquired universal meaning and has for centuries been used to justify a way of life that gives anyone the status of neighbour and treats them as such. The way in which this story has been used is an instance of how the divine demand for pastoral care based on *shalom* cannot be restricted.

Shalom is a practical concept. The well-being of individuals and communities is to be aimed at and can be achieved. But this is only part of pastoral care. The term is also symbolic. It speaks of God's nature and his demand for justice and requirement of moral behaviour. Recent writing on pastoral theology, therefore, also emphasizes the connections between the proclamation of the Gospel of divine demand and pastoral care offered to all. The failure of those involved in this discipline to acknowledge their political and social presuppositions is one of Pattison's criticisms (Pattison 1988; 1994). Campbell, too, has stressed the importance of proposals that will lead to, among other things, altering 'the style of life of individual Christians within the "secular" structures of society, and for the renewal and reforming of the secular structures themselves' (Campbell 1972, 226). He had already referred to adjustments in the Church as another consequence. In all of this the writers are working with the theme of *shalom*, although they do not necessarily use the word. The bridge is built with political and social action that lies beyond concern for the individual alone (Browning 1976; Selby 1983).

A major new context for pastoral care is the contemporary range of behavioural sciences. These have a profound impact on many disciplines. They will be prominent in all the subsequent chapters. But in handling them we need constantly to be aware of two points: they are neither the first new context for the Church's ministry nor are they without their own presuppositions. The vision of *shalom* may assist us to keep these two issues in mind.

1 *Shalom* is down-to-earth. Pastoral care has always been, and has to be, exercised in specific contexts. It could scarcely be otherwise, since it is concerned with people's lives as they are lived. And the settings, therefore, have always affected what the Church has meant by pastoral care and consequently by pastoral theology. The impact of these studies, therefore, while significant, is no more unique than that of other new contexts in which the Church has had to believe and act.

2 *Shalom* extends across the ages, arising in Jewish thought but being appropriated and developed in the Christian

Church. The behavioural sciences happen to dominate the present context. But it does not follow that they inevitably must. Pastors and theologians should never settle for any set of assumptions, however predominant, but always remain alert for any change.

For an illustration of the first point we may turn to seventeenth- and eighteenth-century England. This generally was not a good time for public Christianity. The prevailing picture of the Church of England, for example, is that such pastoral care as it offered was usually inadequate. But it is dangerous to generalize. There were exceptions to this overview, some magnificently faithful (Hinton 1994). However, it was generally true that the clergy of the Church of England were neither as spiritual nor as socially aware as they might have been. Nonconformist pastors provided care mainly to members of their churches. Towards the end of the seventeenth century, however, we can discern the stirring of change. Groups of Christians became sensitive to two contexts. These were, first, that of a God whose demands were stronger than the churches were acknowledging. The laxity of many Christians, particularly the clergy, caused such concern that it led to a revaluation of the meaning and implications of faith for all. Second, social needs began to impress themselves. Putting the two together we have the recipe for the revitalizing of faith through the twin types of pastoral care - spiritual renewal and direction, and social action. These were products of a specific context. The churches were transformed and enriched. Interestingly, too, we can date a renewed professionalizing of the clergy from this period (Russell 1984).

The second point - the influence of the behavioural sciences - is especially observable in the emergence of pastoral counselling in today's world. (A comprehensive series of discussions about the range of pastoral counselling may be found in Wicks, Parsons and Capps (1993).) Later we shall examine why pastoral counselling offers a deficient model of Christian ministry. It is, however, so widespread an approach, both in society at large and in the churches, that we need to pay it specific attention in considering pastoral care and pastoral theology.

Since the Second World War many disciplines have been altered by the influence of the behavioural sciences. One outcome has been a shift in the churches from spiritual direction, whether traditional or psychologically informed, towards a secular model of pastoral counselling. This can be clearly discerned if we take the five traditional tasks that are basic to ministry and explore them briefly in relation to the model of pastoral counselling. The five are healing, sustaining, reconciling, guiding and nurturing (Clebsch and Jaekle 1975).

PASTORAL COUNSELLING AND THE TASKS OF MINISTRY

Healing

Freud's† 'talking cure' revolutionized thinking about healing. His discovery that people could be changed by talking as much as, if not more than, by physical interventions has transformed thinking and activity in many fields. It has spawned a host of generalized talkative healing. Indeed it sometimes seems that for some people the talking for its own sake is more significant than any need for healing (North 1972). Many therapies have evolved. Some ministers have undergone training in psychotherapy and then set up as independent counsellors. Many others have employed psychotherapeutically derived insights in their pastoral practice, sometimes to good effect. And there are some avowedly Christian therapists. Few people, pastors and the pastored alike, are not influenced at all.

Sustaining

Some ministry is concerned with helping people through crises in their lives and relationships. This seems to be becoming increasingly a problem for all in the caring professions. Ministers are not immune (Stone 1995). Counselling models are often suggested as useful for ministers in determining how to make any intervention. At least being able to recognize a possible neurosis or psychosis and so be alert to what may be going on is crucial. In the mid-1960s Frank Lake realized that clergy needed some basic training in this area. Clinical Theology was the first major training that was widely offered to ordinands and ministers. It subsequently became known as a therapeutic approach in its own right (Lake 1966).

14

Reconciling

This dimension is prominent in all Christian activity. It relies on the belief that God's basic work is always that of reconciliation. The distinctive aspect of counselling that follows from this often appears in work with families in distress or when marriages are dissolving (Walrond Skinner 1988).

Guiding

Spiritual guidance is historically the essential ministerial function. How it is offered varies from church to church. But priests and pastors alike are expected to be able to offer it. In the context of pastoral counselling this theme expands to include, for instance, the educational work of preparing people for marriage or family life. Less obviously it is a point where ethics and counselling impinge on each other. Some counsellors believe that they can adopt a value-free approach to their work, although this is a point of contention among practitioners. But even if this were possible for counsellors, ministers can never present themselves as morally neutral. They always represent the idea of a moral stance, even if their own hold on it is tenuous, and are relied upon to be able to offer moral guidance.

Nurturing

This side of pastoral care as counselling is seen in the way that enhancement groups for improving people's quality of life proliferate. Some are Christian, but again the churches in promoting such events are conforming to today's world. Marriage enrichment seems especially encouraged, possibly as a way of trying to stem the tide of breakdown (Kirk and Leary 1994). The Church's public moral stance and personal spirituality thus coincide.

Obviously not all these aspects of pastoral counselling are found in every church. Nor does every minister engage in them. But these emphases can be found when the churches are considered overall. They can, as with the idea of pastoral care, also be found widely offered elsewhere. But four marks distinguish the Christian dimension.

PASTORAL COUNSELLING: THE CHRISTIAN DIMENSION

The context

Christian pastoral counselling is offered from the Church. It may take place on church premises. But the idea of the Church as a context for pastoral counselling is larger than the question of place or even the public role of the counsellor. It refers to a belief held by the counsellor, which the client is invited to share, that there is something significant about the Church as an institution. (This notion is examined in detail in Chapter 8.) 'Church as institution' is used here to describe the complex of ideas associated with 'church' that is in the mind of all involved in any pastoral encounter (Shapiro and Carr 1992). It must not be confused with institutionalizing. Here 'Church in the mind' covers that mix of fact and fantasy, rationality and irrationality, belief and unbelief which emerges in different ways when 'church' is mentioned.

The religious resources

Prayer is the most obvious resource, but we may couple with this the whole Christian tradition, including Scripture. Christians disagree about how to use these in pastoral ministry. But there is little disagreement that they are resources. Some pastors use prayer, tradition and Scripture to inform their work as counsellors. They help them to orient themselves in the encounter, although they will not be overtly invoked. Others believe that they should be openly used in any session. The minister will often quote Scripture and usually pray with the person being counselled. There is no resolving the dispute between the two approaches. But what is done depends on two things.

1 There is the contract between the minister and the person with whom he or she is dealing.[1] 'Contract' sounds formal in the context of most ministerial work. But something is always either implicitly presumed to be in existence or even is actually agreed. There is a discernible difference between American and British approaches to this topic. In the USA the minister is more likely to have a consulting room or office than in Britain. The formality of encounter that such space implies is correspondingly greater.

2 What the minister does depends on the extent to which

he or she can grasp of the client's expectations and what he or she is seeking from the minister by contrast with what any other counsellor might offer.

The counsellor

Pastoral counselling is not the prerogative of ordained ministers. But it has customarily been regarded as one of their duties and is still expected of them. How ministers understand their identity and what training they receive in theology and the practice of beliefs are, therefore, vital topics in pastoral counselling. Underlying all lie the twin themes of holding and of authority. Both of these themes will recur several times in this book. Put briefly 'holding' describes the way in which the counsellor is able to create a sufficiently secure environment for clients confidently to be able to express and address their emotions. The counsellor's authority (like that of pastors in every aspect of their ministry) is a central issue to the encounter. It is constantly being scrutinized, explored and tested. Often in a counselling session the client may be examining his or her relationships with other authority figures – parents, teachers, or even siblings – through their testing of the counsellor's authority. Pastoral counselling is never a one-way transaction from the counsellor to the client. It is always an interaction in which the nature and accessibility of the pastor's own faith is a key component.

The spiritual dimension

Whatever the issue presented and the apparent needs of the person concerned, somewhere in the implicit contract between the pastoral counsellor and the client lurks the belief that there is a spiritual dimension to human existence. In each specific encounter this general belief is given particular significance. Here some contemporary criticisms of religion may emerge. The idea of spirituality may be used as a way to escape the pressure of hard issues of life by removing feelings and experience to a so-called inaccessible realm. We are all adept at such avoidance. But we should also recognize that the reverse may also be true: the use of psychotherapeutic approaches alone by a Christian minister in a Christian context may be a way for him or her to escape having to face an important dimension to the client's own existence and, even more, the minister's.

17

PASTORAL THEOLOGY

Neither pastoral care nor pastoral counselling constitute 'pastoral theology'. What happens in them is crucially relevant. But pastoral theology is a discipline in its own right (Dyson 1987). A series of terms is used in this field. Sometimes they can be differentiated, although they overlap. We note four in particular.

APPLIED THEOLOGY

This branch of theological study holds its place for academic rigour alongside the other disciplines such as biblical, systematic, natural, fundamental and philosophical theology. The strength of the term lies in its emphasis on theology and the importance of every sort of theological thinking being subject to scrutiny. One weakness, however, is that the idea of 'application' may become dominant. There is a risk in applied theology of beginning to think of theology as a set of truths that can be discerned. Once articulated they can then be applied to human situations. Some pastoral teaching seems to imply such an approach. But even if this position were once tenable, it can no longer be sustained. Today in every field interactive notions of learning prevail. These stress the provisional nature of any belief or stance. What is more, the concept of praxis (see Chapter 5) has shown the importance of what is 'applied' to the discernment of truth. Neither thought nor action precede each other. They fuse.

PRACTICAL THEOLOGY

This phrase has traditionally been used of the way in which the Church's ministers were trained. There were four parts to the programme:

1 *homiletics*, training in discerning the Word of God and how to proclaim it;
2 *liturgics*, the study of liturgy and how to conduct it;
3 *catechetics*, the educational dimension to ministry, especially how to teach and train the young;
4 *poimenics*, the pastoral guidance of and care for individuals.

These terms are not common today. But many programmes

still follow a similar pattern. When the Christian Church plays a dominant role in people's lives, this approach has a sound rationale. It aims to produce competent professional clergy. In England the custom used to be that practitioners would pass on their accrued wisdom to the young learners. Experienced ministers were invited to colleges to talk about their work. Today's emphasis by contrast is on learning through placements. Until recently Anglican theological colleges were often presided over by a parish priest with no particular academic pretensions but who possessed the wisdom of experience. In the United States, by contrast, practical theology has placed more reliance on the acquisition of professional ministerial skills. Experts in a range of disciplines, often led by the behavioural studies, have staffed departments of practical theology.

As with applied theology, however, much depends on the attitude lying behind the description. Applied theology might give too great a significance to an academic concept of 'theology' which is applied to human situations. Practical theology might avoid theology in favour of the 'practical', which then becomes a series of anecdotal descriptions of what has been done. Both, however, when treated carefully can be understood as critical theological disciplines, enquiring into what sort of faith is being expressed in practice and where the Church is drawing the boundaries of faith.

PASTORAL STUDIES

Within the curriculum of those being prepared for the ordained ministry the term 'pastoral studies' is most in vogue. But the phrase has only recently become prominent. It seems to have been used (and may even have been coined) by a group at Birmingham who worked with R. A. Lambourne in about 1963 (Ballard 1986). They stressed the careful study of the practice of ministry. It was a response of its time. Everywhere an experiential approach to learning was then emerging. Pastoral studies include a range of experiences such as those found in community work, and exploration of the political dimensions to the Church's ministry and casework. The emphasis is on interdisciplinary study and exchange of skills. But while practical activity is essential, there is also an academically creditable accent on being able to conceptualize and argue about what occurs. Although the word 'theology' is not used, the discipline of pastoral studies includes a genuine theological task. The distinctive theological stance that is associated with pastoral studies is theological reflection (see Chapters 6 and 7 for a full discussion of this process).

PASTORAL THEOLOGY

The key word in the phrase 'pastoral theology' is theology. The emphasis is less on how to do pastoral things than on the theological study of the action of the Church in respect of people's lives, both as individuals and in society. The central question, therefore, always concerns how at any moment God's activity is discerned at any moment and responded to. This process in recent years has become known as 'theological reflection'. It is a new discipline, less in its component parts than in the way that they are integrated. Indeed, 'integration', as in the phrase 'an integrated theology', is a fundamental theme (Baelz 1983).

Pastoral theology is difficult to define. It presents itself as an autonomous academic study with its own distinctive standing and disciplines. One of its major problems, however, is that it is inevitably interdisciplinary. Tracy, for instance, suggests that such theologies will

> ordinarily analyze some radical situation of ethical-religious import ... in some philosophical, social-scientific, culturally analytic or religiously prophetic manner ... In terms of truth claims, therefore, involvement in transformative praxis and a theological articulation of what that involvement entails will be assumed or argued as predominant over all theological theories. (Tracy 1981, 58)

Most importantly, however, today the idea of pastoral theology links traditional theological studies with the behavioural discoveries which have become so prominent in the twentieth century. Some integration between these might be possible if there were any agreement about the content and nature both of theology and of the behavioural sciences. But both disciplines are under continual and sceptical scrutiny, not least by practitioners in each. Thus while we may theorize about what pastoral theology as a discrete discipline might be, in practice it is probably impossible to define.

Even when the academic standing of pastoral theology is emphasized, it retains its vocational dimension. The Church's activity with individuals and society has to be performed by someone: it is not abstract. So the data which pastoral theology uses must include what is actually done, by whom, when, where and why. And since the Church's ministry is exercised by both authorized ministers and lay people, the question of how the Church is understood is also central to this study. Inevitably, therefore, the focus of any piece of work in pastoral theology will oscillate: there is on the one hand the need to reflect on day to day activity and on the other the academic requirement for disciplined thinking and argument.

The concept of pastoral theology by comparison, for instance, with that of pastoral care implies that its study encompasses normal human life, not simply crises or even abnormality. It links studies, such as counselling, with traditional skills, such as confession and absolution, spiritual direction, evangelism and sacramental theology. The problem, however, is where the limits of pastoral theology are drawn. There is no church activity which cannot be described both as pastoral and as theological. The cardinals made that public in 1978. Yet if everything that is thought and done is pastoral, is there any distinctive activity of pastoral care? And how can pastoral theology lay claim to academic respectability?

THE THEOLOGICAL RESOURCES FOR PASTORAL THEOLOGY

It becomes clear, therefore, that any attempt at pastoral theology is likely to encounter the accusation that it is employing insufficient data, or a relevant specialism is being overlooked or ignored. The discipline, nevertheless, is primarily theological. So it is appropriate to consider the sort of theological stance that might be required. As a basis for this examination we may take the theological foundations offered in the Anglican tradition. This is not offered as an ideal. Other churches will place their emphases differently according to their polities (see Chapter 8). But it is a useful starting point for two reasons.

1   It is specific. In England the pastoral ministry offered by the Church of England is usually more publicly exposed than

that of other churches because of the amount of common religion (see Chapter 10) that it handles. It has, therefore, inevitably had to develop its distinctive theological stance with a pastoral slant. The role of the authorized minister may take more prominence than in some other traditions, and this will have to be held in mind throughout. On the other hand the customary distinction between 'congregation' (the gathered worshippers) and 'parishioners' (those who may claim, should they so wish, ministry from the church) is useful, since it holds together the two foci of pastoral activity – the Christian community and the world around.[2]

2   The three pillars on which Anglican thinking rests are Scripture, tradition and reason. All three themes are also found with varying emphases in the pastoral theology of other churches.

Scripture is an obvious basis. It is the foundational material of the Christian faith and, although different values are assigned to it, there is nevertheless general agreement that Scripture and the Church belong together. Tradition is more disputed, often with regard to its standing in relation to Scripture. But tradition means more than the ancient tradition of the early church. In pastoral work, for example, it includes what occurred the last time ministry was offered to a family or community. Reason reminds us that pastoral theology is not just about actions. It demands thought and reflection, the use of the mind. Pastoral theology is located at the wisdom end of human reason.

SCRIPTURE

Few Christians now operate with the idea that the text (or even more a text) is a sufficient offering in pastoral work. Few also now use Scripture without realizing that there is a hermeneutical question. This goes beyond the meaning of text. It is about the dynamic interchange between text and reader: how is this text to be read and by whom?

Like pastoral theology, biblical hermeneutics is as old as the writing of the texts themselves and yet has become a distinctively new study. Teachers and preachers have always publicly interpreted the texts. It is sometimes forgotten that, whatever the leaders of the Church might have believed or hoped, the same is true of many ordinary Christian people.

They, too, encountered the word and understood it in their own way. William Tyndale (1494–1536) famously translated the Bible for 'the boy that driveth the plough'. But prior to this much of Scripture had been 'read' through stained glass windows, monuments, pictures and drama (Duffy 1993). The new hermeneutic arose at about the same time as the modern approach to psychology and other behavioural studies. Friedrich Schleiermacher† is widely regarded as the father of this movement. He argued that interpreting a text was an art. The reader brings together data (what the text says) and his or her psychological capacity to understand. Wilhelm Dilthey† took this further and proposed that hermeneutics was the foundation of all the human sciences. Others have since refined and elaborated these basic ideas. But for our purposes we may note three points:

1   In the study of the new hermeneutics the question was raised whether it was an art or a science. This precisely matches similar debate in the field of the human sciences about the extent to which notions of 'science' are appropriate or misleading.

2   The key issue is interpretation, not merely reading or understanding. Hermeneutical study focuses on the interchange between reader and text. This is never a one-way exchange. The point is sometimes expressed in the form that there is no such thing as a presuppositionless interpretation.

3   This interchange has been structured as 'the hermeneutical circle'. This idea has also been used to explore the way in which encounters occur between human beings.

Although the phrase 'the hermeneutic circle' is widely used, there is no norm of the circle or one meaning (Thiselton 1980, 104f). It is better thought of as a spiral. By engaging in the process the reader (and, through that reader, others) furthers his or her understanding and moves to a new plane from which to take another step by repeating the process. There are two meanings to the phrase:

1   the process of putting questions to the text, as a result of which the questions themselves are reshaped and asked anew;

2   the process of understanding a piece of literature by understanding its component parts, which can itself only be understood by reference to the whole piece in the first place.

In practice, however, the processes are similar (Figure 1). There are five steps:

1 Approach the text: here questions of data are raised.
2 Get inside the text: the reader translates it into a language.
3 Become involved in the meaning: the reader expounds it to him or her self and possibly also to others.
4 Be transformed: the interchange is now allowed to affect the reader in some fashion.
5 Prepare to approach the text anew: as a result of this process, the reader starts all over again but now with different questions.

This circle (better thought of as a spiral to allow for the significance of point 5) is also the basis of pastoral ministry and learning in pastoral studies, especially through placements. In those contexts we substitute either 'client' or 'placement' for 'text'.

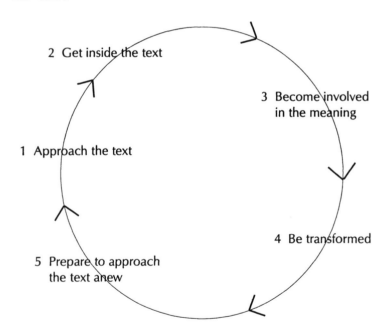

Figure 1: The hermeneutical circle

A philosophical discussion about what a presupposition-less reading of Scripture might be is the core of modern hermeneutics. By contrast, however, pastoral practice exposes us relentlessly to the assumptions that we each make about ourselves, others, the world and God. And it constantly questions them all. Therefore studying presuppositions and the way in which we and others employ them is central to pastoral learning. This perception may in turn contribute to the exploration of the way we use Scripture, especially in pastoral theology. It is possible to identify a specific presupposition, acknowledge it and then work consciously with it. Geoffrey Wainwright, for example, has done this with presuppositions about liturgy. He acknowledges that worship has formed his vision of faith. On that basis he advocates a systematic theology. Thus when referring, for example, to contemporary intellectual problems, he writes:

> Religious statements are in a worse case even than ethical or aesthetic claims, for religion deliberately refers to a transcendent dimension and asserts the ultimacy of the values which it claims to be grounded in the transcendent. As to transcendence, for my part I can do no more than propose the living experience of worship as evidence of the rootage of created reality in a creative Reality and declare that I remain unpersuaded by reductionist interpretations which allow psychology or sociology to explain away that irreducible experience. (Wainwright 1980, 2)

A pastoral approach acknowledging presuppositions would include the following marks:

1 Pastoring is always to do with people. They may be in specific need, but not necessarily so. Whatever doctrinal view of Scripture is adopted, all acknowledge that the Old Testament, Gospels and Epistles are not only written and assembled by people. They are also about people. There is, therefore, scarcely a passage which is not potentially addressable with the presupposition that whatever else it may say, it will speak to the reader and hearer about themselves and about others as human beings. Psychology did not begin in the nineteenth century.

2 A second dimension is the way that people are categorized. In the books of the Bible the emphasis is sometimes on

the chosen people of God, an exclusive stance. It addresses us in the role of religious believers and bearers of a tradition. At other times it speaks of humanity in general and confronts us as members of the whole human race. The distinction is in practice rarely as obvious as this.

An example of how Scripture seems to face us in both these ways is found in the parable of the Last Judgement or of the Sheep and the Goats (Matt. 25.31–46). As we have seen, the phrase 'the least of these my brethren' has been the subject of detailed enquiry. There is no consensus, but it is possible that it technically should be construed as a reference to Jesus' disciples. This would make the story exclusive, one about the way in which Christians respond to their fellow believers. It speaks to the Church about its internal relationships. Yet there are other indicators in the story even as it is told in St Matthew's Gospel, apart from the questions of its origins and subsequent use. These suggest that the parable is not as precise and limited as it seems but is inclusive: it refers generally to anyone in distress. This is not a matter of sentiment: the reading can be argued for. The passage is an exercise in reading with pastoral presuppositions.

It may be claimed that Scripture contains eternal truths. But the texts are time-conditioned. They were written long before contemporary approaches to and understandings of human behaviour developed. Yet in another sense this conditioning is not as absolute as might be feared by some or hoped by others. The history of the Jewish and Christian peoples shows that Scripture has performed a critical function in different cultures and against various backgrounds. One of the main hermeneutical studies is the way in which a specific context may evoke new life from an otherwise apparently dead text. For example, at the end of the nineteenth century scholars and church leaders discussed the possibility of removing the Revelation of St John the Divine from the New Testament canon. The avenging God who appears there was alien to the cultured sophistication of the west. Yet within a generation the language of The Apocalypse was one of the few that could do justice to the horror of the World War. This raises a perennial question for pastoral studies: to what extent is the way that pastoral care is offered and accepted culturally conditioned? (See also Appendix 3 for another aspect of this incident.)

Thinking on such topics with a pastoral presupposition will make theologians ask a specific question: how across a time-conditioned series of different beliefs about people can Scripture still function as a critique (but not a condemnation) of the assumptions that we make about ourselves and about others? The outcome is that when read round the hermeneutical circle, with the pastoral presuppositions acknowledged, Scripture can address pastors in new ways. It is, however, important to note two points.

1 Scripture chiefly addresses the pastor, not the client. There may be occasions when explicitly to quote Scripture is a significant pastoral act. It would probably depend chiefly on how the sensitive pastor discerned the client's view of authority. But to cite Scripture in a pastoral encounter is more often likely to divert attention from the point of meeting. In addition, as will be discussed later, if the pastor is the bearer of the tradition (including Scripture), the way in which he or she does that exemplifies what the Gospel tradition is. And whatever else this may be, it is concerned with embodiment. The incarnation is the classic instance. But pastors embody much for the client, not least what is being projected onto them.

2 While there are similarities between the hermeneutical circle and the process of theological reflection, they are not identical. The point is discussed at length below (see especially Chapter 6). Here it is merely noted.

Scripture, then is a vital resource for the pastor. But the form of its use has to be congruent with pastoral activity itself. But employed in this fashion Scripture informs both the pastor's ministry and other aspects of his or her Christian experience and life.

TRADITION

In theological thinking tradition is often considered, though not explicitly, in terms of the text of St Vincent of Lérins†, the Vincentian Canon: *quod ubique, quod semper, quod ab omnibus creditum est* [that which has been believed everywhere, always and by all]. The Canon was widely discussed in the nineteenth century, although English writers then often misquoted it to emphasize antiquity ('always') before ecumenicity ('everywhere'). Since, however, it is obvious from even a cursory glance at history that nothing has been universally held, theologians have had a problem with this concept of tradition. It is difficult to bring together belief and history, as the Canon tried to do. Nevertheless, not least in ecumenical dialogue, the Vincentian Canon has offered something to which participants might aspire, even if it could never be demonstrated that it was ever achieved.

J. H. Newman†, among others, pointed out that the Canon could not be simplistically used. The way that people reflect on their faith within the Church and the way in which societies alter and environments change imply that in a living church some sense of development in doctrine is inevitable (Newman 1845). Today, in the light of the modern human sciences which inform pastoral theology, the Vincentian ideal, already difficult, becomes even less possible to sustain. The problem of whether there was ever a public form of such belief is compounded by awareness of the unconscious dimensions to belief. In theory the Canon could offer an objective test for Christian faith. But even were a creed affirmed everywhere by all (itself unlikely enough), we should then come up against the next problem. What do these people actually believe as opposed to what they say they believe? This is always the issue facing the pastor. It is also a topic for pastoral theologians. They have to take into account not only history and aspiration but also human behaviour with particular reference to this century and the unconscious processes of which we are becoming aware.

This does not, however, mean that the concept of tradition is to be set aside in pastoral theology. As with Scripture, pastoral theology may suggest different approaches to thinking about tradition, since it focuses upon the experience (both conscious and unconscious) of people. Two points may be considered in such an enterprise:

1 What is it that Christians affirm and what are they doing to themselves and others when they express and live this belief? Here tradition becomes something akin to the idea of a stream of shared consciousness. We align ourselves with this in dynamic interchange. The phrase in the Apostles' Creed, 'I believe ... in the communion of saints', illustrates the point. The popular view today is that as they say this Christians align themselves with the long line of believers, some famous and most less so, in whose footsteps they walk.

Both in ancient and modern times some have suggested that 'saints' (*sanctorum*) should be translated 'holy things' and that it refers to the Eucharist. This is unlikely. But it is a good example of reading texts with theological presuppositions: there is, so the argument goes, no reference in the creeds to the second dominical sacrament. But there ought to be one, so it is found and linked with baptism. But even more interesting is the way in which the phrase seems originally to have been added to the Creed to humanize the idea of 'church'. Standing between 'church' and 'forgiveness' it provides a way of locating Christian experience at any moment within a tradition of experience of belonging and needing forgiveness (Kelly 1972, 388ff). Such a humanized tradition is one with which believers may wish to associate. But today we are also more aware of our wish often to dissociate. The phrase offers this option, too. Hans Küng, for example, sees use of the phrase 'communion of saints' in the context of their veneration. He suggests that this is possibly a way by which Catholics might oppress Protestants and the Roman Catholic Church continue its medieval tradition of triumphalism (Küng 1993, 141ff).

2 The question of tradition, however, becomes more interesting when it is raised in a pastoral setting. It is there less about the affirming believer but becomes concerned with half-believers, those with little or no faith who nevertheless look to the Church for some pastoral ministry. At first sight tradition may seem to be the concern of those who formally subscribe to it. Yet the experience of ministers is that the religious concept of tradition is probably stronger at the fringe or among those explicitly outside the Church. This tradition is not that found in the creeds. It is more an amalgam of church buildings, half-remembered prayers, odd hymns and 'proper' ways of behaviour (the significance of this for the pastor is discussed in Chapter 10). Here we may note that the idea of Christian or Church tradition is not exclusive to those who belong to or attend the churches.

Behind these approaches two notions of 'tradition' can be discerned: tradition as deposit and tradition as dynamic force.

1 The idea of tradition as deposit is found explicitly in Jude 3: '. . . I found it necessary to write, appealing to you to contend for the faith which was once for all delivered to the

saints.' The Greek is more emphatic, referring to 'the once for all handed over faith'. The writer assumes that there is an agreed amount and content of belief which can be handed on intact. This is not the only place in the New Testament where this idea is found. St Paul's teaching about the Eucharist, for instance, implies a similar idea. He refers to the tradition which he received and handed on (1 Cor. 11.23). In that case it was the action and words of institution in a particular form, although we know that there were other 'traditions' around at the same time. Nevertheless this is an example of a deposit which has been handed on. For while St Paul would probably not recognize much in contemporary Christianity, he would still hear the words of institution in recognizable language.

2   There is, however, another idea, that of tradition as a dynamic, creative force running through human life. This is best thought of in terms of an artistic legacy. The skill of a great painter, for example, is discerned not only in his or her own work. It can also be seen in that of the painter's pupils. In order to continue the tradition of the master these apprentices not only display signs of continuity; they also have to demonstrate their own distinctive creative skills.

> The persistence of literary creativeness in any people ... consists in the maintenance of an unconscious balance between tradition in the larger sense – the collective personality, so to speak, realised in the literature of the past – and the originality of the living generation. (Eliot 1944, 14)

These two concepts of tradition are neither opposed nor mutually exclusive. They represent differences of emphasis. In theology the discussion of tradition has usually been based on history and systematics. But pastoral theology has a contribution to make here. For it focuses on the experience of people, both those who hold the tradition and the other key category of those who look to it. At times of stress Christians may tend defensively to try and define the deposit of what they hold. Jude, for instance, seems confident in the power of such a faith to defend the Church against the infiltration of pseudo-Christians. Issues to do with orthodoxy are always around, whatever is happening in and to the Church. They feature more or less prominently according to the context in which the Church finds itself. That is true in history, where the process can frequently be discerned. It is also a significant factor in contemporary Christian living. There is a coming and going dynamic between experience and feelings on the one hand and on the other hand the belief, whatever form it takes, that both stimulates and informs them. Pastoral theology always stresses that the context of tradition is not solely historical: it is also dynamic, part of the here and now of Christian ministry.

> Can the word [tradition] be rescued . . . and refurbished so as to fit the facts? For it does, after all, express something in which people are commonly engaged, whether in family, school or university, or in social and political affairs; while the processes of handing over and receiving, which constitute it, are already there however far we can penetrate into the origins of the Christian gospel. (Evans 1977, 149)

This quotation exposes several themes of pastoral theology – everyday life, social, political and personal contexts, processes and gospel. The answer to Evans' question, therefore, must be affirmative. Otherwise the Christian faith is removed from the realm of human experience. When, therefore, we consider tradition as a foundation for the theological enterprise, we are not invoking a fixed point of reference – a deposit – but acknowledging a distinctively Christian stance on life. The deposit is part of that, but not the whole. And those who look to the Church for some ministry in particular expect this distinctive stance.

REASON

Scripture and tradition pose problems. Reason, it might be thought, would be simpler. In fact, reason possibly creates even more difficulties for the pastoral theologian. There is a long history of the struggle to bring reason into contact with faith in an appropriate fashion. As Tertullian (*De praescriptione haereticorum* 7) put it,

> What indeed has Athens [the home of reason] to do with Jerusalem [the city of faith]? What has the Academy to do with the Church? What have heretics to do with Christians?

Our instructions come from the porch of Solomon [by contrast with the porch (or *stoa*) in Athens where philosophers taught], who had himself taught that the Lord should be sought in simplicity of heart. (Wis. 1.1)

This ancient suspicion has been compounded by the British and American tendency to prefer a pragmatic approach to an intellectual one. There is, however, a practical purpose behind applying reason to pastoral theology:

It is said that souls are not saved nor the Kingdom advanced by academic rigour, intellectual openness or the need to ask the awkward question. True enough. But without the infrastructure of rigorous theological exploration and intellectual openness, evangelism and mission are all too likely to run out into the sands of irrelevance or superstition, bigotry or fanaticism. (Baker 1983, 963)

This is especially true of pastoral activity. Because this is always an engagement with people and because contemporary approaches to human experience are so complicated, there is always a risk that the Church will lose its distinctively Christian perspective.

Pastoral theology, like any other branch of theology, requires the application of reason if it is to continue as a critical enquiry. But in addition it explicitly endorses a dimension of reason that may be lost in other fields through a restricted understanding of the notion of science. Pastoral theology stands at the 'wisdom' end of the spectrum of understanding human reason. There are two causes of this.

1   Since pastoral theology is concerned with situations in human life, both social and individual, it has an inevitable interest in and involvement with all the human sciences. This phrase 'human sciences' is itself disputed. An example is the debate which has continued through much of this century about Freud's work. It revolves around the intellectual status to be assigned to psychology and even more to psychoanalysis. Links with art, religion and imagination take some in the direction of analysis as an art rather than a science. Others persist with the more determinist view of libidinal drives and the psychic apparatus of the mind, a more scientific approach, or at least so it is believed (Schafer 1976; 1978;

Farrell 1981; Rycroft 1985). The discussion is not concluded and probably cannot be. But because it is taking place pastoral theology cannot escape it.

2 The second reason has already been mentioned. Although the human sciences and pastoral theology have both become distinctive disciplines in the twentieth century, neither their subject matter nor their approaches are especially contemporary. Joseph and Daniel, for example, interpreted dreams before Freud. Awareness of the unconscious is implicit in, for instance, many of the Psalms. Pastors and their activity precede pastoral theology. Reason in pastoral theology is heavily influenced by the idea of wisdom. The wisdom tradition which is found in the Old Testament is ratified by Jesus in his style of teaching. It is also adopted by St Paul and refined into his concept of 'Christ, the wisdom of God' (1 Cor. 1.24). Such wisdom is not merely accumulated folk lore, as in a collection of proverbs, parables and wise sayings. It is also a genuinely intellectual stream of thought (Crenshaw 1976). The belief that underlies wisdom is that God gives people, both his chosen ones and others, insights into the way that men and women do, can and should behave. The wise then deploy these, as we might say, pastorally. They interpret the lives of individuals, societies and nations.

It is worth noticing the way in which the development of modern psychologies, although sometimes seen as discounting religion and even as anti-religious, have often had their religious connotation recognized. For example, Freud's relations with the Judaism of his youth have been studied (Klein 1981). It has also been suggested that there was greater Christian influence on Freud than either he or his biographers recognized (Vitz 1988). Whatever the case, we know for certain that one of the first people to appreciate the value of Freud's work was a Swiss pastor, Oskar Pfister. He used Freud's insights, by today's standard crude but at the time liberating, in his pastoral ministry. He also corresponded with Freud, advising him and discussing the relation between religious faith and Freud's approaches (Freud and Pfister 1963). Jung's fascination with religion is well known and was also a subject of correspondence with Freud. Similar interest and enthusiasm persist among some psychologists and therapists.

CONCLUSION

Any definition of pastoral theology is problematic. It might even be a methodological error to begin by seeking one. The discussion in the rest of this book will propose what the components of such a theology might be. We shall also try and see how the resulting amalgam holds together and, even more importantly, remains in contact with other branches of theology. As Tracy says:

> . . . it becomes clear that a radical if not chaotic pluralism of paradigms on what constitutes theology as a discipline and thereby on the public character of theology is likely to occur. It is necessary, therefore, to study more closely what kinds of arguments cross the more radical lines of difference, and then what kinds of public discussion of the remaining major differences among various types of theology can profitably occur. (Tracy 1981, 58)

In a sense it might even appear that the wind is just now in favour of the discipline of pastoral theology. Tracy's emphasis on the public domain draws implicit attention to the fact that all theology must issue in some sort of action, whether praxis, prayer or worship. For example, there is an increasing interest in the idea of 'doing theology', an approach through which every theological idea is at least tested for its usefulness. And what is reflection for the Christian but a form of prayer? These trends may lead to a reductionism which inappropriately applies the test of relevance to every thought. But if sufficient rigour is applied to pastoral theology, it is a way in which this discipline will in new and vital fashion link theological thought to Christian practice and such practice to theology. If theology is to be a living discipline, it must interact with the living.

34

PART ONE

Tools for Pastoral Studies

In this section the four major disciplines that contribute to pastoral studies are considered:

psychology

sociology

dynamic theories

theology

Each chapter is not a full excursus on the subject. Rather it attempts to introduce enough of the key facets of the discipline for students to orient themselves in these worlds.

CHAPTER TWO

Psychology and Pastoral Studies

Crucial for any pastor is the enquiry, 'What is it to be human?'
The question may be treated as existential and given a philosophical or theological answer (Macquarrie 1982). But as a
result of studies which have largely developed during the
twentieth century even such answers now involve empirical
study. The human sciences hold a key position in pastoral
theology. Pastors cannot ignore them. If they do, four unfortunate outcomes result:

1 Pastors lose contact with those to whom they are trying
to minister. Ways of seeing people and their needs are not
techniques. They are assumptions that together make up the
dynamic setting within which the encounter takes place. A
penitent may seek various responses and types of help from
a priest. But among these she will reasonably expect the priest
to appreciate when she comes to confession, for example,
that the loss of her baby some years back may still be affecting her behaviour (including her religious belief). The priest
cannot pretend otherwise. He or she may not be particularly
adept at handling the consequences. A wise decision sometimes might be to suggest someone else counsels the person.
But this does not set aside the relationship between priest
and penitent and the priest's responsibility for facing the
woman with her expectations.

2 Religion becomes separated from everyday life. If
religious belief is not at least amenable to investigation by
contemporary psychological approaches, then it is claiming a
privileged place in the world. But this defeats the basis of the
Christian gospel itself, which is explicitly about the way that
God does not seek immunity from human investigation but
invites it. Those who believe in God should expect similar
scrutiny.

3 The people among whom the churches minister, whether in pastoral activity or evangelism, begin to think that Christians do not speak their language. Language is more than jargon or words. It represents attitudes or commonly shared positions, which are the basis upon which dialogue takes place. This is not to defend 'psychobabble'. Because, however, so much popular language about behaviour makes psychological assumptions, the sensitive minister needs to be aware of what may lie behind it.

4 Pastors may lose contact with reality about themselves. They may begin to forget that they, too, are human. They may retreat behind a false professionalism, whether as priest or counsellor. Or, even if they try to avoid this pitfall, they may be unaware of the underlying dynamics which permeate all human exchanges. If so, as pastors they are likely to lose much of their effectiveness.

Pastoral theology, therefore, cannot be done without some basic knowledge about psychology in its broadest sense. In this chapter we shall briefly consider types of psychology and its relation to religion, as well as applied psychology (including psychotherapy) and especially the influence of psychoanalysis.

TYPES OF PSYCHOLOGY

During the twentieth century the general discipline of psychology has, like other studies, diversified into a range of specific types. Today 'psychology' is rarely used without some qualifying description. Basically, however, we may discern six fundamental categories, although different terms may be found to describe these approaches.

STRUCTURALISM
This stance is essentially a hangover from the nineteenth century. It seeks by careful examination of the self to discover the basic contents of human consciousness. Today its main connections are with linguistics and anthropology.

FUNCTIONALISM
By contrast, this approach, as its name suggests, studies the way in which the mind works, putting the stress on mental

states and activities rather than underlying structures. It is more concerned with processes than with describing experience or behaviour.

GESTALT

Gestalt is German for 'form' or 'pattern', drawing attention to the integration of parts into a whole. Gestalt psychology (the German has not been replaced in English) resists separation of experiences and attitudes into elements and tries to sustain a holistic approach. It stands for the belief that the whole is more than the sum of the parts. The approach arose in opposition to the increasing tendency of psychologists in the early years of the twentieth century to atomize behaviour by analysing its components. Gestalt psychologists argue that the nature of the parts is determined by the nature of the whole. To study aspects of human behaviour, therefore, it is essential to start from the concept of a human being in context.

ASSOCIATIONISM

This type of study is now outmoded. It used to examine bits and pieces of the psychological elements in behaviour, such as experiencing or sensing, by connecting them with one another in various categories. Its empirical approach was specially congenial to English psychologists.

PSYCHOANALYSIS

The central exploration is of the relationship between conscious and unconscious data. Strictly speaking psychoanalysis is a therapy, psychotherapy being its practical outcome. But the term has become associated with a series of postulations chiefly about the concept of the unconscious or unconscious mind.

BEHAVIOURISM

This is the experimental area of psychology. It emphasizes what is believed to be objectifiable elements in behaviour. The aim is to generate a proper science of behaviour by observing, recording, hypothesizing and testing. Opponents argue that the approach is reductionist. Proponents see themselves at the beginning of a revolutionary scientific enterprise.

Of these categories (and any others) the last two remain distinctive. Students of pastoral studies are most likely to meet these, although under different guises. For example, social psychology may employ one or more of these approaches in its examination of the psychological conditions that underlie the way that social groups emerge and act. The others now merge into a different mix of psychology and some are becoming obsolete.

One key question, however, remains: to what extent can psychology be considered a science? It may have dissolved into a number of interconnected approaches because, while the general field of study is recognized – the human mind or human behaviour – no agreed conceptual framework has emerged. Indeed, some psychologists might claim that their 'agreed conceptual framework' is not to have one. The complex issues of human behaviour are best addressed by the eclectic use of different approaches. Such a stance, however, is impossible for pastors. They have to deal with people as entities and as they are, without the luxury of academic categorizing. Hence, as will be later argued, integrative models are essential for pastoral ministry, albeit informed by aspects of psychological study. The pastoral task, therefore, is itself a form of selection as to which approaches to psychology are germane to ministry. Because the field is vast it does not follow that the pastor has to know it all, although some sense of how complex it is may induce humility.

THE PSYCHOLOGY OF RELIGION

The study of religion from a psychological perspective goes back to the roots of faith and is not a modern study. The psychology of religion involves reflection on those inner and transcendent experiences which make up the religious life and, therefore, the phenomenon of religion. In the Old Testament, for instance, some of the Psalms, the Book of Job and perhaps chiefly the Confessions of Jeremiah are examples of this.

> The characteristic of the Confessions is that in the form, sometimes of monologue, but more frequently of strangely ingenuous and arresting colloquy with God, they lay bare

the inmost secrets of the prophet's life, his fightings without and fears within, his mental conflict with adversity
and doubt and temptation, and the reaction of his whole
nature on a world that threatened to crush him and a task
whose difficulty overwhelmed him. (Skinner 1922, 202)

In the New Testament similar reflection occurs in the Fourth
Gospel's portrayal of Jesus, notably in John 17, the Prayer of
Jesus. In St Paul, too, inner anguish erupts from time to time.
His personal struggle around the primacy of covetousness, an
interior force, is expressed in Romans 7. From St Augustine
in *The Confessions*, via John Bunyan in *Pilgrim's Progress*, to
the popular paperbacks of today, reflection on inner experience is central to religion. That sort of psychology of religion
is as old as religion itself.

The contemporary study of the psychology of religion,
however, is a distinctively recent development (Brown 1987).
The first modern publication is reckoned to have been by
E. D. Starbuck† in 1899. The Gifford lectures, *Varieties of
Religious Experience*, published in 1902 by William James†,
are a landmark in the field. Attempts at the scientific study of
religion declined during the 1930s but revived after the
Second World War. Two theoretical perspectives have vied for
supremacy: phenomenology (the study of reports) and
empirical study (discovering whether and how it might be
possible to measure religious behaviour and attitudes). It is,
however, improbable that the complexity of 'religion' can be
adequately addressed solely by one or the other.

Psychological study of religion is marked by six areas of
concern and study, whichever framework is employed. They
may be listed for convenience, but attention to one does not
preclude its being employed with others.

MEASUREMENT

What distinctively constitutes religious behaviour? The answer
will be to some extent determined by prevailing cultural
presuppositions. For example, William James emphasized the
feeling aspect. Between the two world wars greater emphasis
was put on people's conscious awareness as expressed
through religious observance. Unconscious processes were
not a focal issue. The method of issuing questionnaires, which
Starbuck originated, has been taken up with enthusiasm.

Religious behaviour and how people personally and emotionally seem to benefit (or not) from participating have been widely studied. But the basic question – what is it to be human? – cannot be fully answered from within this discipline alone. It is too complex.

DEVELOPMENTAL ISSUES

The question of the origins and roots of religion takes two forms:

1 How does religious consciousness arise in individuals?
2 What factors contribute to the origins of religious consciousness in human society?

Question (1) has had its most practical outcomes in religious education. The work of Jean Piaget†, for example, has been particularly influential. In some ways, however, the more interesting material for pastors is found in the work of Erik Erikson† (1958). He was a psychoanalyst who interpreted Martin Luther's† religious, social and moral development from a psychological perspective. But the nature of the question of how an individual's religious consciousness arises and develops is such that any answer is likely to be suspect. To consider it can often be stimulating. But it is doubtful how illuminating any answer is. A psychoanalytic approach to religious people from the past, whose beliefs are no longer accessible but whose significance has been filtered by history and culture, is sometimes attempted. But such psycho-history or psycho-biography needs to be treated with caution. It reduces the complexity of a person's contexts, historical, social and personal, to a single model of interpretation. Question (2) connects individual psychology with social issues, the next category.

SOCIAL PSYCHOLOGY

The psychology of group behaviour is obviously relevant to the study of religion. The philosopher A. N. Whitehead† once said, 'Religion is what I do with my solitude'. Religious behaviour, however, in practice is always social. Freud's work began with the individual. But it eventually led him to discuss topics in social psychology (Freud 1930; 1939; Badcock 1980). This area overlaps psychology, especially analytic approaches, and the sociology of religion. The key point to note is that attention to the individual in isolation from social factors is insufficient as a way of trying to understand.

TYPES OF PERSONALITY

Superficially we might assume that there would be discernible connections between personality types and religious convictions and behaviour. The topic, however, is more subtle. In particular, it is not possible to divorce the individual from his or her social and cultural context. And religion contributes to that. This type of study is also dependent upon the assumptions which at the time prevail in psychology itself. Recently this has moved generally from a preoccupation with drives and inner motivations to the broader study of the interactions between people and their effect on one another.

One area of the study of personality types with which pastors may come into contact is the Myers-Briggs workshop (Myers and Myers 1980). These have been adopted by a number of training bodies in the churches. The workshops are based on Jung's† theory of psychological types (Jung 1921; Samuels 1985). This proves attractive to some Christians because of the way in which a spiritual dimension, while not essential to the study, can nevertheless be included without contradicting the process. This typology, however, does not make direct links between the personality types that are categorized (and which are themselves disputable) and specific religious tendencies.

ALTERED CONSCIOUSNESS

One of the most intriguing aspects of any religion is the nature of religious experience and of those experiences that, it is claimed, it promotes or induces. Some studies have demonstrated that experiences which may be described as religious are more prevalent than might at first appear. Although not strictly a psychological approach, we should note here the work associated with Sir Alister Hardy†. He searched for a biological basis for religious experience. The Centre named after him has continued his attempt to draw up a taxonomy of such experiences. The type of question asked is: 'Have you ever been aware of, or influenced by, a presence or a power, whether you call it God or not, which is different from your everyday self?' (Hay 1990, 54).

David Hay and his colleagues have produced statistics

43

about the prevalence of experiences which people themselves call religious (Hay 1987). He has also shown that people often feel obliged to deny any such religious experiences. This difficulty is another reminder that individuals cannot be isolated from their contexts. Hay suggests that people in today's western society live in the classic setting for creating a taboo. On the one hand they are aware that they have experiences that are for them religious and value them. On the other hand there are powerful social inhibitions, because of the predominately secular assumptions of the age coupled with the public ineptitude of religious institutions.

> [These experiences] are therefore both desired and forbidden, sacred yet illusory, the source of meaning and madness. In this way, rather oddly transmuted, the industrial West has recovered the great original taboo, which early anthropologists used to define as 'The Sacred, perceived ambivalently, as both holy and dangerous, pure and impure'. (Hay 1987, Preface)

Other areas of contemporary enquiry into altered states of consciousness include the significance of drugs (Bowker 1973), the relation between religious states and such mental disturbance as psychosis (Jackson 1992), and the study of near death experiences (Badham 1980; 1982). Here they merely need to be noted as evidence of a widening and continuing interest in this aspect of the psychology of religion.

RELIGION AND MENTAL HEALTH

Studies in this area are vitiated by two difficulties:

1 Freud's influence has been disproportionate to the amount of evidence he adduced. He held a pathological model in his study of religion. In an early paper he linked religious activities with obsessions. There his basic stance was stated: 'In view of these similarities and analogies one might venture to regard obsessional neurosis as an individual religiosity and religion as a universal neurosis' (Freud 1907, 126). Such a view leaves no room for a more mature use of religion by anyone, the point that the pastor Otto Pfister emphasized in his response (Meissner 1984).

2 It is difficult, probably impossible, to measure whether the mental health, either of an individual or of a group, is

improved or worsened in direct relation to their religious activity. Not only is the change difficult to quantify; the responsibility of religious belief, whether of the patient or of the healer, for that change lies beyond our capacity to measure.

Anecdotal evidence is strong that people do change as the result of a religious conversion. But there are dangers in assuming too much from them, as Brown notes:

> It is an exaggeration to reduce the forms of psychopathology simply to psychosis and neurosis. Even the 'bad' kinds of religion might have positive effects on those who have found nothing else to rely on. The unanswerable question is, therefore, What would religious people be like *without* their religious beliefs? (Brown 1987, 60)

APPLIED PSYCHOLOGY

As an academic study psychology has grown greatly in the twentieth century. But its most remarkable expansion has been in application. Educational psychology, for example, is familiar to many, as is the application of social psychology in industry. Psychometric testing is widely used. But nothing is more widespread than psychotherapy. This term merely describes a method for treating people using psychological means. But this single broad heading disguises a proliferation of therapies that often compete with one another.

The reasons for this expansion are undoubtedly complex. But the fact itself is significant for pastors. Maurice North describes it in this way:

> Ever since the unified enchanted world of Christendom was destroyed and man's certitude with it, man has been alone with no one to mediate between himself and God. The characteristic feature of man's situation in technicized society is not that he is alienated but that he is *isolated*. Technicized society is inhabited by isolated man. Given the impossibility of a return to older forms of religious belief, the therapeutic ideology is the only creed available that can give man the illusion that he is not totally alone, that even if God's grace is not vouchsafed to him, then man's is. (North 1972, 291)

45

Although the range of psychotherapies is so large, the under-lying approach of all may be described as analytic, in that the treatment employs mainly verbal, and usually direct, commu-nication with the patient. Indeed, psychoanalysis itself is an instance of psychotherapy. Three major theoretical concepts underpin the psychotherapeutic approach: the unconscious mind, transference (and its corollary, counter-transference) and projection or projective identification. Pastors need a grasp of each of them, for three reasons:

1   The assumptive world of those with whom the pastor deals has been deeply influenced by these concepts. For example, modern approaches to mothering can be regarded as originating with Benjamin Spock. He was a paediatrician who in 1946 published *The Commonsense Book of Baby and Child Care*. The title was disingenuous. The theory was not based so much on commonsense as ideas derived from the application of psychotherapeutic ideas. Spock popularized these and by so doing transformed the attitudes and behav-iour of parents with their children. His book also spawned many others. But behind Spock's success (his book has sold over 26 million copies) lies a new assumption. Child rearing is no longer a matter of applied experience but a skill to be acquired. Mothers can learn this by becoming familiar with some popular psychology. The same is true of much contem-porary life. It is assumed that behaviour can be explained, often simplistically through half-grasped ideas, and then that people will live more competently.

2   Pastoral work with people requires skills. The efficacy of a religious nostrum is no longer self-evident. Indeed, one effect of the modern study of human behaviour has been to reduce certainty about what we are doing with each other and to expose some of the damaging activities in which we unwittingly participate. This is especially true of relationships in which power, whether believed or actual, is involved. It has become commonplace to think of gender relationships in this way, especially in marriage. Another such relationship is that between minister and client.

This perception was, for instance, the foundation of the Clinical Theology movement. This, although much of the original theory has been abandoned by most people, intro-duced a generation of ministers to ways of seeing those who came to them which were neither so 'spiritual' that they were devoid of psychological insight, nor so therapeutically oriented that no spiritual dimension was acknowledged. In particular Frank Lake, the movement's founder, expounded the difference between neurosis and psychosis (see p. 267 n.3) and the risks in getting involved with a psychotic individual.

3   Ideas derived from applied psychology, however, reach far beyond pastoral activity and psychotherapy. Today's intellectual culture is suffused with psychoanalytic ideas. This is largely due to the work of Freud and Jung, as well as their successors, who extended their reflections to other disciplines. Most important for the pastor, therefore, both in pastoral practice and in theological thinking is the impact of ideas that derive from this source. This area of psychology most impinges on pastoral studies and pastoral ministry.

THE IMPORTANCE OF FREUD

Sigmund Freud is known as the founder of classical psychoanalysis. But his importance for all aspects of contemporary thought reaches far beyond this specific discipline. His role in modern culture is controversial. But students of pastoral theology need to be acquainted with his seminal thought.

As a physician in Vienna, Freud specialized in the nervous system. His initial studies were into hysteria, at the time a fashionable area of research. However, he gradually parted from mainstream thinking as he developed his ideas about word association and dreams. These themes lay at the heart of his discovery of psychoanalysis. His first subject was himself: he performed a self-analysis. The development of his thought was elaborate and much, if not all, remains debatable. It is not easily simplified. But the marks of the analytic process include the following:

DRIVES

Freud devised a model of mental functions, which included a theory of instincts. For him no piece of human behaviour is casual: it always represents something of psychological significance. All human activity has not only apparent motives but also some motivation of which the person acting is unaware. The popular instance of this is found in the so-called 'Freudian slip', when a chance remark or false word is taken to represent something more than a mere error. It also means that the rational, thinking, conscious self is less in control than we like to think. The unconscious can always break through the defences of the ego.

The terms 'ego' and 'id' and to a lesser extent 'super-ego' have become widely used. They are, however, controversial and precisely what Freud meant by them is debated. Roughly speaking, however, 'ego', which means 'I', is that part of the person which is conscious and reflects upon (and defends against) the experiences of the senses. It is contrasted with the 'id', which means 'it'. This refers to the energies which we call 'unconscious'. The 'super-ego' ('super-I') judges the work of the ego. For Freud conscience and the forming of ideals are examples of the function of the super-ego. Students should be aware of these terms, but would on the whole be unwise to employ them.

GROWTH

Human growth from birth, through childhood to adulthood is a process. There are no gaps in it: something is always happening. Freud discovered that early experience influences later behaviour to a degree which had hitherto gone unrecognized. His reference to Oedipus finds its significance here. He suggested that as part of normal male development a child has sexual impulses towards his mother and correspondingly murderous feelings towards his father. The guilty feelings which result produce conscience. As with all Freud's ideas, this theory is disputed. But the notion of psychological connections between childhood and adult behaviour is today acknowledged by almost everyone, even if the precise form of these connections remains unclear.

THE CREATION OF BEHAVIOURAL SCIENCE

Freud began with self-analysis and worked through the analysis of patients towards generalized theories of human behaviour in groups and society. Although psychoanalysis has subsequently tended to be restricted to the consulting room and the work between the analyst and the patient, it is important to recognize that Freud always regarded his insights as having wider social importance. He wrote on religion as well as society and aspects of anthropology (Badcock 1980). The wider influence of his thought was perceived quite early. His books, for instance, were burned by the Nazis in Berlin and psychoanalysis was forbidden in the Soviet Union. Freud himself escaped to London towards the end of his life to escape persecution.

The early analysts, like the adherents of any cult, soon fell out among themselves and established their own schools. Jung and Alfred Adler† both eventually rejected Freud's theories of infantile sexuality and his understanding of growth. Jung in particular explored religious symbolism as an aspect of his theory of the collective unconscious. Some Christians have felt that Jung's thought, in spite of his tendency towards Gnosticism, is intrinsically more sympathetic to religious belief than Freud's. However, the student of pastoral theology may find the Freudian style of thought (though not the detail) more testing and more sharply critical of religious assumptions and, therefore, ultimately more useful. Of central importance are the key ideas of the unconscious, or the unconscious mind; transference; and projection.

THE UNCONSCIOUS, OR THE UNCONSCIOUS MIND

'If Freud's discovery had to be summed up in a single word, that word would without doubt have to be "unconscious"' (Laplanche and Pontalis 1973, 474). But unconscious activity was not discovered by Freud and his colleagues. Prophets and seers have always worked with dreams and people's imagination. And it was on the basis of the interpretation of dreams that Freud developed his theories of unconscious activity. He called dreams 'the royal road to the unconscious' (Freud 1900). But although some treat Freud as if he were either a prophet or a charlatan, he should not be confused with the ancient diviners or seers. Nor should modern psychology be compared with the arts of divination and interpretation. For it is not the discovery of the unconscious that marks contemporary thinking, but the idea that this dimension of human mental activity may be systematically explored.

The phrase 'the unconscious' is now widely used. But its vagueness indicates the difficulty in defining precisely what is being considered. This awkwardness is compounded by the way in which the word has come to be used both freely and imprecisely. Today the idea of processes that are not conscious covers a very large field. Freud used the term to refer to that part of the human system where primary processes, that is, those of which we are scarcely aware and on which we do not reflect, operate. 'Primary processes' are unlike those which make up our usual thought processes. They are best regarded as the sort of 'thinking' that goes on when we dream. Before Freud, dreams had been thought of as a state of mind which had its own logic. They could be interpreted, but as if they were addressing the dreamer or others. They come *to* people from somewhere mysterious but they do not necessarily come *from* them. So, for instance, Joseph, one of the noted dreamers of the Old Testament, interprets Pharaoh's dreams. He shows that they are a warning both to him and to the nation. Freud, by contrast, argued that dreams are connected with our usual thought processes, although they, as it were, slide about within them.

The technical argument about the concept of the unconscious continues and probably will. One difficulty is that to postulate another entity within us seems unnecessary, especially as we move away from nineteenth-century mechanistic views of the way that human beings function. We may better think of ourselves as 'people who think, imagine, feel and act, sometimes consciously, sometimes unconsciously' (Rycroft 1985, 26). There is no longer a profound distinction between behaviour of which we are consciously aware and which appears when we make our more rational decisions and unconscious activity which emerges as irrational behaviour. That distinction is too dualistic. We now recognize that human beings have ways of being which are not always conscious, although in some circumstances they can be brought to consciousness and explored. This understanding (we might even describe it as 'belief') is the basis of psychoanalysis. With the aid of the analyst a patient may get in touch with unconscious parts of him- or herself and articulate them consciously. They can then be explored and addressed.

A prevailing belief that follows from Freud's work is that

unconscious activity is at least as important in our everyday life as conscious reflection. It includes many dynamic elements which make up our personality. But whereas in theory (it is unlikely in practice) we could become fully aware of our conscious selves, the same is not true of our unconscious selves. For these are connected with experiences in infancy and childhood, which are in many senses no longer accessible. If to this we add Jung's suggestions about the collective unconscious, the ramifications become even greater. But from time to time the unconscious dimension to our behaviour becomes prominent. For example, we may not necessarily accept Freud's theory about the interpretation of dreams. But most of us dream. From that we may become aware that processes are at work in us which relate to who we are but which are quite different from those decisions which we take deliberately.

Acknowledgement that there is an unconscious dimension both in individuals and in groups is crucial for pastors for two reasons.

1 This is part of our contemporary culture, both at the intellectual level and at the level of everyday living. Even if the concept were proved to be falsely defined, as it is from time to time, some familiarity with the phenomenon is necessary for pastors. Otherwise they will be out of touch with aspects of those with whom they minister.

2 There is sufficient evidence from the way people behave, both as individuals and in groups, that whatever we call it and however we understand it, there is a dimension to human beings that is other than conscious. In fact the evidence now seems so overwhelming that the arguments are less about the postulation of an unconscious mind than about the way in which it might or might not be addressed or articulated.

TRANSFERENCE

If unconscious activity is to be made conscious, so the theory goes, then transference will be involved. In the setting of a psychoanalytic session, the analyst becomes the focus for the patient's transference. The patient is encouraged to displace thoughts, feelings and images from others to whom they originally and maybe even properly belong onto the analyst. He or she encourages this process, bears it and interprets it. As a result patients may again live through experiences that they have had with other people, most likely members of their family. Freud did not discover transference. Indeed at first he regarded it as a hindrance to treatment. Later, however, he realized that it could be a powerful therapeutic tool.

The popular picture is that by transference the patient turns the analyst into father, mother, uncle or abuser. But people do not through this process relive actual experiences. That would be a straightforward repetition, which is impossible. The conditions of any experience cannot be replicated. Transference is the way in which deeply unconscious wishes and memories are addressed, usually in unexpected fashion. In the relationship between the patient and the therapist powerful feelings of love, hate or resentment build up. They are greater than the occasion ostensibly calls for. This is itself evidence that the patient does not simply love or hate the analyst. The depth of these feelings indicates that the relationship is carrying more significance than is superficially apparent. 'Acknowledging, bearing and putting in perspective' are the tasks of psychotherapy (Semrad 1969). As the therapist and patient work, feelings and attitudes which are derived from childhood relationships, and which are affecting the patient's behaviour, become addressable. If the idea of the unconscious mind remains controversial, that of transference is even more so. As with most, if not all, aspects of human behaviour, we know that there is something there but not precisely how it works. Its therapeutic value is also, as with many aspects of psychotherapy, still disputed. But pastors need to be alert to the phenomenon since its effects are not confined to therapy or counselling.

Three key facets to transference require pastors to attend to it: the importance of feelings; universal transference; and countertransference.

FEELINGS

During the twentieth century close attention has been paid to the emotional dimension to human life and behaviour. It has not, of course, ever been absent from religion, although sometimes expression of feeling has been frowned upon. The theological significance of feelings, however, has been more problematic. A classic context of dispute, for instance, has been the doctrine of the atonement. One set of arguments has been marked by deliberately non-emotional theories which emphasize God's objective achievement. Another group has emphasized the emotional force of the saga and images of the crucifixion have brought to the fore the significance of the feelings that it arouses (Carr 1993).

The reasons for this resurgence of concern with feelings are not wholly clear. But we may note at least four factors which have contributed:

1   The end of the twentieth century is marked by a sense that the legacy of the Enlightenment is coming to an end and that we are entering a post-Enlightenment age. We are losing the sense that all things are ultimately measurable and manageable. Consequently more attention is given to the uncontrollable aspects of human life, among which feelings and emotions predominate.

2   The impact of wars in the twentieth century should not be underestimated. There was no time between the First and Second World Wars for the nations involved to recover their equilibrium. Indeed in retrospect it increasingly appears that there was a Thirty Years War (1914–1945) punctuated by a pause. Throughout this period there was a considerable and varied output of poetry and music. This may represent a pervasive sense of unresolved emotion.

3   Third, the impact of psychology, especially as it became more popular, legitimized the expression of feelings in a way that hitherto had not been expected. Feeling has become a distinctive and publicly legitimate point of reference for people.

4   A specific example is found in the general behaviour of the churches. Noel Annan describes the process in the post-war period:

Nothing will ever stop people demanding large-scale explanations of the world. Religion supplied some of them ... There were interesting theological disquisitions from Ian Ramsey, reminders abroad from Barth of the terrible images of the Christian faith, billowing clouds of transcendental philosophy from Tillich in America who assured us that it was as atheistic to affirm the existence of God as to deny it. If God is so difficult to know and hence to love, should we not obey the second commandment at Holy Communion which is at least clear – to love one's neighbour as oneself? Thus began a transformation of the Christian message. The liver and lungs were torn out of the old theology leaving the heart still beating. Compassion came from the heart, judgement disappeared. (Annan 1990, 299)

While questions of the value to be assigned to feelings in the theological enterprise remain acute, their significance for pastoral theology is indisputable. Transference is specifically about the meaning of feelings in any relationship. It is not a theoretical stance alone.

UNIVERSAL TRANSFERENCE

The discovery of transference was primarily the result of Freud's clinical analyses. But he and his colleagues soon recognized that the phenomenon had a wider relevance. By 1925 Freud could remark that Transference 'is a universal phenomenon of the human mind ... and in fact dominates the whole of each person's relations to his human environment' (Freud 1925, 163).

There may be a touch of hyperbole about this claim. But it is essentially correct. If transference is concerned with everyday feelings and emerges so powerfully in the intimate relationship between analyst and patient, it is probable that it is an underlying dimension to all human activity. This is always composed of relationships, whether believed, imagined or actual. There is no such person as an isolate who is or can be divorced from these. Even hermits can be viewed as in some relationship with others, although they have nothing to do with them. They have an impact: the hermit is by choice not in touch with those others of whom, however, he or she knows. The reverse is also true: people know about hermits, even if they have no contact with them. There is, therefore, a relationship of some sort. And, as is obvious, each of us is born into relationship. Everyone has parents.

COUNTERTRANSFERENCE

The way in which transference is discussed sometimes suggests that it is a one-way process. But feelings never work in one direction only. Even if at one time it was thought by some that in therapy the analyst was like a blank screen for the patient to use as he or she wished, that idea has long been abandoned. Obviously the counsellor is human, too, and, however well and in whatever way trained, remains so. In any human encounter there are various sets of feelings and these are reciprocal. 'Countertransference' describes the feeling response of a person who is a focus for transference. Freud hardly considered countertransference. But since his time it has been increasingly recognized and attention has been paid to it.

Some therapists try to minimize countertransference; others try to use it; and others go further and give their own countertransferential reactions as guides for their interpretations. These theoretical questions are also important for pastors. Just as transference is a universal phenomenon, so is countertransference. The pastor's work is always in less structured contexts than that of, for instance, a counsellor or therapist. As a consequence, there is more space for unexplored transference that can obscure what is going on. Pastors, therefore, need to be aware of their own feelings and predispositions and how these may be aroused as countertransference, if they are to grasp what people are doing with them. As will become clearer later, the key question in any encounter often is not 'What is the matter with him or her?' but 'What is happening to me?'

Transference and countertransference are not vaguely theoretical ideas. They are ways of describing fundamental human behaviour that occurs when people meet or groups come together.

PROJECTION

The third key notion is 'projection'. In some ways it looks like transference, but there is a difference. Transference involves bringing something from the past by imposing it on someone who is present. So, for instance, deep and unexpressed love by a child for its parent may appear as affection for a counsellor. Projection is a facet of present behaviour. The word describes the way in which we disown parts of ourselves and place them in others and deal with them there. As might be expected, the part of ourselves that we wish to disavow is usually something negative. But this is not necessarily so: we can project desirable parts of ourselves, too.

When, for example, we think someone is being hostile towards us, the chances are that they are. But that may not be all. They may also represent part of our own aggressiveness which we do not recognize. The emotions which follow are curious but powerful. If we deny our aggression, the other may actually feel more aggressive towards us, but he or she may not know why. It is as if they hold our feelings and we deal with them there and not in ourselves.

This sort of projective behaviour is especially prominent in intimate groups, such as a family. Feelings there whirl around. Many will be familiar, for instance, with adolescent aggression. This is natural as part of the process of growing up. But it can be compounded by the way in which the parents project into their child parts of themselves which they cannot face, such as their anger with each other or their envy. The theme of the scapegoat is a classic example of projection. In the ancient rite the people projected onto the scapegoat all the parts of themselves (their sins) for which they could not take responsibility. The modern use of the concept is similar: in a family the members conspire, often unconsciously, to load parts of themselves that they cannot face onto a vulnerable member. The process is so widely recognized that the verb 'scapegoating' has been generated for it.

As with the other themes, projection is a universal phenomenon which is not confined to a few relationships. It is a characteristic of many organizations. For example, hospitals stir up powerful feelings in people. They represent sickness and death, both of which arouse disturbingly intimate emotions. As a result, different groups which have their place in the treatment programme may be used for other covert purposes. Thus, doctors may wish to disown the unscientific and messy aspects of their treatment. So they leave it to the nurses. They hold to a sanitized view of healing and project the residue of messiness onto others. As with all projection, there is something apparently legitimate about this. It is truly nurses' work. But it is also part of the doctors' responsibility to acknowledge the bits of their treatment with which they do not feel comfortable. By projecting these into the nurses the doctors may feel a little better, but the work of the nurses will suffer. The outcome is that the hospital's overall effectiveness may be damaged (Shapiro and Carr 1987).

Pastors need to be especially aware of projection, not least in an era when one of the prevailing models of the church is that of the family, that home of powerful projections.

CONCLUSION

The study of psychology exposes both its value for pastors and its limitations. Psychology in it widest sense is a primary intellectual setting for today. Its influence ranges from philosophy to the arts, from history to anthropology. But even more important is the way in which it has permeated popular thought. Pastors who are not at least familiar with the themes of this discipline will find themselves disadvantaged.

The limitations of psychology as a study for the pastor, however, also begin to become apparent. Taken alone it is always likely to push towards the individual. That is largely what happened in one period when pastoral studies were emerging as a distinct discipline (Campbell 1985; Pattison 1988). Even if a person is thought of in context, a purely psychologically-informed approach reduces complexity, at least from the pastor's perspective, to an inappropriate simplicity. Pastors need a way of interpreting not just individuals and families but also their social context. And even more they need an integrating way of holding the disparate data together. We turn, therefore, next to consider the way in which pastors might think sociologically, before attempting to find a sufficiently useful integrating model for ministry.

CHAPTER THREE

Sociology and Pastoral Studies

Sociology is the second major human science which has a profound impact on pastoral studies. Technically, however, it predates modern psychology. The word 'sociology' and the discipline are both nineteenth-century innovations. In a more general sense, however, its roots go back to earlier ages. It is a dimension of that humanism, belief in progress and emphasis on scientific enquiry and rationality that characterized the Enlightenment. Sociology is linked with economics, anthropology, psychology, political science and religious studies. At one time these were not separate studies, but all regarded as part of general learning and culture. They have only become specialisms in the last two hundred years. Yet even now it is not possible to draw hard and fast divisions. But they have this in common: all take as their subject matter the study of human social behaviour.

'SOCIOLOGY' AND AUGUSTE COMTE

The word 'sociology' was coined by Auguste Comte†. His story illustrates the roots of this discipline. He was a philosopher, a founder of positivism. Although he had lost his own Christian faith, he considered religion the means by which ideas and beliefs were created and sustained. He could hardly have done otherwise. At that time people still widely assumed that religion and theology were integral to a society. Indeed later in his life he tried to establish a new 'religion of humanity'. Comte also coined the terms 'positivism' and 'altruism'. His aim was to replace theology with sociology as the way of interpreting religion as a social phenomenon. The enterprise had three parts to it:

DETACHMENT

From Comte derives the idea that any student of human behaviour not only may, but should, work from a detached stance. Hitherto it had been assumed that students of human religious behaviour would themselves be believers, at least in public. Sociology was a new science, which was to be aligned with the emerging natural sciences. For these methodological scepticism was the presumption, and so this would also apply to sociology.

DIFFERENT QUESTIONS

The customary theological approach to questions of religious behaviour had been first to ask about God, doctrine and belief. After this the second enquiry was into the behaviour which followed from that belief. The sociological study of religion reversed this order. Comte and his successors scrutinized people's behaviour for data. On the basis of these observations they explored the way in which beliefs may or may not develop. This approach remains fundamental to sociological study, although it has, like other sciences, had to alter the way it thinks about itself in the light of more recent discoveries and the new philosophy of science.

A PROGRAMME

Later students have tried to stress the objective and dispassionate nature of sociological study. Comte and other early sociologists of religion, however, included commitment to a programme of social change as part of their study. The ideal of value-free enquiry, sometimes held as the intention (and by some the achievement) of sociologists, is not achievable and never was. Recent social studies have had to pay more attention to this dimension. But some sociological writing still implies that its discoveries are the result of objective observation and evaluation alone.

THE DEVELOPMENT OF RELIGION

Comte himself proposed a theory of three stages of development in religion:

The theological era

When theology was dominant, all knowledge was interpreted in its light. Theology was the queen of the sciences, since it addressed every aspect of life and learning and not an isolated area. Social organization was hierarchical. The associated idea of God was that as 'Almighty God' he was the head of that hierarchy.

The metaphysical era

During this period there was a search for abstract notions which hovered between the old theological views and the need for data. It was marked by the emergence of a democratic social structure which held egalitarian ideals. God in this setting undergirded rather than dominated society. He was best thought of as 'The Ground of our Being'.

The scientific era

This third stage was the one to which Comte and the early positivist thinkers aspired. Sociologically educated experts would now be the rulers. A scientific study of data was crucial and would only be possible if, like the natural sciences, social studies separated themselves from the control of religion. The result would be definitive understandings of the world which would liberate people from the tyranny of superstition and religion – at least the old style of religion. The God of this new world 'religion' would be conceived as perhaps 'The Great Architect' (Hill 1973, 21). This era would be marked by a belief in and experience of progress, disenchantment (the removal of magic and mysticism) and the triumph of rationality.

Today it is easy to pick holes in this scheme and expose its underlying motivation. But Comte's approach should be considered in its historical context. The early nineteenth century was a period of exploration and categorization. Most sociologists were working against the background of the Darwinian revolution. This, too, was marked by the acquisition of vast quantities of data and the desire to create schemes that would provide a total interpretation of all this newly acquired evidence. We should not underestimate the way in which these two original intentions intertwined. Technical developments in all the sciences have opened up debate about the meaning of objectivity in ways that could not have been foreseen by the pioneers. But today, especially in discussions about sociology, most would acknowledge that as a discipline it is marked by the intermingling of theory and intention. Indeed the process itself is one of the pieces of data that must be taken into account in any sociological enquiry. Because of this the claim of sociology to be scientific is sometimes queried. Others go so far as to dismiss it altogether. But what some may regard as a negative point against it may in practice, as we shall see later, be a positive one in its favour.

When considering psychology we noted the influence of a series of individuals, such as James, Freud and Jung. The sociological study of religion is even more examined in terms of individuals and what they distinctively represented. There is, however, widespread agreement that after Comte the founders of the modern sociology of religion were Emile Durkheim and Max Weber.

EMILE DURKHEIM

It is a mark of Durkheim's significance that so much critical attention has been paid to his theories. Few of them have survived this examination intact. Yet they remain ideas with which anyone interested in religion as a social phenomenon must grapple. The title of one of his major works, published in Paris in 1912, *The Elementary Forms of the Religious Life* (Durkheim 1954) sums up Durkheim's approach. He was intrigued by the way that religion functioned. A man of his age, he assumed that an evolutionary principle was at work in societies. Primitive societies would evolve into more complex ones. But in his process their primitive aspects did not completely disappear. Durkheim discerned two marks of such residual primitiveness:

1 a profound distinction is drawn between what is sacred and what is profane;

2 people have a dependent longing for something that lies beyond or transcends their immediate experience in society.

In order to examine these hypotheses, Durkheim tried to explore people's attitudes towards what they regarded as transcendent or supernatural. He studied primitive tribes, most famously the Arunta in Australia. He considered that primal attitudes would be less likely to be overlaid in such societies than in the west. He was especially intrigued by the idea of the sacred. He noted that sacred objects were used in many societies. Yet considered objectively it was obvious that such sanctified things were ordinary. The quality of sacredness, therefore, must lie somewhere in the attitude taken by a tribe or people towards the object and not intrinsically in the item itself. But since such attitudes were not solely those of individuals but represented some sort of implicit agreement among people within a society to treat such objects as sacred, then these sacred objects were not the private possession of the religion itself. They were symbols of the society that practised that religion. Thus Durkheim came to one of his central themes: religion performs a social function. Religious ritual is one means of reinforcing social cohesion in a society.

But what is such religious belief dealing with? Durkheim was working in a Europe which lay in the philosophical shadow of Immanuel Kant†. Kant had died half a century before Durkheim's birth, but his legacy dominated intellectual thought. The conclusion of *The Critique of Practical Reason* (1788), his study of morals, might almost be the philosophical text for Durkheim's sociology: 'Two things fill the mind with ever-increasing wonder and awe, the more often and the more intensely the mind of thought is drawn to them: the starry heavens above me and the moral law within me.'

Durkheim perceived that rules and values within a society seemed to exist as independent entities. They also appeared to endure through changes in that society. As such, therefore, these rules and agreed values possess a power which is both desirable and awesome. It is desirable because it sustains shared attitudes within a society, thus producing social cohesion. It is also awesome since, when logically considered, such rules and values seem to have no obvious basis. One function of religion, therefore, according to Durkheim, is to preserve the idea of sacredness. It does this through rituals. Such religious activity is designed to preserve a right relationship between people and the sacred and only makes sense in the context of the sacred. Religion, therefore, is a powerful social reinforcement. It not only derives its power from social solidarity but also in so doing strengthens it. The question of the truth of any religion is thus determined by the degree to which it effectively promotes confidence and well-being in society.

Implicit in this account is the principle of social conformity. This is always likely to be an outcome of any evolutionary approach, which Durkheim shared with many of his contemporaries. He expected sociology to become a body of knowledge which would inform social planning. Within that process, the aspect of each dimension of a society, including its religion, could be examined and in principle determined. Prior to the profound shock of the First World War thinkers were often optimists and Durkheim was no exception. By the end of that war, however, he had lost a son, his work seemed in decline, and the French intelligentsia was decimated. A new and more cautious era had begun.

Towards the end of the twentieth century both Durkheim's assumptions and his reasoning are suspect. There is a circular touch to his argument. He thinks of religious patterns of behaviour as symbolizing 'society'. But he has already defined society in terms of patterns of religious and moral belief. Sometimes he shifts from what he thinks ought to be the case to treat it as if it were the case. In a modern plural society the role of religion is more complex and manifestly not cohesive. We are less convinced by the idea that human societies are evolving for the better. The optimism of the nineteenth century has given place to the anxiety and pessimism of the twentieth. We may say that Durkheim represents modernism, but that his approach no longer works in a postmodern world. Yet in four ways Durkheim's thinking remains important for the sociology of religion and for pastoral studies.

1 While standing in the positivist tradition which derived from Comte and which has continued to be a mark of sociological analysis, Durkheim seems able to 'feel' the significance of religious activity while observing it. His writing is essentially sympathetic. As a man of his age he seems to have held utopian ideals about the human capacity for change. Yet he acknowledges that there is more to the experience of religion than is summed up in the cold concept of religion as a social function.

2 Durkheim pioneered the imaginative use of statistics. His fundamental stance is that every individual act has a

social basis. One famous study of his was an enquiry into suicide (Durkheim 1952; Worsley 1970, 74ff). He took this most individual of acts and assembled the official statistics throughout Europe. He then examined them and showed that any explanation in terms of individual psychological types alone would not suffice. The weaknesses in the thesis have since been exposed. But for all the problems of evaluating with statistics, they remain a key tool in the work of sociologists. The pastoral theologian cannot ignore them. An example of how Durkheim's approach prevails may be found in some recent studies of the theory of secularization. David Martin, for instance, acknowledges a Durkheimian frame in his *A General Theory of Secularization*. The first sentence of this quotation could have been written by Durkheim. The second indicates how great is the changed attitude of a sociologist at the end of the century.

> I should stress that this is an empirical theory and I believe such theories have an appropriate and honourable place in the economy of science. I have not attempted to touch on the transformation of science, the shifts of paradigm, or the mutations and revolutions of ideas and I have definitely eschewed any hint of the philosophy of history. (Martin 1978, 13)

3 A key distinction which Durkheim examined is that between religion and magic. This is important in itself but also particularly significant for practising pastors. For Durkheim the difference between the two is social. Religion holds the sacred on behalf of a society and does so by creating a church or company of people. Magic by contrast is the work of the magician and individuals who consult him. He has only a clientele. The distinction is difficult to sustain, but Durkheim rightly indicates a felt difference between religion and magic.

4 The final influence is worth noting here, since there has been a mild resurgence of the sort of approach that Durkheim exemplified. In the late 1960s in Western Europe and the USA there were major social upheavals and riots. The anti-Viet Nam war protests in the USA coincided with the student-led riots in Europe, especially in Germany and France. The issue that they have raised is not only whether any western form

of society has a future. The larger questions are those of the relation between the individual and society and of social and personal identity. Thomas Luckmann† argued that relations between the individual and the social order had entered crisis (Luckmann 1967). He and Peter Berger† produced further sociological studies about this crisis (Berger and Luckmann 1966; Berger 1980). They have especially explored the actual and potential role of religion in such a context. Their work exemplifies ideas that were originally pioneered by Durkheim, especially in his thinking on the importance of the sacred and the inevitable sense of dependence which is felt by people in a society.

We revert to some of these ideas below. For the present, however, we are reminded that religion inevitably has a social function of some sort, even if it is difficult to define. No student of pastoral studies, therefore, can ignore Durkheim's influence on the sociology of religion.

MAX WEBER

While Emile Durkheim was working in France, another pioneer of modern sociology, including the sociology of religion, was developing different theories in Germany. Each was acknowledged as great in his own time, although curiously there is no evidence of any direct contact between them. They worked with different mind sets. Durkheim adopted a rational approach, full of ideas and attitudes; Weber by contrast took a more historically oriented approach. His studies were more empirical than Durkheim's and ranged over religions throughout the world and not just Christianity in the west or supposedly more primitive tribal religions. And there was a third thinker whose ideas parallel those of Weber. This was Karl Marx†. His thought on religion is probably best known through his famous dictum: 'Religion is the moan of the oppressed creature, the heart of a heartless world, the soul of a soulless environment. It is the opium of the people.'[1]

Both Marx and Weber were historically minded and studied human processes by studying history. Marx was a European Jew, with all the inherited tragedy of that tradition. He and his colleague Friedrich Engels† wished to discover how the early Christian movement, a sect within Judaism, had emerged and how that process was linked to the class struggle. The key, so they thought, lay in issues of ownership of property and the means of production. These were the same issues as Weber identified. For him the answers to the emergence of religious bodies lay in the way in which societies organize themselves and create bureaucracies. In retrospect it might seem easy to expose the weak foundations of both Marx's and Weber's approach. But it is important to remember the context within which they emerged and to note that both continue to exercise a major influence on sociology, including the sociology of religion.

Two questions preoccupied Weber:

1 Why did capitalism develop in the west and in the context of Christian faith and not in similarly sophisticated societies and religions such as, for example, in Asia?

2 What is the connection between social class, economic activity and religious expression?

The two questions persistently emerge in his preoccupation with the nature of authority and its exercise, especially domination; what it is to be rational and correspondingly irrational; and what is the connection between ideas in a society and material interest, especially between religious ideas and economic activity. All these themes are summed up in the title of one of his most famous books, *The Protestant Ethic and the Spirit of Capitalism*, first published in 1904/5 (Weber 1952).

The main shift that Weber brought about in the focus of the study of religion was from the central notion of religion and church, which had preoccupied Durkheim, to the periphery. He explored the points where social class, economic activity and types of religion coincided. These were also issues for Marx and Engels, although in a less systematic fashion. Such study required four basic approaches, which have become the hallmarks of Weber's analysis:

1 An historical perspective was an essential prerequisite for taking such an overview. Weber moves easily between different times and different cultures as he elaborates his theories. This gives his approach some of its strengths, but is also a weakness. For his arguments are always susceptible to

a revaluation of history. His basic hypothesis, for example, that there is an intimate link between Calvinism and the Protestant work ethic has been questioned. Other reasons can be adduced for capitalist developments, for instance, in New England where the same doctrinal basis is found. Similarly, further work has shown that Calvinism took strong hold in Scotland and Hungary, but without the accompanying economies that might have been expected. On the other hand, because Weber works with this historical perspective, his thinking is rarely arid and is often warmly human.

2   This observation connects to the second point. Weber realized that the positivist tradition of sociology established by Comte had an intrinsic weakness. When dealing with people and their behaviour, questions of attitudes and ideas necessarily softened the hard edges of positivist notions of data. This is a fundamental discussion in the field of sociology in general. Nevertheless, it is important for pastors to recognize that in observing and hypothesizing about people's behaviour, data is critical but the nature of that data is equally significant. Data in the human sciences can never be solely statistical (see Chapter 4).

3   Although Weber never precisely defines what he means by religion, he examines religions across a very wide field. He makes broad generalizations about Judaism, Christianity, Islam and Buddhism. This gives excitement to his thinking and makes his arguments captivating. But it also leads to the distinctive contribution of Weber to the study of religion – classification or typology.

4   Weber offers a number of typologies and these may be his most enduring legacy. They have been used by many subsequently and even if not technically understood they offer pastors a useful framework for considering their ecclesiastical context. The most famous list is the structural comparison of 'church', 'sect' and 'mystic group'. But he also examines the different nature of authority that derives from priest and prophet from a sociological perspective.

The typology of church structures was not Weber's own creation. Between 1894 and 1914 the theologian-philosopher Ernst Troeltsch† lived in Weber's house. His *The Social Teachings of the Christian Churches* (1908–11) dates from this period. In it he applied sociological methods to the study of history and theology (Clayton 1976). He also introduced the typology of church-sect-mystic group. A 'church' takes its message and in order to proclaim it accommodates itself to the realities of human life and the world in which the church is set. His model was the Roman Catholic Church in Europe. A 'sect' also proclaims the gospel but emphasizes its other-worldliness. It aspires to a higher moral and spiritual level, usually aiming at perfection. For Troeltsch the Protestant churches generally exemplify such behaviour. The third classification is not formally a group. It is composed of associations of individuals who seek their private communion with God. They set aside structures, sacraments, doctrines and orders of ministry in order to seek direct contact with the divine.

This way of classifying religious groups has been subject to intense study. But it has proved seminal in the study of sects. Weber took over this categorization but added other categories. For instance, he was fascinated by the way in which authority was exercised. This, too, he classified. There is a traditional form, whereby the elders possess a wisdom and are assigned leadership. Contrasted with this we find charismatic leadership by which an individual is chosen to bring about change. He (not, I think, according to Weber, she) is believed to possess a magic or a religious power that can transform people's worlds. And behind these obvious forms lurks a legal or rational approach to the exercise of authority which emphasizes the need for laws and norms.

A third area in which Weber has permanently contributed to the study of religion is his differentiation of 'priest' from 'prophet'. This is a facet of Weber's concern with change in the social order. How does this come about?

> The priest is the servant of an existing order, the prophet is the centre of a new one. The priest typically receives regular fees or maintenance; the prophet depends on gifts and alms, for his new message is of criticism or even rebellion against the established order, from which he must assert his independence. To the degree that he is successful he must attract and organise a new community. Thus prophecy lies at the beginning of congregational religion. (Scharf 1970, 151)

This concept demonstrates both the strengths and weaknesses

of Weber's approach. It is vulnerable in the sense that we have only to find a society in which this way of categorizing religious leadership does not apply in order to falsify his argument. Not surprisingly this has in fact happened. Yet at the same time the categorization, at least for Christians and especially for pastors, carries a message which is intrinsically fascinating and demands response. In particular, even if not wholly accurate, Weber's theory challenges Durkheim's argument that religious systems reinforce social patterns in society. Whereas, therefore, work built on Durkheim has tended towards generalizations about dependence and the way in which it is institutionally managed, that following Weber has been attracted to the sectarian side of religion and matters of intense belief and counter-cultural expressions.

One obvious question arises, which has been widely debated: does Weber, at least in principle, predict the so-called secularization debate of the second half of the twentieth century? His well-known phrase 'the disenchantment of the world' (*die Entzaüberung des Weltes*) has been taken to indicate the decline of religion as a more rational world emerges. It seems, however, that at the beginning of the twentieth century Weber was not predicting western secular, pluralist societies so much as pointing to the imminent end of magical ideas. For Weber magic and religion were not identified. He stood in that stream of sociological and anthropological thought which held a class-ridden and intellectualist attitude to religion and magic (Frazer 1911–15). Religion, as represented chiefly by priests, was a veneer over a morass of magical expectations, which is held by the populace. Intellectuals distance themselves from both. As a result there is a tension between religion and magic which is worked out in the tension between the priest and the people. But Weber, like Frazer, did not identify religion with magic. The later debate on secularization, however, took a different perspective.

SECULARIZATION

It is impossible to undertake contemporary pastoral studies without reference to secularization. This topic also lies at the heart of the sociology of religion. The word 'secularization' is widely used. The adjective 'secular' is frequently employed both in technical and popular senses. One result is that the discussion, which is central as to how religion and the Church are perceived, becomes confusing. Sociologists range from those who make a theory of secularization the core of their work (for example, Bryan Wilson) to those (notably David Martin) who question the usefulness and validity of the concept. Some clarification is necessary.

Michael Hill (1973) proposes the six senses to the term which have been discerned by Larry Shiner (1967). These are not mutually exclusive, some more obviously being related to others. But it is a useful list of the range of uses which are frequently confused.

1   The most widespread and general sense is that secularization describes the *decline of religion*. It is appealing for a number of reasons, not least because it is simple: 'By the term *secularization*, I mean that process by which religious institutions, actions and consciousness lose their social significance' (Wilson 1966, 149).

This sense also feels right for different groups of people. Those with a positivist stance will feel that this is what ought to occur. Religious believers tend to feel that their faith and beliefs are not as significant, especially for others, as they would wish them to be. The notion of 'decline', therefore, fits experience. We need, however, to ask 'Decline from what?' The idea of a time in the past when things were better than they are now is itself not so much a religious belief as a basic human longing. There is no need to be scientific about this. Discussions among football supporters, academics, parents or any other group tend towards the belief that things once were better. The same is true of sociologists. They are inclined, as anthropologists sometimes indicate, to postulate a point in social development which did not necessarily exist – such as the idea that primitive people are more religious than sophisticated or that at one time magic prevailed throughout the ancient world. This generalized working meaning to secularization, therefore, appears more abstract and scientific than it really is.

2   An alternative is to speak of how adherents of religion shift from *an other-worldly* to *a this-worldly motivation*. Again, there often feels to be some truth in this. As an example we

may take developments from the nineteenth century to the present day. There has been a widespread loss of belief in eternal damnation. Any idea of the after-life plays today less of a role in Christian belief than at some other times. There is also a tendency towards pragmatism in morals. Some sociologists include the churches' movements towards institutionalized ecumenism as evidence of a loss of self-belief and a shift towards a this-worldly notion of corporation. The question, however, that arises for the Christian, especially the theologian, is why such a fuss is made of the two poles. Christian belief necessarily draws attention to the intimacy between heaven and earth which may lead to oscillation between the two but can never be seen in terms of a straightforward progression from one to the other. The shift to pragmatism in morals and administration seems matched by a greater awareness of the need for mystery in other areas. The growth in church bureaucracy, for example, has been paralleled by an increased interest in retreats and spirituality.

3 A third definition of secularization is that it describes the way in which *society disengages from religion*. This way of seeing begins from the mind set of the society rather than church-related activity. The thesis runs that in an industrial society – and, we should now add, the post-industrial society in much of the west – there is a structural abandonment of formal religion. The Church and its beliefs no longer function at the centre of society. Religious institutions are marginalized. Again, in a sense this states the obvious. Western societies have developed in such a way that the place which the Church historically occupied has not been assumed by another institution but dispersed among several. But, as is becoming clearer, a decline in religion and belief does not necessarily follow. In the highly industrialized society of the USA, for instance, public religious belief seems to flourish in a way which many in Europe envy (Bruce 1992). Yet even in Great Britain, the persistence of belief is remarkable, even if it is not so public (Hay 1987).

4 A further refinement of the last definition is that secularization describes *the transposition of religious beliefs and activities away from religious institutions*. For instance, during the twentieth century the Communist Party in the USSR became the focus for much quasi-religious activity in place of

the Russian Orthodox Church. Between the two world wars fascism similarly carried religious overtones, notably in Germany and Italy. In each case the religious feelings of people were mobilized but their point of reference was explicitly not divine but secular. The issue here, both for sociologists and practising pastors, is mostly one of language. The fact of the process seems indubitable. But is there any defining limit to the term 'religious'? For instance, we may allow that the Nazi ceremonies in Nuremberg were religious activities. The assembled congregation expressed its belief and worshipped at its shrine. At one level that seems a reasonable description. But if we allow all such activity to be considered religion, then there is nothing left that could be secularized.

5   The fifth suggestion is that secularization refers to the way in which *the world is progressively deprived of its sacral character.* 'Sacral' refers to the way that the world which human beings inhabit is itself to be held in awe. It is suffused with magic and the way to deal with it is by employing rites, rituals and magical skills. By contrast, so this argument runs, the secularizing process steadily removes this facet of the world. Then people cease to hold the world in awe and learn to manage and manipulate it. Magical ways of handling the world are abandoned and scientific or managerial stances become the natural way of thinking. This concept is, however, weak in at least two ways. First, it assumes (as we have seen earlier) that so-called primitive man had an essentially religious or magical attitude to himself and his environment. But there is no clear evidence that this was always and in every instance the case. Second, it also assumes that there is a development (note the implication of progress) in the way that human beings understand themselves and their world. This belief, however, may prove to have been itself more culturally conditioned than has been acknowledged. We are today, for example, witnessing a widespread attempt to resacralize nature. To be 'green' is almost to be an adherent of a new religion of the environment. It is certainly a key social convention: to be credibly green is a political expedient. Spiritual and religious overtones are explicitly assigned to attitudes to the environment by New Age thinking. And at both a popular and a more serious level interest and belief in

astrology also give the lie to taking this understanding of secularization at face value.

6   Lastly, secularization may refer to *a straightforward shift from a sacred society to a secular society* – the phrase that we hear most frequently. It is used to suggest, for instance, that rural communities are likely to be less secular than urban ones. In the former, the traditional ties which make up a small community remain stronger than in the latter, however much they may be idealized. Again, it is noticeable that such a belief can easily be felt. But implicit within it are assumptions about the nature of communities and especially the comparison between 'primitive' and 'sophisticated'. This often may owe more to everyday longings and assumptions than to sociological classification and clarification.

After such a catalogue it might be thought that we should avoid thinking about secularization at all. In the hands of some the term is used ideologically. Nevertheless, in spite of the problems of definition and the way that attempts at clarity may sometimes lead to unclarity, overall the range of topics outlined in Shiner's six definitions still offers a reasonable agenda for thinking about religion and society at the end of the twentieth century. The list was produced in the 1960s, which was a time when the secularization debate was reaching one of its peaks. However, because this debate does relate to the way in which pastors and theologians perceive the context within which they are working, awareness of it and sensitivity to the assumptions which underlie it are essential.

One warning, however, should be noted. There is a danger that the *process* of secularization may be confused with the *theory* of secularization. There seems little doubt about the process. When, however, discussion of that is developed into a grand theory or overarching narrative, we are firmly placed in the modern world, that which stems from the Enlightenment. The question at the end of the twentieth century is whether we are now entering, or indeed already inhabit, a postmodern world. The point should be noted and may become increasingly important for the pastor. For it would seem that while modernism, as exemplified in most sociological studies, is committed to ideals of objective truth, to be postmodern is to be without commitment and possibly sub-jectivist – the point is disputed. But having noted the issue, possibly too much should not be made of any supposed divide between modernism and postmodernism, at least in pastoral thinking. Gunton quotes Ziauddin Sardar: 'Whereas modernism tried to come to terms with the "other" by excluding it, postmodernism simply seeks to render it irrele-vant. The underlying fear of it continues unabated' (Gunton 1993, 69).

The 'other', whether God, our neighbour, the client or parts of the self is a preoccupation of the pastoral theologian.

THE SOCIAL CONTEXT OF THEOLOGY

In two books Robin Gill has explored the context within which theology has to be done (Gill 1975; 1977), especially in the light of modern sociological studies. He has not explicitly considered pastoral theology, but his arguments are impor-tant for this discipline. In particular he has emphasized that, if theologians are to develop their ideas and communicate them, they have to take into account the context in which they work.

After examining the secularization debate and its alterna-tives, Gill proposes what he calls 'an alternating model'. One difficulty in engaging with the debate on secularization is that the evidence adduced can be variously interpreted. This makes it difficult for those outside the professional circle, such as pastoral theologians, to grasp the whole. It also appears to encourage some participants first to define their theory and then to seek evidence to confirm it. The comparisons between various types of society, whether contemporary or historical, suggest that religion is something different in each and that therefore no accurate comparison is possible.

Yet when all the caveats have been entered and the evi-dence scrutinized, the result, when considered in not too technical a fashion, feels (the word is important) relevant and true. Gill concurs and suggests that while overarching and total explanations are bound to be deficient, sociologists of religion, and consequently theologians concerned about their context, can work with limited and proximate tasks:

An alternating model of secularization and de-secularization is essentially prosaic: it does not refer to 'historical sweeps', . . . it remains agnostic about the *overall* status of religion. Nevertheless, it does suggest that there are processes of both secularization and de-secularization apparent within contemporary society, and possibly within all societies. Whether or not either of these processes will finally obliterate the other must remain a matter for speculation, though at present it might seem an unlikely eventuality. (Gill 1975, 128)

Gill's observation is relevant to pastoral studies. He argues that a sociological method must be as value free as possible. It works, therefore, on the basis of an 'as if' mentality, moving from hypothesis to hypothesis and avoiding sweeping generalizations. By contrast, theology is explicitly not value free. Theologians of whatever sort do not confuse faith with religiosity or false certainty. They, too, operate a similar 'as if' mentality. For faith always moves from belief to new belief. The theologians' work is thus complementary to and not at odds with the contemporary scientific mentality.

This observation has obvious consequences for pastoral theologians. Since they are dealing with human behaviour, it will be important that they work with interpretations of that behaviour and not with sweeping generalizations about it. The sociological approach offers much, but always includes this danger. Yet without some awareness of society, however difficult that is to define, pastors will become cocooned in their own estimate of human nature and behaviour. They risk losing the immediate 'as if' both of their theology and of the lives of those with whom they are dealing. Pastors who are alert to sociological factors will also become aware not only that their theology is being done within a social context but also that it is interacting with that context. It will, therefore, be assuming the form of a contemporary social structure. Again, however, whereas the sociological interpretation is concerned with the analysis of what is happening, the theological one will include some sense of the potential in any situation and of the consequences that may follow from any interpretation and decision.

A recent example is found in some of the studies that occurred around the Church of England's report on urban priority areas, *Faith in the City* (1985). Ahern and Davie (1987) examined some of the social reality behind figures which suggested that over 70 per cent of British people believed in God but that less than 10 per cent attended church. This is not merely an interesting sociological statistic. It is also a theological issue, which needs both theological investigation and practical decisions about ministry to follow. What does such a figure imply about our knowledge of God, the world and the Church? How is the Church to structure itself for ministry and mission in the light of such a discovery? Davie later drew attention to the connection between believing and belonging (Davie 1994). The discussion, like all sociological exploration, can be disputed. But even if the interpretation is questionable, the fact that such data has been assembled and that such a construction has been put upon it challenges the pastoral theologian. He or she may be able to offer another, even a better, understanding. But without first engaging with the proposed hypothesis, pastors will be deprived of a key stimulus to reflection and ministry. And without that, pastors are unlikely to be able to grasp what is happening to them at moments of ministry (see Chapter 9).

SOCIOLOGY AND MINISTRY

Historically the study of sociology has seemed to tend towards determinism. What apparently is the case can easily be confused with what ought to be or ought not to be. The shift from description to prescription is not always subtle. Some work on religion has tended to be less value-free than the authors have thought. The use of statistics may at times have been casual, especially in the way that like has not been compared with like. But all these strictures can as easily be applied to theologians. Nineteenth-century writers, for instance, may have had a tendency to think that their scheme was somehow self-contained and in an absolute sense 'true'. The debate about the place of theology as an academic discipline which has taken place throughout the twentieth century and is still not ended raises the issue of the extent to which theology itself is an autonomous – we might say 'value-free' – study (Farley 1988). Nevertheless, awareness of the sociological interpretations of religion and of society will remind pastors

76

of three obvious aspects to their ministry, which are easily overlooked.

1   All ministry takes place within a specific social context. This, however, cannot be defined by reference to the here-and-now alone. It is easy to convince ourselves that we understand the past. This is sometimes, especially by religious people, taken to be obvious. Sweeping generalizations about the present may result. But as the complexity revealed through sociological analysis makes clear, these are often erroneous and always inadequate. The warning for practising ministers is that they are less in control of what they themselves signify than they may realize. For instance, one-to-one pastoral counselling may be thought of in psychological terms. But that aspect to interpretation cannot be used to exclude one at the sociological level (Selby 1983). Unless pastors are aware of the multiple dimensions to their activity, when one alone comes to their attention they are likely to be flummoxed. The inevitable response then is more likely to be denial than learning.

2   One interesting effect of the wide generalizations which occurred in the early sociology of religion has been that subsequent work has been more precise. It is in some ways less bold and often less entertaining. However, this precision is important for pastors. A sociological approach to ministry might, for instance, direct attention to the wide-ranging idea of the priest. The associated themes of power in society, influence and authority, as well as the current weakness of the priest's role, may all emerge. Whatever a minister's personal theology of ministry, such a general description of the role of priest may be both helpful in enlarging horizons and challenging in questioning assumptions. There is, however, a negative side. It might so widen the believed scope of ministry that any vision is felt to be beyond grasp. At this point the theologian allies with contemporary sociological tendencies and becomes specific and precise. Some of the limits to belief and activity are provided by the fact that these are *Christian* ministers, that is, they have a specific vocation with distinctive ways of thinking about themselves and what they are doing.

3   The extent of ministry is continually drawn to the pastor's attention, he or she remains aware of a sociological perspective on ministry. A major insight from this way of thinking

is the extent to which all human activities are interactive. Early sociological and psychological approaches in terms of cause and effect were simplistic. But they do not apply when dealing with people. The minister is affected by, even changed by, any encounter as much as the client. What is more, their meeting comes about without a precise beginning which can be defined. For in each of them there is a long and unknown (and usually unknowable) history. Similarly it is without end, in that the impact of the moment may have (we probably can be more sure and say, will have) subsequent repercussions.

For the theologian these three perceptions have immediate theological resonances. Here they can only be indicated. They will be explored in later chapters of this book, especially Part 3.

1   The idea that ministers control events less than they think points to the fall and to the nature of the sin of pride. There is a necessary perversity in human relations which it is a pastor's duty to recognize. 'Septic human relationships cannot survive in an antiseptic bath of psycho-social formaldehyde' (Kavanagh 1979, 14). It is also the pastor's role to speak of salvation. This is not about taking control but about locating ourselves in a multi-dimensional world within which and over which is God.

2   Sociological awareness leads to specificity, not generalizations. The oscillation between what is general and what is specific is the daily concern of any thinking Christian. One who, for instance, regularly repeats one of the creeds will be reminded of broad generalizations: the succinct statements are underpinned by tracts of theology. At the same time, the brief statement is a reference point for reflection and action in specific situations. We may believe, for example, in salvation. But what this means – what it means to be 'saved' – for ourselves and others in any situation has always to be worked anew. While, therefore, in daily life general terms such as 'religion', 'the divine' and 'God', have a necessary place, the pastor will also be driven to consider what in any circumstance is the particular application of the Christian message that 'God was (and is) in Christ'.

3   Lastly, the interactive nature of ministry both raises questions and arouses insights about the momentary nature of the gospel. Good news is generated in particular moments and has an effect beyond that encounter. It also encourages

reflection on the way in which, perhaps, the Holy Spirit is not discovered in isolation but always somewhere in the interstices of human life. 'The God of the gaps' used to be spoken of disparagingly and rightly, since the phrase was used of a God who was invoked to fill holes in human knowledge. On the other hand, since gaps – interactive spaces between people – are the essence of human encounter as revealed through sociological insight, we have here a new version of that idea which the pastoral theologian can profitably explore and illuminate (Taylor 1972).

CONCLUSION

Psychology and sociology are complementary. The relationship between each and both of these disciplines can be explored with comparative ease. They employ similar methods of study and the object in both cases is human behaviour. When theology is added there is a tension. The object of study, even in pastoral studies, is not human behaviour for its own sake. It is that behaviour within the context of a belief system about God and his world. Practitioners of the human sciences adopt a stance of methodological atheism. But this option is not open to the pastoral theologian. It is not, therefore, surprising that some see an irresolvable tension between the 'believing' work of pastors and theologians and the unbelief of sociologists and psychologists. But this is not helpful to the pastor, who can benefit from the provocation of the behavioural sciences. It is essential that pastors and pastoral theologians struggle with these tensions.

However, a practical point now arises. The amount of work required to be abreast of any discipline today is phenomenal. Practising pastors certainly cannot keep abreast of developments in these disciplines. In so far as, then, they feel the need to be in touch with insights from the human and theological sciences, they also need a coherent model by which to hold these together in such a fashion that they can be used. It is, therefore, to the search for such a model that we now turn.

CHAPTER FOUR

Dynamic Theories and Pastoral Studies

A dream of twentieth-century science has been the discovery of a unified field theory. This would hold together the basic laws of physics. Two fields may be linked, such as gravitation and mechanics in the general theory of relativity. But so far no theory seems capable of combining more without diminishing the importance of some piece of data or without illegitimately comparing like with unlike. The same is true in behavioural studies. Psychologists, anthropologists and sociologists have produced a vast amount of data and many theories about the same basic material – human behaviour. From time to time one or other of these disciplines enlarges one of its fields and combines into something new. One instance would be the way that social psychology emerges and allies with sociology. But still there is no unifying theory of human behaviour.

For some engaged professionally in any one of these disciplines this might be a cause for regret. For others it will be a stimulus to research. Pastoral theologians and ministers, however, are denied both luxuries. They have to absorb the insights of these various disciplines and hold them sufficiently together to be able to work with people. But they also have to avoid so canonizing one theory or stance that they exclude others. As we have already seen, psychology and sociology are for the student of pastoral studies complementary disciplines. So ministers require a way of holding these disciplines and theology together. This aspiration need not be a dream. It is possible to find one, provided we recognize that it will inevitably be incomplete and that we keep it under constant scrutiny from both the behavioural and the theological perspectives.

STUDYING GROUP BEHAVIOUR

From the study of the psychology of the individual we have learned about unconscious motivations. From sociology we have been alerted to such large dimensions as culture and society and their impact on people's behaviour. To hold these perspectives together the pastor needs a way of thinking that pays due attention both to unconscious behaviour and to the social dimensions of life. The obvious point at which the individual and social dimensions coincide is the group.

A significant aspect of research in the twentieth century has been the study of behaviour in groups. Some studies arose from dissatisfaction with the limitations of individual therapy. Group analysis and therapy began, bringing together the social and individual dimensions (de Maré 1972). Research was also stimulated by the two world wars. After the First World War many felt dissatisfied with the diagnosis of cowardice or shell shock to describe the behaviour of some soldiers. Among mass casualties, why pick out a few individuals? Later, in the Second World War, more sophisticated weapons were man-ufactured. These placed greater reliance on the individual soldier. Consequently the focus of study became the collabo-ration that was demanded between men in a unit. Each individual soldier had to be affirmed, but as a member of a team. For this sort of fighting new styles of leadership were required. Changes were, therefore, brought about in the way that officers were selected. Leadership, it was perceived, might not be so much a gift or charism as a function of the way that a person and a group interacted – several articles describing this story may be found in Pines (1985).

Parallel to these developments, industrial societies, both the old ones of the west and the emerging ones in the east, were being built on the basis of new social assumptions. Workers refused to be treated as a commodity. But if they were to be given individual recognition as people, how were complicated industrial organizations to be made to work? All these factors combined to make the second half of the twentieth century a period when close attention has been paid to the group as a point of interaction between the individual and the social aspects of people's lives (Sofer 1961; Rice 1963; Jaques 1989; 1991; Miller 1993).[1] The interaction of social systems and individual psychology has been carefully examined (Jaques 1955; Menzies 1967). Many churches have been caught up in this learning and have altered their selection processes and augmented their programmes of lay and clergy training.

Study developed quietly during the 1930s when, after the great depression, people in the new public social and health services hoped for change in society, both its leadership and management. Simultaneously a new generation of psychoanalysts was exploring child development from the earliest years. Classical analysis dealt with adults and explored their remembered and fantasized early experiences. These analysts, however, were dealing with young children whose parents were still actively involved in their lives. These studies were pioneered by Melanie Klein†, who published *The Psychoanalysis of Children* in 1932. More original work on groups occurred after the Second World War. Several models emerged. There was interest in groups for their own sake. How does a group adjust internally as it responds to a changing environment? Questions of leadership in organizations explicitly explored how individuals take assigned or assumed roles in groups. Other researchers studied how people make choices within groups. What is the relationship between an individual's wishes and expectations and the behaviour of the group as a whole? As in most fields of study of human behaviour, there were both major conflicts between people working in the same field and more common purpose and discovery than this outline might suggest. In this climate arose a rich and new interest in groups and in social interaction. This still potentially provides a unifying model by which we may consider pastoral activity without denying respective importance of theology, psychology or sociology.

Studies in the application of thinking about groups diverged into two general directions, which should be distinguished:

BASIC SKILLS TRAINING

This approach emphasizes the group as a supportive context for affirming individual self-learning. The style of study is widely known as the 'T-group'. It arose in the USA, where the National Training Laboratory in Group Development held summer workshops in Bethel, Maine. These began in 1947 and still continue. The model has been taken over by others and is widely employed in industry, education and the churches.

A T-group consists of 12-25 members, together with a trainer and often an assistant. The aim is to learn about groups and how to become more effective in them.

There are two main goals of the T-Group which can be indivisible in operation: (1) that group members become more aware of the enabling and disabling factors in decision making in groups and of their own behaviours and feelings in groups; (2) that group members utilize the group as a crucible for increasing their repertoire of skills in managing group processes and their own behaviours in groups. (Bennis 1964, 272)

GROUP RELATIONS TRAINING

In this approach the group collectively attempts to develop itself into a distinctive culture or society in which the members may learn about the contexts in which they work and so become more effective in them. The phrase 'group relations training' is used because there is no other proper description of the alternative direction that group studies took. But it is inadequate to describe the richness of consultation and interpretation that this stance has spawned. The T-group tended towards support for the individual. By contrast group relations studies became more concerned with authority and how it is exercised, with roles within groups, and with groups as microcosmic societies or cultures. A similar laboratory method emerged, in which, however, the members of a learning conference were offered a range of groups to which to belong (Rice 1965; Miller 1989). The approach is distinctively associated with the Tavistock Institute of Human Relations in England, the A. K. Rice Institute in America and similar institutes throughout the world.

Underlying both models, however, is the belief that the group itself has intrinsic importance. Although there are disputes about the relative emphasis to be placed on the group and on the individual, the crucial discovery was the impact of the group on the life of individuals and an increasing recognition that the individual cannot be separated from his or her context. Psychological and sociological perspectives cannot be divorced and have to be held together: 'The individual is a creature of the group, the group of the individual' (Miller and Rice 1967, 17).

Two names should particularly be noted, Kurt Lewin† and Wilfred Bion†. They did not work together. But their separate insights have subsequently been combined to produce a way of considering individual, group and society congruently. It also offers an approach that is sufficiently unifying to be used in pastoral studies and by pastors. The term which is usually used to describe this development is 'group dynamics'. As with every aspect of the behavioural sciences, the phrase is often misunderstood and can be misleading. Thinking about groups, however, was taken up by others who worked with organizations, including the churches. Organizational consultancy is one of the applied sciences of the twentieth century. It has usually comprised a mix of concern to maximize workers' efficiency and attention to their welfare. A. K. Rice and E. J. Miller, both anthropologists by training, collaborated to produce seminal thinking in this field and developed what has become known as the 'socio-technical approach' (Miller and Rice 1967; Silverman 1970). The ideas have been applied to a wide range of institutions (Miller 1976; Lawrence 1979; Miller 1993;[2] Obholzer and Roberts 1994). The reason for such wide application is threefold:

1 Attention is paid to human behaviour, whatever the context in which it occurs. Since there is no institution that is not made up of human beings, all institutions can be examined using this model as a starting point;

2 Care is taken to address not superficial presentations but the underlying processes that they represent. Whatever the form of the organization, therefore, and whatever its distinctive task, it can be addressed;

3 The issues which emerge are usually those of authority and how it is exercised, leadership and where it is located, formally and informally, and the organizational structure that results. These problems are common to any institution.

A GROUP APPROACH

Lewin initially worked in Gestalt psychology in which the key idea is that an organized whole may possess qualities which are different from those of each of its components. The parts are therefore secondary to the whole. Much of the first experimental work in Gestalt was on perception. Lewin, however, saw that the theory could also be applied to human behaviour. After 1933 he spent the rest of his life in the United States. There he developed ways of exploring the complex processes of social interaction through laboratory experiments with groups and individuals. His seminal insight, now largely taken for granted, was that a person's behaviour is a function both of individuals and of the way that they perceive their environment. The two aspects are inseparable. In 1944/5 he founded the Research Center for Group Dynamics (possibly the first use of this phrase) in order to study the forces that may assist or resist change in groups.

Although not as well known as Lewin outside the fields of group relations and psychoanalysis, Bion possessed a seminal mind. From 1948 onwards he published a series of papers which were later collected in *Experiences in Groups* (1961). He developed a series of ideas about groups which addressed several issues which were becoming apparent to researchers at the time and which remain central to any group experience. These are (Thelen 1985):

1 That groups have periods in which they are dominated by different moods. However much we may try and predict what may happen, it often seems that unpredictable behaviour follows from nothing other than a mood. This behaviour is not explicable. It is a commonplace of human experience that sometimes a group 'works' and sometimes it does not.

2 That the concept of the group as an entity in itself rather than as a collection of individuals is essential when we think and behave as social beings. This, too, is an everyday experience. We often find ourselves caught up in something that seems to involve us profoundly even if we do not give our personal consent. A mob is an obvious instance, but many less intense instances occur. The only way of beginning to speak about and interpret them is to assign primacy to the group.

3 That the laws, if there are such, which govern group life will be about change. They will be concerned with the continually shifting balance of forces in the group and the constantly changing culture of the group. 'Culture' means here the group's assumed values and purposes. These need not be expressed but are nevertheless adhered to by the members.

4 Lastly, that feelings – what is sometimes called 'affective behaviour' – are a direct means of communication. Members of a group sense them non-verbally and feel them with uncanny directness. This implies that emotions become primary data rather than something that lies behind so-called objective behaviour. Again, on reflection, there is little startling in this: most people have felt unexpressed emotions which do not seem directly to belong to them but which are felt corporately in a group or by individuals on behalf of the group.

Bion's original studies were with therapeutic groups. He soon moved, however, to consider groups of strangers by giving them the obvious, but until then not considered, task of studying themselves. One problem then, as in all subsequent work on the same basis, was the unclear notion of task that this implied. 'What are we here *for?*' was and is a frequently asked question. But the absence of the familiar ideas of task and aim enabled Bion's groups to explore some of the underlying and unconscious activity that goes on in every group of human beings. From the 1940s links were established between Lewin's Center and Bion's work, which led to a new approach. The chief outcome of this study has been an approach to thinking about human behaviour which links in a coherent frame the individual, the groups to which we belong, and those larger units such as society.

THE INDIVIDUAL AND THE GROUP DYNAMIC

Bion discerned that any group of people in principle functioned in the same way as the individual. He took the basic discovery of the unconscious and some allied ideas and related them to group behaviour. People function essentially at two complementary but separable levels: conscious activity and unconscious motivations. For most of the time the two are in some sort of harness, often uneasy but essential for living. When the link breaks down in the individual the conditions arise for a debilitating neurosis or a dangerous psychosis.[3]

The same applies to people in groups. A group works with its conscious intention – why it has formed and what it wishes or intends to achieve. Bion called this the 'work group'. But simultaneously the group is also operating at an unconscious level with what he called 'basic assumptions'. This term has not been bettered, but it can be misleading. The idea of an 'assumption' may seem to imply the deliberate adoption of a stance of which we may be aware. But 'basic assumption' refers to unconscious activity of which the members of a group are not usually aware but which can be interpreted when attention is drawn to it.

> ... no individual, however isolated in time and space, can be regarded as outside a group or lacking in active mani-festations of group psychology, although conditions do not exist which would make it possible to demonstrate it. Acceptance of the idea that the human being is group animal would solve the difficulties that are felt to exist in the seeming paradox that a group is more than the sum of its members. The explanation of certain phenomena must be sought in the matrix of the group and not in the indi-viduals that go to make up the group. Time-keeping is no function of any part, in isolation, of the mechanism of a clock, yet time-keeping is a function of the clock and of the various parts of the clock when held in combination with each other. There is no more need to be confused by the impression that a group is more than the sum of its members than it would be to be confused by the idea that a clock is more than a collection of the parts that are necessary to make a clock. (Bion 1961, 132f)

As with the individual, there is a constant tension in every group between its work and its basic assumption life. Some congruence between the two aspects of the group's life produces reasonable harmony and competent activity. If there is not, however, disarray ensues.

Bion discerned three basic assumptions. A full exposition goes beyond the scope of this study. They need to be noted, however, since the theory provides pastors with a way of integrating individual, group and larger contexts such as organizations or even society.

DEPENDENCE

This basic assumption prevails when a group believes that its members have come together to gratify their own needs for reassurance. The emotion takes the group corporately back to the primitive individual need for assurance, which is most obviously shown in the mother/child relationship. The growing child needs sufficient certainty to feel secure enough to take risks, such as that of venturing into an unknown world. This basic assumption is a good example of why they are value-free. Dependence is necessary. Human beings cannot exist or grow without it. Yet there is always the danger that as it is invoked it may become irrational and destructive. When this happens an individual or an institution (such as a church) or an idea (such as a gospel) can be treated as if it were ultimately the sole source of all gratification. Then individuals surrender their responsibility for themselves and become in the pejorative sense 'dependent'. Most ministers will have experienced this in a group. It is particularly prevalent in churches, where, for instance, the preaching of people's necessary and appropriate dependence upon God can be transformed into an infantilizing and debilitating holding of people in a collusive form of dependent weakness.

FIGHT/FLIGHT

The members of a group where this predominates feel that they are gathered either to confront or escape from any leadership. Work is ignored as this struggle takes over the group's energy. This is a double assumption: it is not either 'fight' or 'flight'. In everyday language the two are opposites. But in the unconscious activity of a group the underlying dynamic of both attitudes is the same. To run away or to attack are both unconscious responses to a situation which feels threatening. Fight or flight are both ways of self-protection. Under the influence of this basic assumption the group feels ambivalent. It is impossible to be sure what it will do, since the feelings involved are usually intense and individuals within the group are volatile, ambitious but also invigorating.

PAIRING

When a group's life is founded on this assumption, it believes that if the group can produce an idealized pair, they will generate a miraculous solution to the problems facing it. In a sense pairing is an aspect of dependence. A dependent group seeks an individual to remove its problems of authority. When pairing prevails it looks for a pair to produce the longed-for messianic or saviour figure. When serious divisions occur in a group it may not so much look for a person or institution on which to rely as to some pair to resolve the problems.

AN INTEGRATIVE APPROACH

The theory of basic assumptions uniquely links irrational and rational processes both in the individual and in the group. The group may be any size, from the first organization which we experience, the family (even when only one parent, for whatever reason, brings up a child, in the mind of that child there are two parents and something called 'the family'), to vast concepts such as society (Khaleelee and Miller 1985; Shapiro and Carr 1992). This theory is not a complete explanation of human behaviour. That claim would be both foolish and grandiose. But it provides pastors and theologians with a means of holding together, both theoretically and practically, those insights into the individual and society which have been generated by the behavioural sciences during the twentieth century. Specifically, when this approach is adopted – and even more when it becomes instinctive – six things follow:

1   The pastor is forced to hold together in his or her mind both the individual and the social context in which the encounter is occurring. Ministers cannot sacrifice one or the other. What is more, this approach always enlarges the context of meeting. It may appear to begin, for instance, with an individual. But it is happening in a specific context and that setting, too, is part of a wider social or cultural context. The pastor cannot, therefore, oversimplify the encounter.

2   The minister is constantly reminded of the context. Since there is no such person as the individual apart from the context, then in practice a large perspective is essential. This, as we shall see, does not mean that it is offered always

to the client. But it is part of the minister's working tools for two basic reasons. First, it is a reminder of the reality that however intimate the meeting may appear (for example, a formal act of confession), it is always more than that. Second, this approach prevents the minister losing his or her theological perspective. For in any meeting the minister represents the context of belief, of God and the Church.

3 That which feels disparate – and we should not underestimate the disarray that pastoring sometimes induces – is brought together. The approach brings together those parts of human life which are integral to the minister's activity but which often feel disparate. For example, what at any moment is the relation between the individual and the group? Or, as pastors might consider, how do they connect individual belief and idiosyncrasy with the corporate expression of faith in the Church? The question is endemic to Christian belief. It cannot be finally answered. But the pastor has continually to address it. Or again, how do we evaluate claimed faith and belief in relation to psychological tendencies or even types? Is there a connection between feelings and faith? And what psychological or sociological function do we assign to belief? These are both major questions for the theologian and day-to-day material for the pastor. And what about the notion of 'the Church'? What is the connection between the organization which is necessary to produce an institution and the Christian imperative to freedom? Ministers, for example, may only be allowed to do their work in so far as they let themselves be seen as representatives of an institution – the Church. Yet often they will wish as a pastoral stratagem, or even in response to their own experience of pastoral ministry, to distance themselves from that church.

4 Because the minister is aware of so many levels of activity – especially the unconscious behaviour of the individual and the way in which that can be a factor in the basic assumption behaviour of the group – he or she will always be encouraged to listen for that which is not being said. This is not to cultivate scepticism but to adopt a stance that is sympathetic to the fact that the client has come in the first place.

5 The Church, as we shall see, is an important 'institution in the mind' when someone meets a pastor, especially an

ordained person. This approach takes seriously the organizational context in which meetings occur and, what is more, the impact of those meetings in contributing to the developing shape of the organization.

6 This approach draws attention to the importance not just of the people involved in ministry but to their roles. It is here that the working difference between lay and ordained ministers can be explored in terms of ecclesiology and ministry instead of ideologically.

CONCLUSION

How all these areas are worked is the substance of the remainder of the book. It would be naive to suggest that Bion's theory of the individual, the group, society, basic assumptions and work groups and its elaboration magically solves such problems. It would also be nonsense. Yet pastors need a working framework by which to hold together as best they may the disparate aspects of their activity. These ideas are useful for that purpose. In particular they draw attention to the way that every human being lives within a set of human institutions which can each be thought of in a systemic fashion. For example, a family is a system of interacting parts. Members are not only themselves; they also represent facets of that system. Anyone, therefore, working with a family needs some sense of this model and a way of holding the various aspects together without losing sight of the whole. The systemic approach derived from the theory offered in this chapter is one way of doing this. Work with dysfunctional families that is called by some 'family therapy' is today increasingly being thought of as 'systems intervention' (Box et al. 1981). Similarly a church, whatever its distinctively denominational shape, can be thought of as a functioning system in a state of some sort of dynamic equilibrium.[4]

One mark of the socio-technical approach is that theoretical writing on it is quite difficult to grasp, whereas case studies are very illuminating. It is the same with the study of groups and social systems. During the process many lively moments occur. But if these are subsequently written up they either seem obvious or obscure. Instead, therefore, of taking this discussion further here, we shall turn to the final resource for the pastoral theologian, theology itself. The way in which dynamic theories inform pastoral studies will then emerge in the practicalities of the chapters that follow.

CHAPTER FIVE

Theological Resources
for Pastoral Studies

It would be strange in a book on pastoral studies not specifically to include theology among the tools. Theology is ministry's ultimately distinguishing discipline. Counsellors and social workers utilize the insights of the human sciences. They are expected to know about these things. When ministers employ these skills to inform their pastoral activity they are not expected to be noted for their knowledge of the behavioural sciences. But they are required to know about God, that is, to be theologians.

What are the distinctive theological resources of the pastor, whether lay or ordained? This question is difficult. In one sense all Christians, whatever their vocation and activity, are theologians: they think about life and their existence by paying specific attention to belief in God and an eternal perspective. For most of the time the matter is probably given little thought, although in worship and prayer it becomes overt. Or a crisis may direct them to the question, 'What is it to be Christian now?' That is not just a matter of applying faith: it is a theological question, the response to which may not only affect the lives of people involved but also add to the body of the faith. In other words, it is, however humble, a theological activity.

This observation, therefore, leads to our asking what the professional distinction in theological learning may be for the ordained minister. This lies not in the amount or quality of theological knowledge. In many cases people who are not pastors, and certainly many who are not ordained, will have greater theological learning than the authorized minister.

The difference lies in the expectations that are held of them. A theologically learned lay person may have many expectations invested in him or her. But in the last resort he or she will not be required to represent the Church and its theological tradition in the way that ministers are believed to do, however inadequate their learning. Pastors, whether they choose or not, are theologians, less because of any knowledge than because the belief focuses in them that they represent the Christian tradition. The pastor's theological resource, therefore, is the whole Christian tradition, not only as it is (if there could ever be such a summary) but also as it is believed to be – a much more complex issue. In this chapter, therefore, we shall consider that resource in principle. The elaboration of detailed doctrines is the minister's work of a lifetime.

The days when theology, the 'queen of the sciences', united and transcended all knowledge are long gone. It now has to struggle for recognition as a discipline among the range of sciences. Many of these, as we have seen, are not new. Much that they incorporate has in previous ages been subsumed under the heading of philosophy or theology. They have become new in the way that they have been refined and used in the last two centuries. The danger for theologians, however, especially pastors, is that in response to this array of '-ologies', including those which distinctively impact on the pastor's ministry, theology might be simplified into something that it is not – a unified body of received learning.

THEOLOGY IN PASTORAL STUDIES

In pastoral studies theology has often been considered as much a matter of approach as of content. Applied theology naturally puts considerable emphasis on the context within which it is being generated. Four main emphases may be discerned, although there are many variants on them. They are not discussed in any order of priority.

THE BIBLE AND TRADITION

What the Scripture or the Church (whatever form that authority takes) has to say on a topic has been universally reckoned important. This tends to produce a one-to-one approach to theology and pastoral issues. The question is first asked: 'What does the Bible (tradition) have to say on this topic?' The answer is as best as may be applied to the current situation. This stance is simplistic but understandable. Amid the confusions of human life it retains the believed objectivity of the Scripture or the tradition. Its weakness, however, is twofold. First, the question being asked may not be one that either Scripture or tradition has ever addressed. As a result the response, if not odd, is at best general. It is often expressed in terms of love, grace or judgement. On the whole the Bible and tradition are not clear guides to the detail of contemporary living. Second, this approach overlooks the developments in hermeneutical study. Apart from fundamentalists and those approaching that position, Christians everywhere have recently explored much more how Scripture and tradition are to be interpreted. Pastoral activity is not immune from this learning, or at least it should not be.

NARRATIVE THEOLOGY

This approach emphasizes the importance of story. Its theological foundations lie in contemporary biblical studies and the way they employ discussion about the basic structure of human experience. The biblical authors use a range of literary devices to invite their hearers and readers to share in the story being told (McKnight 1988). In pastoral work there are two main stories: that which generates the situation being addressed and that from the tradition which is brought alongside as the interpretative tool. If the biblical approach is marked by excessive attention to the supposedly objective criterion of Scripture, this one is in danger of too much subjectivism. The story from the situation inevitably involves both the subject who tells and the one who hears. The selection of the narrative aspect of the tradition as an interpretative vehicle is also subjective. The approach, therefore, risks becoming collusive as the material used is selected. The challenge is to bring alongside the situation something, another story, so that the tradition can function critically. A problem, however, is that the tradition, including Scripture, is not all amenable to being thought of as story. The result is a restricted use of the tradition. Nevertheless there is a distinguished tradition of such story-telling in theology and pastoral work, and as a pastoral activity there is much to commend this way of thinking.

CORRELATION

This has become increasingly popular as a way of doing pastoral theology. It has much in common with the praxis stance which is found in liberation theology and its derivatives. It owes much of its theological legitimacy to the work of David Tracy (1981). The explicit application to pastoral care has been particularly worked out by Donald Browning (1976; 1983; 1991). The emphasis is shifted from right thinking to proper action. Correlation pays attention to the human sciences, using them as a means of bringing together – correlating – a specific pastoral situation and the Christian tradition. But unlike the two previous approaches, on this basis both the experience presented and the tradition invoked are interpreted through these human sciences. Different insights are derived from different sources. So, for example, three aspects of the 'tradition' are brought together.

1 The Bible, although this will be read not as obviously authoritative but as performing a normatively critical function for believers to test both their adherence to the faith and their present understanding of it.

2 The tradition itself. The Christian faith has not only evolved over the 2,000 years of its history. It has also grappled with different demands on it, especially those arising from new and different contexts. Knowledge, therefore, of the richness of this history, not as dates and facts but as instances of interaction between the Church and its context, is essential to this approach. It encourages pastors to contextualize themselves and what is happening in the pastoral situation.

3 The pastor's felt experience, not least his feelings about what may be happening between him and the client or even in the client alone.

Scripture, tradition and experience are thus brought together, coalescing around the presenting issue that the pastor is dealing with. And this approach must always issue in action. It is sometimes suggested that this stance assigns insufficient prominence to the gospel. This key issue is discussed later. But unlike the previous two methods, the purpose of the pastor's theology on this model is to inform him. It remains covert. Its public expression is in whatever the pastor does or recommends and in the action that results from the encounter. The pastor does the correlating to himself so that he may be used by the client.

A GOAL-ORIENTED APPROACH

When the question is asked why think theologically at all, the answer is not as obvious as might be hoped. Some pastors, for instance, seem to be quite effective as counsellors without displaying knowledge of any theology. And pastoral care and concern has been effective for centuries without pastors being theologically or behaviourally literate. It is, however, no use longing for such a past or believing that it can be recreated.

One effect of the growth of knowledge since the Enlightenment and of the increasing compartmentalizing of learning into different disciplines has been that knowledge itself has become fragile. Theology is not immune. Farley offers this definition of theology:

> *Theology is the reflectively procured insight and understanding which encounter with a specific religious faith evokes.* Note the elements of the definition. First, it presupposes the historically incarnated or determinate character of religious faith ... Second, understanding is the sort of thing theology itself is. Accordingly, theology is primarily an understanding and only secondarily a science or a discipline ... Third, theology occurs in a reflective mode. It is not simply the spontaneous insightfulness that may be generated by participation in or encounter with a specific faith. Theological understanding is *considered* understanding ... Finally, that which evokes the understanding is encounter with the faith. (Farley 1988, 64f)

This distinction between a science and an understanding is useful. It connects theological learning, especially that needed by the pastor, with wisdom and the experiential foundations of faith – prayer and worship. It also reminds individuals that they are part of a community of faith. For encounter with the faith must involve meeting in some way the community of those who have held and of those who still hold that faith. Such a meeting is, as we shall later explore, the essential quality of many pastoral encounters. In an earlier work Farley (1983) called the aim of such theology '*habitus*'. This term originated in anthropology (Bourdieu 1977) and refers to the assumption of a way of life that consistently brings to bear in considered understanding the experiences and the tradition with which the Christian lives. According to this approach the goal of any theological activity will be a new or different way of life as much for the pastor as for the client.

AN EXAMPLE OF THEOLOGY IN
PASTORAL STUDIES – PREACHING

We may take the instance of preaching to illustrate these different approaches. This is a pastoral activity, in that it involves interpretation of life. Unlike what is often assumed to be pastoral work it takes place not with the one-to-one meeting but in a large group setting, that is, over approximately twenty people.

THE BIBLICAL APPROACH

Using the biblical approach the preacher would quote texts. By so doing he or she announces that they have an intrinsic authority. The act of quotation itself conveys the message. Such preaching can still be heard. But for it to be effective the predisposition of the hearers to invest the quotation with such meaning is vital. Hence in some churches the congregation is expected to exclaim 'Amen' or 'Alleluia' throughout the sermon as the familiar language resonates with them. This one-to-one approach with Scripture (and with appropriate modifications it is also true of those who preach on the basis of what 'the Church teaches') is unlikely to reach much beyond the community of believers. Its strength is that by reference to the Bible the preacher is likely to have God in mind. The weakness is that such biblicism may lead to a worship of the book or at best irrelevance to the contemporary lives of the hearers.

THE NARRATIVE APPROACH

This style of preaching appears when the preacher tells a

story from current life and brings a biblical story or some-thing from the creed alongside. The emphasis is frequently on the Kingdom of God and the stories are usually taken from the Gospels. Parables lend themselves to such analogical use, as they always have (Jeremias 1963). But the rest of Scrip-ture (especially the more dogmatic material) is less accessible and so less often used. Such preaching is often subjective, the story being the preacher's own story. Harry Williams fam-ously determined never to preach about anything that went beyond his experience. There are great strengths to this preaching, as Williams's writing show (Williams 1969; 1972). The limitations are that the preacher may end up addressing only himself.

THE CORRELATIVE APPROACH

Most preachers probably adopt this style today and it is expected by most hearers. Steeping themselves in the Bible (often as selected given by a lectionary), studying the tradition (by following the text through commentaries) and listening to the voice of their own experiences (through the pastoral ministry of the week), such preachers expect to engage their hearers. They frequently do. The point of engagement is chiefly around what the people, having heard all this, are now to do. A good example may be found in the sermons of John Bowker (1991).

A GOAL-ORIENTED APPROACH

The fourth stance produces preaching which oscillates between the life of the community of faith, as expressed in the past and the present, and the contemporary experience of people. It is likely to begin with the latter, so that these experiencing people (the abstract notion of experience for its own sake is eschewed) may be brought into contact with the faith. The medium may be preaching, although this form is a characteristic of broadcast addresses. But often it will be liturgy – the process and content of worship and prayer. Through such experiencing of two worlds – life and the com-munity of faith – new faith is generated and custom (*habitus*) develops.

THE THEOLOGICAL TOOLS

When practising ministers discuss theology they sometimes imply that pastors only need enough theology to see them through. Academic theologians are dismissed to their ivory towers. Working ministers disclaim any need for much technical learning. They may also suggest that they have little or nothing to contribute to the Church's theological enterprise. The supposed sophistication of the professor is contrasted with the rough working theology of the pastor. No amount of resisting this dichotomy seems to have much effect. Yet every type of theology takes some starting point. There is no such thing as 'theology' in the abstract. This discussion, although familiar, is always suspect.

Theologians, wherever they are working, have two assigned tasks: to elicit doctrinal development and to elucidate doctrine. These tasks go hand in hand. The theologian – defined for the moment as someone who thinks about the faith professed – is responsible for development in the tradition. As contexts change and understandings differ, so there is the need constantly to reinterpret the faith, discovering what developments are afoot and critically examining them. In so doing the theologian will also, especially through this examination, elucidate doctrine. The two approaches may be seen as aspects of the two concepts of tradition that co-exist in Christianity (see pp. 27ff, above). What is handed on (*paradosis*) lies at the heart of the faith. No-one today believes from cold. They believe because others have already believed. The content handed on is given formal expression in the creeds and other documents of the faith. These demand the second theological task, that of elucidation. Elucidation follows from the content of what is handed on; development pays closer attention to the process of handing on and receiving. Both these senses of 'tradition' occupy all theologians. They stand in a tradition which they have received, and so elucidate it, and at the same time contribute to it, and thus ensure development. The two tasks are complementary, neither has primacy. Obviously some thinkers will tend towards one or the other. But no theologians are immune from both senses of the tradition that they handle.

On this basis types of theology have over the centuries

been categorized. The different categories overlap and there is continuing debate about them. But among them we may usefully list six, each of which has relevance for pastors:

NATURAL THEOLOGY

Thinkers may seek to discern what may be thought or known about God by human reason. This approach was powerful from the earliest apologists to the high point of medieval scholarship. It was, however, largely rejected by the Reformers. That disdain has been reinforced in recent times by Karl Barth† and his followers. For pastors, however, the principle of natural theology remains important, whatever its precise status. Much of the intuitive feeling after the divine or God which they encounter in ministry is more natural than revealed. In particular, the place of experience in theology is an essential dimension to the pastor's theology. Indeed, it may be that this is an area in which pastoral studies have a distinctive contribution to make to the Church's theological enterprise.

> Since living reason develops the content of experience actually had by an individual, consideration of the arguments for God from this standpoint will have to be approached in a way somewhat different from the usual. The question of the formal validity of the arguments is by no means the only question to be raised; more important is the discovery of the concrete experience behind them and the sort of intelligibility they lend to experience ... If we are to understand the full import of these arguments we cannot afford to ignore either their religious import or their foundation in experience. If these two aspects are kept in the foreground, the arguments will not be reduced to logical exercises by means of which philosophers express their secularity in refuting the arguments or their piety in defending them. (Smith 1968, 121)

SYSTEMATIC AND DOGMATIC THEOLOGY

Systematic theology, by contrast with natural theology, is more the Church's own work than that of philosophers. Believers of all types and abilities try to order the elucidation of what they believe. Pastors, therefore, are expected to be systematic. They represent the Church in such a way that as a result others, as they deal with the mixture of belief and emotion that constitutes their experience, may not have to be so systematic. The main difference between dogmatic and systematic theology is that the dogmatic emphasis is to explore what the Church teaches and has taught rather than what people have believed and do believe. But the distinction is minimal.

FUNDAMENTAL THEOLOGY

As the term implies, this approach goes behind systematic theology and investigates basic themes. These include revelation, inspiration, hermeneutics, what faith is and how it is formed and by what authority it can be articulated. Christians are regularly thrown into the realm of fundamental theology. And because pastors experience so much of religion (not especially Christianity) and of other people's experiences, they are likely to come up against the themes of fundamental theology on a day-to-day basis. Yet, as they often feel, the work which raises these issues itself reduces the time and inhibits the development of the technical ability to explore these topics in depth.

PHILOSOPHICAL THEOLOGY

This stands in particular relation to fundamental and to natural theology. The main difference is that the philosophical theologian pays more attention to the presuppositions which are made before the theological enquiry begins.

APOLOGETIC THEOLOGY

The argument for faith in general and the Christian faith is the stuff of apologetic. It is discussed in more detail in Chapter 9.

APPLIED THEOLOGY

This is what has customarily been thought of as pastoral study, together with a study of the social, political and ethical aspects of theology. As compartmentalized disciplines break down, however, it has become clearer that all theology is ultimately applied. Just as philosophy has had to take into account the more precise human sciences of the twentieth century, so theology is now required to have some sort of application. This may issue as pastoral theology, the underlying thinking that pervades the ministry of the Church. Other possibilities include more recent phenomena such as liberation and political theologies or the theology of hope. The traditional dimension of ethics remains important and is a continuing, though difficult, concern for the pastor.

There are other theologies which might be mentioned – biblical, liturgical and doxological, for example. These have generally been in the forefront of the modern notion of 'doing theology', by which is meant thinking and reflection that issues in action.

Because pastors are both Christians and public representatives of the Church, they will not be able to limit their theological endeavours to one particular type of theology. Even less should they believe that pastoral (or applied) theology is their sole concern. For instance, much pastoral work is with people on the margins of or outside the Church. These encounters bring ministers face to face with the boundary between belief and unbelief. This will be partly external, between pastor and client. It will also be internal in the way in which the pastor's own faith and the way in which it is believed and articulated are challenged. Even in the simplest pastoral encounter many if not all categories of theology are in principle likely to be disturbed:

1   What is the argument being put forward by apparent non-believers for being involved here with God, or at least the transcendent? – natural theology.

2   What dimension of the Christian faith primarily informs the minister in this encounter? – systematic and dogmatic theology.

3   What outcome is sought from this pastoral activity? – applied theology.

4   What defence of and argument for the faith (although the minister will probably conduct much of this debate with himself) does the minister offer? – apologetic theology.

PUBLIC THEOLOGY

A distinctive aspect of the pastor's contribution to theological thinking will be attention to the social context. No theology is ever isolated from the world in which it is being done. Social institutions are created through interactions. It is not, for instance, possible to conceive the Church without there being some context which is recognizably 'not-Church'. Through interaction between belief and unbelief, believer and unbeliever, including that between those aspects themselves being held ambivalently by people, the meaning of faith is discovered. An example may be taken from the family. At some point the members of a family determine a boundary at which they can say that something or someone is 'not-family' or 'not-us'. But that boundary is not a barrier to keep the rest out. It is a boundary across which transactions occur. These exchanges generate the particular family: it helps it to define itself and to be publicly acknowledged by others.

A similar process occurs with theology. It has its social contexts. It also to some extent takes on characteristics at different points in history according to the way in which it addresses and allows itself to be addressed by that context. David Tracy argues that one way by which a theological approach may be categorized is by discerning the public to which it speaks. In this he, possibly unwittingly, concurs with the interpretation that the Church is created by interaction rather than being self-defining. The theological enterprise is not self-contained; it is to a degree determined by its various publics. Tracy helpfully distinguishes three main contexts (Tracy 1981, 57ff):

THE ACADEMY

The world of the university and academic thought is primarily addressed by fundamental theology. Under this heading are subsumed natural, apologetic and philosophical theology. Such theology is noticeable for attention to what is rational and how an argument can be developed and sustained. It is also marked by an ethical stance that values honesty and enquiry. The integrity of the process is judged by the persistence of critical questioning and answering.

THE COMMUNITY OF MORAL DISCOURSE

This includes the Church but will not be exclusively defined by it. This is the concern of systematic theology. Here the thinking of the Church in its tradition as received and elaborated will be offered to those with sympathy but not necessarily belief. They are invited to subject the thinking to scrutiny and a learning partnership evolves. The arguments will be less publicly accessible than those of the academy. But the work will be one of constant reinterpretation of the faith and elaboration of the tradition in the light of the social context in which it is set. The ethical dimension to this theology will emphasize loyalty to the community of faith and critical fidelity to its ideals and beliefs. As might be expected, recent study of the nature of the congregation as the pastoral agent has drawn heavily on this concept (Browning 1991).

SOCIETY AT LARGE

Practical or applied theology addresses society. Here the issue of ethics, politics and action coalesce. Pre-eminence is given to social, political and pastoral concern, often today with a stress on praxis. The Greek form *praxis* has become more widely used than the anglicized word 'practice'. This is as a result of the influence of theologians who have stressed that true Christianity always issues in 'right action' (*orthopraxis*) rather than, as has customarily been held in the west, 'right belief' (*orthodoxy*). J. B. Metz, for example, a German theologian, remarks 'The orthodoxy of faith must be constantly verified in an operational praxis oriented toward the end of time, since the promised truth is a truth that must be *done*' (Fierro 1977, 21). The ethical emphasis will be on commitment to a cause and action on its behalf.

THE PASTOR'S THEOLOGY

Which of these theologies will the churches' ministers most require and to which will they make potentially the greatest contribution? Perhaps not surprisingly they will need to be conversant with all three major types – fundamental, systematic and practical. (For a fuller exposition of this section see Carr (1992).)

Pastors need to be alert to issues in fundamental theology because in the nature of their ministry they will constantly be presented with dilemmas in this field. Much of the pastor's ministry is about the nature of belief, whether expressed or not. The pastor handles people's capacity for faith, where revelation or truth is to be found, and how to sustain some sense of rationality in the face of irrational demands and expectations. Often the pastor meets people who not only desire to believe but also are unable to. The representative nature of pastoral ministry is most often to do with others' wish to believe. Such people consequently need to be assured that someone can and does so believe. In many encounters the question of the divine and how it (he/she) may be known is raised without reference to the technical issue of revelation. Indeed, the pastor – not least when dealing with common or folk religion – comes face to face with arguments for the existence and activity of God which owe little or nothing to anything other than what people think and feel (see Chapter 10). It may be, given the present sense of disillusionment with the post-Enlightenment world of the west and the equally problematic question of the role of those who claim a revealed faith, that from their experience with people pastors may have something to offer academic theologians. These will continue to address the academy, but will have to do so on the basis of reported and interpreted experience (Montefiore 1992).

The pastor and systematic theology naturally go together. Indeed, it may be here that the greatest contribution can be made and whence the most assistance can be derived. But ministers in their public role are distinctively members of several communities of moral discourse. They represent a known tradition, the Christian one, even if this is neither understood nor explicitly wanted as such. The pastor is expected to be not only a God person (the realm of natural theology) but specifically a believing Christian (the field of systematic theology). It is not possible to be merely religious: the representative figure is an emissary both of God and of the Christian Church. Such ministers, therefore, should be able to stand scrutiny not solely of their personal beliefs but also of those for which they are believed to stand. It is thus not optional but essential that pastors have a sound grasp of that tradition which they represent. But the theological task is both to elucidate and elicit development with the tradition. Therefore it will be on the basis of the specific experiences

within contexts that arise through pastoral activity that systematic theology will flourish.

Practical or applied theology is the pastor's lifeblood. But it
is also the key point of criticism. Pastoral studies sometimes
imply that much pastoral ministry is concerned with individuals in need. Whether it be training in spiritual direction or
in pastoral counselling, the one-to-one encounter is assumed
to dominate. This assumption is also widely shared by
members of congregations. The myth prevails that ministers
are always busy and that they spend an inordinate amount
of time dealing with individuals. In practice, however, most
of them spend little. But even if this were the usual pattern
of ministry, contemporary psychological insights emphasize
that the individual must be thought of in context. Here,
therefore, the two dimensions of pastoral activity that are
sometimes overlooked come into play – political theology and
ethical exploration.

Behind all pastoral activity lurk difficult questions of ethics
and politics. For instance, by handling the ritual element of
life in baptism, weddings and funerals, pastors proclaim a
belief about the order of the world in which birth is recognized, the couple is idealized and the value of individuals,
even if minimal, is affirmed (Carr 1994). Each of these issues
has a moral and political dimension in addition to the
pastoral. The minister may ask why he or she is engaged in
work with a disturbed person or family. It is not sufficient to
say that this is simply a response to the love of God. There is
always the question of for what purpose is this work being
done? Even if a minister does not get trapped in today's
obsession with personal meaning and growth, when counselling individuals he or she will ask what is the point of this
person's journey for the rest of the world (Browning 1976;
Selby 1983; 1991).

PRACTICAL OUTCOMES

The pastor, therefore, has potentially major theological significance for the Church as a whole. From the activity of
pastoring derive data that theologians cannot ignore in both
the elucidation and development of the tradition. Not

enough may suffuse the thinking of those whose task is to address the academy. But in terms of the community of moral discourse and society at large pastors have much to contribute. It is essential, therefore, that ministers make time to think specifically about their theological learning. The ideal of a learned pastor remains a good one.[1] Ministers need to be informed by their primary discipline, a thoughtful Christian faith. But also in them and their work with people the essential apologetic of the Church will be presented to every age.

Realistically, however, it is impossible for most pastors to sustain a consistent and wide-ranging learning programme. The working pastor's theological endeavours, therefore, need to be focused. Three main points, or 'classics', can be discerned. The notion of 'the classic' again comes from David Tracy. He points out that in every culture classics exist:

> We all find ourselves compelled both to recognize and on occasion to articulate our reasons for the recognition that certain expressions of the human spirit disclose a compelling truth about our lives that we cannot deny them some kind of normative status. Thus do we name these expressions, and these alone, 'classics' . . . what we mean in naming certain texts, events, images, rituals, symbols, and persons 'classics' is that here we recognize nothing less than the disclosure of a reality we cannot but name truth. (Tracy 1981, 108f)

Three such classics can be identified within the Christian tradition. The selection may seem arbitrary. But it is made on the basis of the interaction between aspects of the pastor's ministry and the way of life of the Christian Church that he or she represents. The three are incarnation, atonement and creation/resurrection. (This section is condensed. The full exposition may be found in Carr (1992).)

There would be no Christian faith without reference to the incarnation. This is the core revelation from which all else stems. The atonement is about the efficacy of that faith to transform lives, human nature and society. The word usually used for this process is redemption. In the Christian tradition the cross is always in some fashion the way in which this redeeming takes place. The third classic focuses on the wider revelation within which both incarnation and atonement are set. This is belief in God the Creator, which for the Christian Church is inextricably linked with the theme of God the author of the new creation – the resurrection.

These three classics influence the pastor's ministry and are influenced by it.

1 The incarnation is concerned with relationships between God and human beings as this focuses in Jesus Christ. So, for instance, the theme of Jesus Christ as *both* God *and* man is a basic tension for Christians. It cannot be relaxed, however much it is worked over. The crucial questions are: What is the difference between God and man? And how is it handled by God and by human beings? This creatively reflects the way in which we allow differences to be destructive or creative – a major issue for the pastor, not least in view of the way that difference is used in any pastoral encounter.

2 The atonement – bearing the sins of the world – points to projections and how these are borne and interpreted.

3 The underlying issue of creation/resurrection is the playfulness of God and the ordering of creation around him. This theme is ritual – a key element in pastoral ministry – and how it is employed.

Finally, as might be expected, three aspects of life in the Church – the life of discipleship – these classics and their pastoral foundation illuminate. Resurrection and ritual point to worship. Atonement and projections direct attention to what we mean by holiness or spirituality. The incarnation with the use of difference points to the bridging of the gulf through prayer in all its forms, whether as meditation, contemplation or intercession. This brief overview is presented systematically in the following table:

CLASSIC	PASTORAL IMPACT	DISCIPLESHIP
Incarnation	Using differences	Prayer
Atonement	Handling projection	Holiness and spirituality
Creation/ resurrection	Ritual	Worship

CONCLUSION

The resources for the pastor mentioned in this chapter are qualitatively different from those in the preceding three on psychology, sociology and a dynamic approach. Theology is the minister's primary discipline which he or she brings alongside the others. But at the same time it is itself informed by how the pastor uses insights from the human sciences. Few pastors, for instance, are likely to make significant contributions to sociological or psychological study. It is not their calling and for most these are not their special disciplines. To minister they need to be aware of this thinking and to use its results. By contrast, as theologians pastors can be expected to be creative. They need not merely use the work of others but may generate new ideas themselves. Their major contribution is likely to be in the realm of how theology works in different contexts, especially those where the modern disciplines can be applied. Pastors, therefore, are inevitably also theologians. Those among whom they minister expect them to be, whether as apologists for the faith or systematicians who teach it. They will always be required to bè pràctical theologians, involved in the moral maze of people's lives and the political and social consequences of his work with them. And they also have a special role in the Church's dogmatic and systematic theology:

> Pastors as watchers and explorers, bridge-builders and guardians of communal memories and vision, sharing and reflecting back to the rest of the *laos* its own ministry, have a special role in keeping the Church in the way of pilgrimage and in touch with its own nature as a sacrament of God-given humanity in Christ. (Moody 1992, 133)

PART TWO

The Mode of Pastoral Studies

The mode of contemporary pastoral studies is widely, almost universally, considered to be that of theological reflection. In Chapter 6 a definition is offered and discussed. It represents what may be called today's 'standard' mode of theological reflection. This, however, seems weak at the crucial point of the role of the person or body offering pastoral care. In Chapter 7, therefore, the model is developed distinctively taking this into account. The chapters need to be read together.

CHAPTER SIX

Theological Reflection in Pastoral Studies[1]

Theological reflection is today widely assumed to be the appropriate, even the required, mode of work in pastoral studies. The phrase is common in syllabuses and receives widespread approbation. It suggests thoughtful, informed reflection on experience. Yet in practice it is often left undefined. As a result 'theological reflection' may seem vaguely to represent an attitude and not a distinctive and appropriately professional form of learning.

THEOLOGICAL REFLECTION AND THE 'OLD' THEOLOGY

Some presentations of theological reflection imply that it is newly developed in response to deficiencies which have become apparent in previously held ways of thinking. Three arguments are especially familiar:

1 The 'old' theology was part of an educational system which assigned pre-eminence to our rational selves. The mind was affirmed as God's gift. But its use was divorced from those aspects of ourselves with which we have become intensely aware in the twentieth century – those facets of individual and social life which are being studied in the behavioural sciences. Traditional ways of theological thinking and learning, it is suggested, did not and cannot take sufficient account of our emotional side and our irrational selves. Yet these are the aspects of human behaviour that have become more prominent in everyday life. They, therefore, now need to be

given due place in pastoral practice and theology. Theological reflection is claimed as a way of acknowledging this.

2   One effect of the long era of Christendom has been to diminish the importance of the prophetic dimension to the Christian faith. This, in both Old and New Testaments, emphasizes that God's promise and demand address specific situations. These cannot be reduced to generalities. Yet much that passes for theology and proclamation both generalizes and avoids being specific. The Church, therefore, requires a new theological approach that gives proper attention to specific parts of life, if it is to proclaim a prophetic word.

3   Historically, pastoral thinking has been primarily concerned with individuals and their journey through this world to the next. Even when the notion of the next world declined in prominence, personal behaviour and morals remained the dominant focus. Less attention was paid to social issues and to the contexts in which pastoral interventions take place. We need, therefore, a theology which takes proper account of the social and corporate dimensions to all human living. To some extent this is an elaboration of point 2 above.

Each of these judgements could be discussed at length on its own. Each would also be a focus for disagreement. In particular the assumption about the way that 'traditional' theology is done should be questioned. It is too easily dismissed. Nevertheless, whatever the niceties of each point taken severally, together they describe a culture in the Church. This becomes especially notable when we think about pastoral activity and study pastoral theology.

.

THE REASON FOR THEOLOGICAL REFLECTION

One of the 'discoveries' of the twentieth century – and one with which no discipline has yet fully come to terms – is that all learning and exposition is embedded in a specific culture, time and place. We have lost the capacity for thinking in terms of eternal truths but have not yet replaced this with an agreed alternative way of conceiving things. The outcome is the sense of relativism that pervades all forms of discourse, including even those that appear to be the most objective.

The pastoral theologian's work cannot avoid these difficulties. And since the ethos which pervades academic work is also part of the popular culture of the late twentieth century in the west, pastors find an unexpected congruence between theological problems and the sort of material that they handle when dealing with people. The fascination with theological reflection is itself a function of this complex of practice and theory. It can be seen as a response to two major trends:

1 The stance called 'theological reflection' has arisen because of the crisis of faith in and understanding of God which marks the end of the twentieth century. Those struggling to proclaim and interpret the gospel feel that much traditional theology is not immediately relevant to their ministry. The idea of doctrine is itself often regarded as deadening rather than exciting. There are problems with Scripture and how to use it. A phrase like 'systematic theology' seems to emphasize order and organization rather than the free spirit of discovery. It is easy to caricature. But although the issue is sometimes disguised as a matter of appropriate style – for example, academic versus applied – it is more profound. There is today a crisis in theological understanding. The context for theology is, as with all intellectual disciplines, one of inherent scepticism. Even if the logic of the argument is sound, what is actually being studied? Questions of truth and whether theism is possible are returning to the centre of theological exploration. As a result much traditional work on, for instance, the person and work of Christ, the Spirit, the Church and the major doctrines of the Christian faith, appears weakly based and possibly unfounded. It may be interesting, but in what sense could it ever be known to be true, even if it is?

To be distinguished, but not separated from this attitude, is the crisis of faith. We have already noted that there seems to be more religion in everyday human life than the prevailing assumptions about a secularized world imply. But the core question of faith remains: how can God in any sense be known? People may have feelings of the transcendent or acknowledge a spiritual dimension to their lives. They may be willing, even eager, to call this 'God'. But in what sense can we trust these? However profound our belief that they are significant, are they in the end any more than the product of our own wishes?[2]

When these two crises – of understanding and of faith – are put together, the result is to emphasize experience. This is irreducible, even if it is neither shared not interpreted. The prevailing intellectual scepticism criticizes all stances, including itself. It, therefore, generates the idea that, although this stance itself may not seem to lead anywhere in particular, there is nevertheless no alternative to it. The crisis of faith leads to a similar conclusion. When there are no agreed categories for knowing God, we are forced back onto the testimony of experience. Thus the crisis in intellectual understanding and the crisis of believing appear different. Sometimes they are presented as such. But in practice they tend towards the same conclusion, the idea that experience alone constitutes evidence. These are the conditions which begin to produce the concept of theological reflection. The danger is that this process may become trapped in two levels of so-called 'experience' – that which is merely solipsistic and that which, although it appears more substantial, is in practice nothing more than anecdotal.

2   Theological reflection is a response to contemporary western culture and is, therefore, as ephemeral or otherwise as we judge that to be. This is a major problem, not least because of the dispute about the nature of both culture and thought. The predominate assumption about the modern world, for example, is that it is now to be described as plural. But

> the pluralism of modern culture, of which so much is made in so many places, is a myth, in the popular and pejorative sense of that word, at least so far as the West is concerned. On the surface there is diversity and variety in modern life, but beneath the surface there is a pressure for homogeneity which in effect nullifies them. (Gunton 1992, 84)[3]

These two perspectives – the crisis of faith and the change in contemporary culture – are both important in considering theological reflection. This is not a stance which might or might not be adopted. The idea of process itself lies at the heart of contemporary intellectual and practical debate. Theological reflection is the way by which process is given due place in theology. We may, therefore, expect it to change as ways of thinking and different approaches emerge. However, when all is said on the grand scale, there is little doubt that something like theological reflection is a necessary stance for working pastors who are theologians. For they are simultaneously caught up in two worlds:

1 that of the Christian theological tradition, which both informs what the pastor thinks and does and which he or she also represents;

2 practical activity in immediate situations, rather than (as the word 'reflection' might sometimes imply) the luxury of leisured contemplation of what may be the case and what sort of response might be adopted towards it.

Theological reflection, then, elucidates and focuses some of the central problems for contemporary theology and faith. But at its simplest the Church has two options that become specific as they confront its pastors:

1 They may take the prevailing culture seriously, whatever the technical errors in describing it. Even if that culture, in the judgement of the theologian, is wrongly discerning itself, it is nevertheless the context within which the Church functions and to which it contributes. The nature of this relationship is beginning to become the subject of discussion (Tracy 1981; 1987; Newbigin 1991). The practical risk is that pastoral theology will dissolve into social study and the associated practice into social work or counselling. This is a familiar dilemma for pastoral studies once the theoretical and practical significance of sociology and psychology is admitted.

2 They may ignore these problems and allow the Church, led by its pastors, to become a coterie of like-minded people. Such a course is itself a function of a culture. But it can allow a church to feel that it has a distinct and private identity and its pastors to find a restricted area for their work – the company of believers alone.

In both cases the presenting issue is that of identity. In the first case it is a matter of what is meant by 'culture' and how it is identified. In the second, the identity in question is that of the Church in relation to the world in which it is set. This topic is itself one that underlies all contemporary thinking. It has to a large degree taken over the historical quest for meaning and truth. Part of the problem for the pastor as theologian is that he or she is always actively trying to work

117

with both sets of presuppositions, neither of which is clearly articulated.

THEOLOGICAL REFLECTION – A DEFINITION

Given all these difficulties, there is, however, a recognizable process of theological reflection. There are difficulties in definition. Some that have recently been explored include (Durston 1989):

An interpretation of God's presence and action in the world, making explicit that which is usually implicit (David Brindley).

Reflecting, on the basis of (diverse) Christian beliefs, on events, trends, attitudes of others with a view to forming our own attitudes, guiding actions, reforming the tradition (Gerald Downing).

Exploration or analysis of some area of experience through conversation or correlation between that experience and scripture or the inheritance of faith leading to some judgement about the truth (what God is saying to us) resulting in a new attitude or actions (David Durston).

We may discern two levels to theological reflection. They roughly correspond to the complementary dimensions of what is personal and what is social. The practitioner reflects on his or her experience especially in relation to the other (God or one's neighbour). But this alone would involve the risk of solipsism and anecdote taking over. So there is a parallel process whereby the practitioner also works from his or her role as a representative of the Christian tradition and how this is being used to inform the context in which ministry is being exercised. The two are held together in a working definition, which I think is more precise than those mentioned earlier:

Theological reflection is a constructed, ordered, reflective enquiry on the interaction of one's self (person and role) and one's context (God, the world and the neighbour), which produces a conceptual framework which leads to action. (Carr 1990, 101)

Person (experience) and role (tradition) are brought together with the other (God and neighbour) and the general situation in which ministry is being offered. Like any working definition this statement is compressed. But each component is included for a specific reason. After the following discussion of the theoretical content an illustration is offered.

There are three parts to the definition:

THE PROCESS

1 It is *constructed*. Without acquiring knowledge and being able to make use of it, the pastor cannot engage in any reflection that may confidently be called 'theological'. The tools for building the process of reflection do not consist of a specific amount of knowledge of Scripture, history and doctrine. Nor are they randomly assembled. Pastoral theologians cannot know everything; they are expected to know something. Knowledge is to be acquired in training, which forms the basis on which later learning can be founded. But there is also the question of discovering and embodying new knowledge as the pastor's ministry proceeds. In most churches there is a belief that the minister should be learned. But such knowledge as he or she possesses needs to be constructed into a shape which is congruent with the task of theological reflection.

2 Theological reflection is *ordered*. It is not a *laissez-faire* approach in which the theologian casually considers any experience or feeling. The processes are deliberate, bringing together unknowns and uncertainties. The pastoral theologian brings to bear on a situation that is experienced (which can never be fully understood or in that sense 'known') such knowledge as he or she can muster. An integral part of the process is to be able to acknowledge the feeling of inadequacy that it engenders.

3 *Reflective* is the core word of the enterprise. Reflection is upon data: the question is where these data are found. The answer must be, in the light of those behavioural insights that we have discussed, that pastoral theologians primarily reflect on the feelings generated in them by their experience of a situation. The crucial question in theological reflection, for which some sort of hypothesis has to be generated, is 'What is happening to me and why?' We shall later examine

how this question leads to a distinctive model of Christian ministry.

4   The process is best thought of as an *enquiry*, since in theological reflection the participants are always moving from what is partially perceived (felt and understood) towards what is unknown – namely the outcome of the process.

THE POINT OF ATTENTION

Pastors are most engaged in theological reflection when they are engrossed in normal ministerial activity. Theological reflection is not a special process in which the expert occasionally indulges; it is the basic activity of everyday ministry. So here, as with every piece of ministry, the minister's focus is not on him- or herself alone. Nor is it on the other, whether this be an individual or a group with whom the pastor is dealing. The key point of interest, and eventually of interpretation, is what is happening at any moment between two parties.

The self is one contributor to any interaction. But, as we have repeatedly observed, the idea of the self has today become complex. But even if we allow for the philosophical dilemmas, there remains a practical issue. We are now more aware of two distinct but related aspects of anyone involved in any relationship. There is what we mean by person and what we refer to as role. A pastor, for instance, is whoever he or she is. We can to some extent explore this in terms of their birth, development and growth. But at the same time the pastor occupies the role of pastor. This they may or may not grasp clearly. But it is significant in any interaction. This point is important, since the confluence of person and role is a key piece of data in the context of theological reflection.

The other obvious contributor to the interaction is the 'other', whether this is a group or individual. There is, however, a further dimension to be held in mind – the interaction itself, that new complex which is created by the way that the pastor and the other act together. This is an important concept to hold. We have already considered some of the dangers inherent in polarity. There is a natural tendency towards projection and the apportioning of blame. If a pastoral encounter is conceived solely in terms of the connection between the pastor and the other, whatever importance we

120

may also assign to the context, two key points will be missing:

1   There is the fullness and richness of what is being created in the interaction. Without a sense of this the encounter itself may not (indeed probably will not) be valued for its own sake.

2   The concept of 'the interaction itself' provides within that encounter a sense of something which is both intrinsic to it but which also lies beyond it. In other words, we have here the beginning of a transcendent reference against which each party may test its motivations and intent. This re-emphasizes the importance of something specific – the immediate interaction. In turn this offers a defence against our natural tendency to sustain illusions about the future outcome of a piece of ministry. In theological reflection the pastor is firmly locked into the here-and-now and in that arena has to make some theological sense, however tentative and even incompetent.

THE OUTCOME

The outcome of all theological reflection is always practical and will be varied. Sometimes the minister will seem to change most, as he or she becomes more competent or better at self-understanding. Sometimes those with whom the work is done may become more faithfully Christian in their belief and action. Sometimes, especially when the context is the world of the neighbour, the Kingdom of God may be furthered as a human life is changed. Whatever the specific outcome (and it is unlikely that there will be only one), it will be action through which change may be brought about in the situation which is being addressed. This is another reason why the concept of 'reflection' may be misleading unless carefully considered and qualified.

THEOLOGICAL REFLECTION AT WORK: AN ILLUSTRATION

The following story will be familiar to many ministers and students.[4] It is an Anglican story, so it focuses on the vicar as the parish priest. But *mutatis mutandis* it could be told of other churches in similar environments. In particular where the word 'I' appears there are some churches that would emphasize the role of the congregation as an entity: in that case read 'we'.

The Revd Andrew Martin is vicar of a parish which is dominated by a housing estate. The council and social services tend to rehouse so-called problem families there, although this is not publicly acknowledged. Not many people attend the church for worship. But the congregation is involved with those around in several ways. They help, for example, to supply volunteers for a council-run drop-in centre. Here people can call in for company, advice and access to the welfare services. The clergy are also used to help in struggles with the authorities. And there is a widespread belief that the church is a source of charity and support, especially when other sources fail. Andrew Martin often feels manipulated by these expectations. The inherited patterns of worship and pastoral care do not seem to say much, if anything, to the inhabitants of this estate. Nor do what they do seem to Andrew or the congregation to say much that is obviously Christian. How, then, is he to interpret what the God who called the church is saying and doing among these people?

As the church leader in the situation he could ask himself, either alone or in discussion with the congregation, something like, 'What do I think should be done here?' He has an active Christian faith. He, therefore, instinctively looks to what this faith prompts him to say and feel. He can support his beliefs with argument drawn from the realities of life in the community and from the Bible and Christian tradition. It matters to him that what he decides and does should be consistent with the Christian faith. He might argue, for example, that every individual should be given dignity, respect and identity by the community in which they live. Each is made by God, in love and for love.

One implication of this belief might be that he should encourage the community to express this love in the way that housing, benefits, welfare and employment are managed. This attitude, and the actions which follow from it, will align Andrew with others who share these concerns – social workers, councillors and other groups in the community. Each will have its own reasons for coming to similar conclusions about social involvement. Andrew claims that his faith is the basis of thinking and deciding as he does. But it seems that he could reach similar conclusions if he had no religious faith at all. Yet because he is a Christian it is essential that he ask how his faith in the God revealed by Christ says something distinctive about hope and salvation. It might be argued that what makes Christian faith distinctive is that it is the only legitimate basis for believing any of these things. Others who share similar political and social views could be regarded as discovering (at least in part) God's truth through other insights. This position would not be impossible to sustain. But if he took that route at this point Andrew would by-pass the question of what his situation signified for what God is doing and promising in the community and to individuals caught up in it. What are the implications for putting one's trust in this God here? What are the expectations put upon God?

We may briefly indicate where the six aspects to the definition of theological reflection so far apply. Andrew Martin is a theologically literate priest. The great themes of the Christian faith, such as God the Creator and Redeemer, are not slogans in worship. They are essential as he seeks to (1) *construct* a way of thinking in even the most difficult environment. Struggled with in study and prayer, they constantly enlarge the context of humdrum ministerial activity and so prevent Andrew becoming trapped in it with little or no vision. Allied with this is the matching knowledge that enables him to (2) *order* his reflection. Much of this, for instance the issue of housing benefits, will be to assemble the data on that topic. There is nothing especially Christian about this, but it is an essential part of the process.

(3) *Reflective* (4) *enquiry* involves generating an hypothesis with which to work. This is not a new understanding of the situation: Christians, least of all ministers, do not possess miraculous insight into insoluble problems in social life. But Andrew needs to conceptualize what is happening and why he is involved in it. This step both checks any excessive misunderstanding of oneself and enables some realism to prevail without surrendering to pragmatism. The enquiry based on a working hypothesis will take him into areas of himself (including his beliefs) of which he was unaware, and probably into areas of unexpected involvement and activity. So the minister will not be locked into one level of interpretation

and behaviour alone. He or she will, for example, have to be alert to the social dimension as well as to the particular needs of the individual, which the minister might legitimately feel always according to the Gospel take priority. As a result, Andrew will lastly explore the (5) *interactions* which he is having with different groups and individuals. These, once examined, may enable him to decide where to put his energies and maybe those of his church. Whatever the case, some sort of (6) *action*, political, social or even religious, ensues. In practice there is more likely to be a series of actions.

This story, however, both illuminates the process of theological reflection and exposes some of its limitations. In particular it highlights two questions:

1   What do I as a Christian minister (or, as noted earlier, we as a Christian congregation) think and decide and what attitudes, insights, decisions and plans do I have in these circumstances?

2   What attitudes do I, or might I, have which arise out of my Christian commitment and faith and which I can express in this situation in such a way that my faith makes a distinctive contribution to the experience and activity of others?

The first question is a predicament which has been familiar to Christians through the centuries, although today it is sometimes described as theological reflection. There is, however, nothing distinctive about it. The second leads to an instance of that crisis in theology which underlies much that now passes for theological reflection. We need, therefore, to reconsider the practice of theological reflection.

THE PRACTICE OF THEOLOGICAL REFLECTION

The main components of theological reflection now emerge.

ACKNOWLEDGING A SITUATION

The above story reminds us of what we all know instinctively: every human situation is complex. As we also noted earlier, permeating any so-called 'situation' there is a range of unconscious activity. This will reside in the individual psychology of the participants and in the group and social dynamics that prevail. This fact makes any idea of 'understanding' dangerous and even erroneous. The notion of a 'situation' to be explored is fundamental to theological reflection. But it runs the risk of being confused with a diagnostic model of working. Diagnosis, however, with its suggestion that there is someone who can precisely grasp what is happening and respond to that, is alien for these purposes. The first step in theological reflection is simply to acknowledge that there is a situation. To a large degree it does not much matter which aspect of it is first addressed. Often, of course, there will be a presenting issue and, although it may at first sight seem simplistic, that is in fact the first point onto which to latch. It may later be abandoned, but it will provide as good a starting point as any.

This may seem like a recipe for indifference. But at this stage all that is being discussed is the way by which the first step into engagement can be taken. Once a point is grasped the process of assembling data can begin around it. But here, too, we need to beware a false scientism. What is data? When dealing with people, singly or in groups, there is a range of data which for the most part is of similar value. There are, for instance, facts that can be elicited and elucidated. In dealing with a situation to do with a church's life there will be information about the building's location and the people who attend that must be noted. These, however, will rarely provide guidelines for action. Statistics are a refined form of fact, although they need to be treated with necessary caution and scepticism. Figures on who comes, how many to which event or service, where they come from, age, gender and so on are valuable and essential. But such statistical data cannot tell the whole story – for a useful example of this, see Gill (1993). The process of theological reflection presumes that the way in which the situation is construed includes anecdotes, beliefs and fantasies about it. For instance, there is likely to be a penumbra of belief around the church of which for the most part pastors and church people are unaware. Only when stories are heard might they begin to recognize that the Church (building, minister and people – in different ways) may represent something beyond statistics in the community. The stories people tell may say more about attitudes than apparently more statistically reliable data.

One myth, for example, that clergy have sometimes heard,

usually when they are already feeling depressed, is that at one time people used to queue to come to church. In a rural parish the new vicar was feeling low after Easter. Only a handful had turned up for Communion on Easter Day, and he could not understand it. He thought it represented a vote of no confidence in him after his much loved predecessor, about whom he had endured hearing for the whole year. The vicar reflected (we can see here the danger of the word) and came to a series of 'conclusions' about his personal inadequacy and the incompetence of his ministry. He invited someone to advise him. Before doing anything else, the consultant took the vicar over to the church to check the records – the one thing he had not thought of doing. Looking back over previous years, this was not the first time that Easter Day had seen an empty church. The register did not give the reason: that became a matter for ministry. But it did provide the first level of essential data from which further work could emerge. That said, however, the fact remained in the present that for some reason people had not attended in this specific year with this new priest. The records were a beginning. But far more work on the situation was needed. To begin that process required listening to the anecdotes and stories that made up contemporary beliefs and attitudes to the Church.

THE PASTOR'S EXPERIENCE

Such attention to the situation generates an unusual mixture of feelings and emotions in the pastor, in addition to any data that is assembled. This mix becomes the pastor's personal experience. All ministry is concerned with people and therefore involves feelings. Whatever use is eventually made of these in theological interpretation, they point to the significance of the faith level of discourse within the process of theological reflection. Pastors and those with whom they deal have to find some shared experience of reality in order to work. But that reality will include those who are present in the situation. Less obvious, but as important, are those who are not present but who are dynamically contributing to it through the unconscious processes that are activated. For example, in any dealing with a family where the father has left, a child's behaviour is as much affected by the absent father as by what the present mother and the other children may do. In Christian ministry that shared experience is not solely a matter of agreeing the data. It also involves finding some common basis for the discussion. Among the contributing factors to such engagement will be the Church's characteristic intellectual activity – theology.

It may seem, however, that when the importance of feelings is emphasized theological reflection is surrendered to subjectivism. This might further suggest that the whole enterprise is erected on a notoriously and fragile aspect of human life. The charge is only true, however, if we accept the underlying assumption that feelings cannot be differentiated and that the subject/object distinction is clear. This stance cannot be sustained. It is worth noting, too, that this concern is not confined to pastoral studies or indeed the human sciences alone. In business studies some consultants are once again recognizing the importance of feelings and there is evidence that unconscious processes are always at work (Cooper 1977).

> Such feelings aren't just the inevitable emotional residue of human work relationships. They are *data* [original italics], valuable clues to the dynamics of boundary relationships. In this respect, feelings are an aid to thinking and to managing; they are a real part of real work. . . . the best managers understand this intuitively. They not only manage with their heads, but also with their guts. (Hirschorn and Gilmore 1992, 49)

CLARITY OF THOUGHT

We return here to the ideal of the learned minister. The emphasis on feelings does not diminish the need for clarity of thought. Reflection of any sort involves going beyond the experience which is provoking the reflection. There is an immediate 'more' of some sort. Experience itself, therefore, is necessarily self-critical. This is an important contribution from pastoring to the study of theology. There is a contemporary tendency to regard experience as self-sufficient, an end in itself. When claimed, experience cannot be gainsaid. But although an experience is always the focus for theological reflection, it also has to be examined critically. The 'I' or 'we' who are reflecting are also because of their roles bearers of a tradition or representatives of something more than the experience. The need for clarity of thought, therefore, lies at the heart of the process of theological reflection. Confusion occurs when 'personal' is identified with 'individual'. For example, the phrase 'personal authority' is sometimes used. When asked why they acted in a certain way, someone may reply, 'I acted on my personal authority'. This sounds fine. It appears to integrate person and role, as expressed in 'authority'. But in practice it may disguise the exercise of power – 'I did it because I wanted to' does not sound quite so legitimate, although this may be what is meant.

This use of 'personal' makes the idea of power or authority private, as if it referred solely to me. But the essence of theological reflection, bearing in mind that it has to issue in action, is that it cannot be private. It is important to recall here the profound change in the understanding of psychology that has come about in the twentieth century. That which is within, and which therefore might be considered private, has been exposed as accessible for examination. The unconscious mind is not necessarily private. Therefore, as the minister goes about his or her work, the process of reflection is available for scrutiny. But because the process is integral to the content, and the content is public since the situation is an agreed one (even if the 'understanding' of it is not), the personal feelings and attitudes which are data must themselves also be public.

THE COMPONENTS OF THEOLOGICAL REFLECTION

We come now to the nub of theological reflection. There is a situation to be addressed; the sort of data to be dealt with is agreed; and the central place of feelings and what is personal is acknowledged. At this point the process begins to jell. For the faith dimension brings to bear the faith that is in the pastor, not in an eclectic fashion but in a way which seeks integrity and cogency. There is no point in this faith being exposed as lacking integrity. If that were the case it could help no one. Nor is there any point to faith that does not possess its inner cogency. This issue lies at the heart of the historic debate about the relative status to be accorded to faith and works.

The content of that faith has to be recognized as more than feelings. Why I believe is a complicated idea with which to cope. Yet without being prepared repeatedly to face this complication as each situation arises, the pastor cannot engage in theological reflection. For without the component of faith the process would merely be one of applying (or possibly not applying) theological *a prioris* to affect-laden human situations. To do that pastors could hunt through Scripture, tradition or history according to their predilections and find a precedent or illuminating story and quote that. But whatever else such action would achieve, it would not require the minister's personal involvement. We should then be not far from a sterile form of advice giving which could never engage with the complexities of the situation.

The pastoral theologian needs to know the traditional disciplines and in addition be aware of how they have functioned and still may. For example, there is little point in knowing the text of the Bible without also having a grasp of how it has worked for different generations. The process of Scripture and its content are both required. The traditional disciplines offer three key ingredients to the process:

INFORMATION

No opportunity for theological reflection occurs in isolation. Every situation is unique. But each occurs in a stream of belief and reflection in which all the participants are caught up. This stream does not provide precedents but is an orientation for the Christian that has been tested repeatedly through the ages. Especially when dealing with feelings in a human interaction, the pastoral theologian needs reference points by which to check not only himself but also his role, that is, what he stands for as a Christian. Personal faith alone will be always in danger of merely colluding with the range of feelings that are generated in the encounter. Pastors, therefore, need to know and keep alive in themselves the boundary markers of the Christian tradition in which they are working and which they are also representing.

TOOLS

Linked with information is the ability to use it. To engage in theological reflection pastors need to be able to use the information that they possess. This is where the behavioural studies take their place. Psychological and sociological awareness, held together by the integrative model of interpretation that the pastor has adopted, interplay with the tradition that the pastor represents. This is less of a problem than it first appears. In the light of modern hermeneutics the processes of reading and using a text are now known to be integral to its comprehension. The same is true of the range of sciences with which the pastor deals. The connection between content and process cannot be severed. These disciplines, as they are employed, consistently remind the pastor of this. The Christian tradition and all other learning is not so much to be reverenced as employed. It often comes as a surprise to neophyte ministers to discover that people expect them specifically to speak religious language. This is not because they understand it, but because they expect the pastor to be able to do so. It is one of the pastor's representative functions to sound religious. And the corollary is, even in today's eagerness for the certainty of understanding, that people also sometimes expect him or her not to be comprehensible or obviously relevant.

CRITERIA

If in theological reflection pastors assess the information that they possess and use it as best they can, then it becomes a self-referring set of criteria to them about how Christian they are being. There is no single way of validating theological reflection, any more than there is within the Christian Church agreed standards of orthodox belief and practice. These are constantly being reformed. The Protestant tradition enshrines this in the tag *ecclesia reformata semper reformanda* ['A reformed church must always be being reformed']. A similar position was espoused in *Lumen gentium*, the Constitution on the Church at Vatican II. Even the most conservatively biblical churches acknowledge that they may become deaf to Scripture and need to hear it anew. In each case the process includes the same components as may also serve to validate a process of theological reflection:

1 Does it feel right? Unless people believe something together as the beginning of exploration, no work can be done. Shared belief is a matter to a large extent of agreed feeling.

2   When first tested by the normal criteria (such as Scripture or tradition) does it seem right enough? There is never likely to be full agreement at this, or possibly any other, stage. But there can be sufficient consensus.

3   Can I, or we, risk action on this basis to test the process? Action is the determining factor.

When the issue involves a major church decision, these criteria become elaborate and long-drawn out. So, for instance, in the case of the Church of England and its decision to ordain women, it eventually felt right to most, was judged sufficiently congruent with the gospel tradition and was finally tested by action. In the case of a moment of theological reflection in a pastoral context, the criteria will almost fall over each other. Feeling, testing and acting may conflate into a sudden pastoral decision. But the process is the same.

THEOLOGICAL REFLECTION AND PASTORAL STUDIES

The situation and associated feelings engender the experience that sets the agenda for any act of theological reflection. But the tradition of faith requires the pastor to check whether the theological responses historically available amount to much in this particular situation. Are they credible? Do they also need to be confronted? Because the experience sets the agenda, the theologically reflecting pastor cannot eclectically select bits from his or her store of tradition. But the nature of the experience enables him or her to assign priorities in the encounter to parts of the stream of tradition in which it is happening.

> We do not move to theology and faith in order to leave other aspects of critical awareness behind. Just as we had to say that faith is engaged at every point from the start, so conversely we have to say that our 'theology' is not detachable from the whole complex of how we experience, understand, clarify, decide and adopt attitudes. It is only for procedural convenience that we might say that we begin with the experience, and then go into a theological reflection on it. If that encourages us to practise a split between the two, then we had better adopt some other procedure. (Ponter n.d.)

This way of thinking links with four points that we have already noted about pastoral studies in general:

1 The central thrust is upon creating working hypotheses which also attempt to integrate disparate but vital material. Such an approach is required for handling the important behavioural evidence. It is also essential for the theological enterprise.

2 The approach does not merely derive from traditional theological thinking; it also contributes to it. Tracy's categories are valuable here. They also elaborate the contribution of pastoral theology, and the way in which, for instance, this offers a way of thinking about tradition as artistic. This could have a significant impact on the way that churches behave.

3 There is in every human activity an innate tendency towards polarization that encourages (or is encouraged by) projection and projective identification. If pastors know that this has psychologically to be resisted, they may also be able to do so intellectually.

4 The process is public. Not only are the minister and the situation both public. The public nature of the exploration and interpretation makes the outcome of such theological reflection, both the action and the changes which occur in the situation and the theological resource for it, a matter also of public truth.

Figure 2 outlines the process diagrammatically. From this diagram the dimensions of the process become apparent. The two normative components, without which theological reflection is impossible, lie at the heart of the system: a coherent theology coupled with the integrity of faith and human awareness linked with critical disciplines. They are there because they each inform and are informed by every part of the process. The process progresses around this core from the first decision through the theological process to the renewed activity that follows.

In this chapter we have examined what may best be called the 'standard' mode of theological reflection as it is generally taught in pastoral studies' courses. Central to such reflection is the concept of experience (see further Appendix 2). But this is a notoriously loose concept. It may even limit the potential for theological reflection, since this is the component in the process which seems least definable, although a great deal depends upon it. Theological reflection as a stance or process is vulnerable around the point which is often not considered carefully enough: whose experience is being reflected upon? We need, therefore, to elaborate this theme.

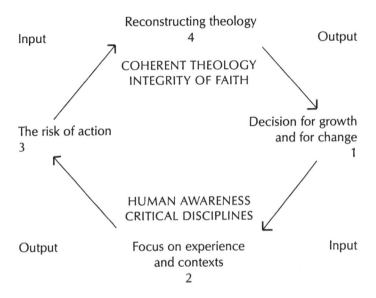

Figure 2: The 'standard' process of theological reflection

CHAPTER SEVEN

The Experiencing Minister:
Task and Role

All students of theology encounter at an early stage in their study the distinction between the Kingdom of God and Church. The two are intimately linked, as, for instance, in the way that the Church is distinctively called to discern the Kingdom and so witness to the gospel. But they can be differentiated. The same is true of the stance of theological reflection and the pastor. The process is not the prerogative of the pastor. Other individuals and communities may engage in it. Yet in ministering especially with those who are not formally members of the Church, it is more likely the authorized, recognizable minister who is expected to embody the gospel. What, therefore, he or she is in that role is a critical issue for theological reflection.

The pastor is both a person and someone in role. And a role is both assigned and accepted or adopted. Thus whenever role is mentioned we focus on the subtle negotiations occurring between the client, who is assigning a role, and the minister who is accepting or adopting a role. For example, John Smith is a local minister. The role of 'vicar'[1] is partly what he thinks it is – something to do with vocation and a general sense of being in the right (or wrong) place. But it will also be what others think a vicar should be. These beliefs may derive from any source, not least the media (especially television) or experience of other ministers. Yet wherever each party's conceptions come from, these have to be renegotiated in every new encounter: the vicar has to sense what he is being expected to be, without necessarily colluding with it, and the clients have to come to terms with the fact that this actual minister does not fit their image. Ministry is possible only as that negotiation takes place.

But John Smith is not a role: he is a person. The connection between person and role is one of the most delicate with which pastors deal. Clearly there is likely to be some connection between who someone is by nature and the specific roles to which they are attracted and which they take up in life. A person with a propensity to care, for example, might tend to find their place in life in caring roles. A technical term to describe this phenomenon is 'valency' (Bion 1961). Each individual possesses personal proclivities that constitute their valency. That may urge them towards professions and roles in life where it is gratified by being mobilized. For example, someone who can cope well with dependence may join a caring profession.

But in their dealings with people pastors go beyond such simple connections between person and role. They also need self-awareness. At one level this is obvious. We have, for example, in our society been made sensitized to the difference that gender makes in a relationship. The churches are finding the same true as more women are ordained and given authority. Whether the pastor is male or female has an impact on the type of ministry that is exercised. Indeed in a society that seems increasingly uncertain about gender the issue may become disproportionately significant. But pastors also need some sense of their unconscious dispositions. Self-analysis, however, is usually superficial. The context for critical judgement is absent and it is all too easy to delude oneself. Something more is needed.

THE PASTOR'S ORIENTATION IN ROLE

People in the therapeutic and caring professions keep self-awareness alive by two means – analysis and supervision. Anyone, for instance, who practises as a psychoanalyst will themselves have been analysed. Many therapists undergo the same procedure. Others, social workers being a good example, submit to supervision by co-workers. Few ministers will undergo analysis. Indeed it is not appropriate to their distinctive vocation. The idea of supervision requires a context of critical teamwork that is rarely available to ministers, even when working collaboratively with colleagues. The distinction between therapy and pastoral ministry must be sustained even here. Although the one can inform the other, it cannot substitute for it (Wright 1980). If Christian ministers are to sustain this essential self-awareness, their resources will lie in the Christian Church and its traditions from which they derive their ultimate authority.

Christians orient themselves through life by prayer and worship. These two activities are held to be ends in themselves. God is worshipped because he is God. Christians pray because they pray. Functional discussions of worship and prayer are discouraged: they also crumble. So, for example, while people naturally are curious about whether prayer 'works', when prayer is subjected to the test of results, it ceases to be what we thought prayer was in the first place. In 1883 Sir Francis Galton conducted a well-known statistical enquiry into the efficacy of intercession. He isolated one aspect of the complex practice of praying. But the result was not only a weak statistical argument. The experiment also so restricted the definition of prayer that the concept itself became unrecognizable (Brümmer 1984). Prayer is an end in itself, whatever all the other motivations may be (Baelz 1968). The same is true of worship.

> In his prayer, as in his moral life, the believer is *practising* his fellowship with God, and not merely *practising for* it. The practice of prayer is not like practising swimming strokes without going into the water. . . . .William Temple is right in emphasising that 'the proper relation in thought between prayer and conduct is not that conduct is supremely important and prayer may help it, but that prayer is supremely important and conduct tests it'. (Brummer 1984, 113)

This is a core idea for pastoring. Just as, for example, the analyst embodies the practice of analysis and therefore goes deeply into it himself, so pastors embody the divine dimension to all human encounters and must be rooted in that themselves. Theology is the pastor's skill. Spirituality is the context which the pastor embodies.

Although prayer and worship are ends in themselves, the practice of both has a practical outcome. They bring the individual into closer relation with God, confirming what is and offering hope for what might be. The old maxim *laborare est orare* ['Working is praying'] is relevant here. It does not mean that to do something adds to the attitude of prayer. It is the belief that action itself is a form of prayer. The connection between spirituality and morality is well-established.

> It would be absurd to think that we could enter through prayer into fellowship with God, if this is not manifested in the life we live. On the other hand it is logically impossible to live a life of fellowship with God, if this fellowship is not established and re-established again and again, and this fact acknowledged in praise and thanksgiving. This is what we are doing when we pray. (Brümmer 1984, 113)

Person and role are both affected by prayer and worship. Pastors become more alert to the transcendent context of all life and specifically of their ministry. Consequently they also become more aware of the self that they are, have been and may become. That means that the individual becomes alert both to personal proclivities and to any meanness of vision in the face of the transcending vision of the divine. Pastors also become more attuned to the roles in which they experience their ministry as they become increasingly aware of the authority which they exercise. But in order to attend to these roles, the minister needs self-awareness and screening for proclivities or tendencies generated by his or her personal valency. The way that ministers achieve this is through contextualizing themselves through prayer and worship.

'Role' may sometimes be contrasted unfavourably with 'person'. It is thought to be cold and distancing. It can be used that way. It may carry overtones of hypocrisy when thought of as performing or acting. Yet to be a pastor is to occupy a role. One way to clarify thinking about roles is through the idea of task. 'Role' and 'task' are intimately linked. A task is what an institution must perform in order to exist. This is not to say that it is always clear. But the concept is central. For example, for a church to exist as a church and not just as a social gathering the congregation must worship God. It is difficult to conceive a church that did not do this. There is, however, often more than one task in hand at any moment. A family might, for instance, have such tasks as trying to earn enough money to survive, to work together to create its distinctive values, or be in the business of allowing particular members to develop. These are not exclusive, although they will vie for prominence. Nor is one task necessarily more legitimate than any other, although sometimes this may be claimed. But at any moment one will for whatever reason be primary (Miller and Rice 1967).

'Role' describes a function of a task that is taken by or assigned to someone. Such everyday ideas as 'father', 'mother' or 'child', for instance, are roles which individuals assume or are given in relation to the task of a family. Without some notion of family, the terms are meaningless and there are no roles. The same is true of a church. The roles of 'pastor' or 'worshipper' are meaningless without the notion of Church and its having a task. This theme may also be discerned in the familiar Pauline notion of the body of Christ. This description of the Church is sometimes used in an anti-institutional sense. The Church, it is argued, is not an organization or institution; it is a fellowship which constitutes the body of Christ in the world. But as Paul makes clear, the idea of the body of Christ is in fact one way of conceptualizing the Church and its task. From this description derive the various roles – arm, leg, eye, hand – and their distinctive contribution to and need for the body derive. In other words, there is no role of pastor without some preconception about the Church and its task (Shapiro and Carr 1992).

The range of possible roles will reflect the complexity of an institution's task. For example, people engaged in pastoral ministry might have particular positions in ritual. Clergy have this function, not least in terms of blessing or conducting baptisms, weddings and funerals. The task of the Church in such instances is about marking transitions in human life. The role of the minister becomes that of bearer of the tradition and conductor of the ritual. Another task of the Church is to do with relationships, both those between God and people and persons in relationship with one another. In the setting of that task the role of the minister focuses on facilitating such relationships – the priest, colleague or pastor. It is, however, also important to note that such roles are not just assumed: they also have to be assigned. Any new minister knows that his or her authority to minister derives partly from their external authorization by the Church and partly from the way in which the people, both within and outside the Church, acknowledge that authority and so confirm it.

REPRESENTATION IN ROLE

The formal role of the public ordained minister, however, relates to one distinctive task of the Church: to represent God. The fact that the Church is a public body enables the topic of God to remain somewhere in people's agendas, even if they mostly prefer to ignore it. Representation lies at the core of the Christian tradition. It is also the essence of pastoral ministry. The Greek preposition *hyper* is the key. It means doing something or being someone on behalf of, but not in place of, another. So, for instance, the actions of Jesus Christ are *hyper* (on behalf of) the world. We receive the benefits of his acts on our behalf but are not deprived of our own responsibility. Christ acts on our behalf so that we can join with him in similar action for others and share the consequences. He does not replace; he represents.

The same is true of pastoral ministry. The pastor does not replace the client but represents them in a context where they are at a loss as to know what to do, how to act or what to think. The critical context is God. When they have some sense of the divine, however tenuous, people become unsure of what is proper. They often become aware of their failings, real and imagined, and experience a consequential sense of guilt. But the pastor does not bear all this for them. The relationship is more subtle. For the pastor not only stands for a God who acts on behalf of people. He or she also embodies that representation by what they do and say. Just as God makes himself both vulnerable and explorable in order to love and serve his people, so pastors embody a similar vulnerability and make themselves available for exploration. This is the area in which the distinctive theological reference of pastoral ministry comes into its own. Four marks of this stance may be noted:

THE PASTOR STANDS FOR GOD
God is only accessible in so far as people believe that he can be found within a specific (in this case, the Christian) tradition.

Bits of half-remembered history and Scripture, coupled with popular songs and children's hymns, produce a muddled notion of tradition. But people approaching a pastor for ministry will come with this baggage and to expect him or her to represent something that is dimly felt to be beyond them. This may be a vague notion of God. But that 'God' is not general: he is specifically located within a particular believed tradition. The pastor cannot deny this and become unspecifically religious, otherwise the client cannot find their point of reference for the encounter.

THE PASTOR STANDS FOR THE CHURCH

People mostly focus their expectations of God in churches. It is important that pastors can hold this 'church in the mind' in an ideal sense and at the same time never allow it quite live up to that ideal. If it ever did, then the Church would prove impossible for people to approach. The aura of perfect holiness would be too great. The Church is the means by which God is earthed in people's minds. That is why any understanding of ministry must follow from a grasp of the Church and not precede it or be divorced from it. This story illustrates this ambivalence about the Church, as well as why any pastor must grasp what he is handling:

> No one in the Church of England is able to be ordained or licensed without a place or parish in which to serve. Immediately a priest is confronted with the responsibilities of leadership. I remember vividly that on the day of my own ordination I was called 'sir' for the first time by a man old enough to be my father. That experience was elaborated by a senior Churchwarden who remarked, when conducting me round the parish as a prospective Incumbent, 'We place Vicars here on a pedestal.' I felt uncomfortable with that assertion and replied, 'I shall jump off.' 'You cannot jump off other people's pedestals, but you can look to your own and then ours will take care of themselves.' (Bowering 1994, 95)

PASTORS HAVE A SYMBOLIC ROLE

All theology has an aesthetic dimension. It must be capable of being taken up in worship and valued because of its intrinsic elegance. Pastors will have to give careful attention to the major Christian symbols which they are handling. But they will do with some awareness of how these function in religion in general. Much of such work will occur around the natural symbols of everyday. For example, every pastoral encounter contains a ritual dimension. Some are obvious, as for instance the rituals of baptism, weddings or funerals. But the request to bless someone or something includes a range of religious ritual. Most pastoral encounters are also likely to include prayer. Whatever prayer may be, in this context it has a ritual dimension. This ritual function is an aspect of the minister's authority. And the aim of the encounter is to get behind the immediate meeting with a vague sense of transcendence to a deeper and clearer approach to God. The minister, therefore, is a symbol in this context. In pastoral ministry most of the discerned social interaction between Church and people, religion and ritual, occurs.

This topic is large and remains complicated. But pastoral activity brings to the fore issues of power and belief about it, as well as how it is to be managed. Pastors thus find themselves at a critical point in the contemporary world. Secularization has not extirpated religion in the way that some predicted. Yet it is impossible to deny that there has been a weakening of the ties of public religion. At the same time therapeutically-oriented thinking has assigned internal emotional states greater importance than they traditionally warranted. The ritual, therefore, of dealing with an authorized minister reflects a time when boundaries, such as those between God and man or between heaven and earth, were felt to be dangerous and powerful. That primitive feeling has not disappeared and it may unexpectedly surface in people's lives. The difficulty for many lies in acknowledging it lest they are thought mad or in finding ways when vocabulary is impoverished to articulate it (Hay 1987). The minister's ritual significance, therefore, is probably greater than he or she either realizes or is allowed to recognize. At the same time the idea of counsel as dealing with an emotional state is the underlying presupposition on which the pastoral encounter is based. At this level symbolic significance gives way to believed professional competence as a counsellor (Douglas 1970, 14ff).

PASTORING HAS AN ETHICAL DIMENSION

We have already touched on this with the mention of power. In every pastoral encounter questions of moral behaviour arise. Some of these concern the behaviour of the person counselled. What should he or she do or not do as a result? And is it legitimate to counsel an illegal or immoral course of action? The problem is well-known, for instance, in the Roman Catholic confessional over the question of contraception. Casuistry may get the priest so far, but there remains not just for him but also for the penitent a moral question. But there are also ethical matters involved in the pastoral approach itself. In the 1960s emphasis was placed on non-directive counselling (Rogers 1951; 1974). This has been well contrasted with the pastor's calling to be unbusy, subversive and apocalyptic (Peterson 1993). It is doubtful whether there is or ever can be non-direction in human relations. But it was discussed. In part it represented a resistance to what was perceived as too great a power residing in a counsellor, especially when this was someone with the additional authority of a priest or spiritual adviser.

But this also raises the question whether there is a specifically Christian style of pastoral engagement. The answer is that there is. It is based less upon counselling in a therapeutic sense than upon the ancient model of confession and absolution. In this process, whether formal or, more likely today, informal, the minister operates somewhere between being non-directive and being directive. It is a stance of modified direction. The minister, being expected to stand for God and the embodiment of the divine in the Church, cannot be unlike that God. Since God appears not to impose his will on his creatures, then in a sense he might be described as non-directive. The invitation to penitents is to make their own mind up and become responsible for their lives after these have been interpreted in the light of divine transcendence. Yet the penitent individual and the Church at large expect the word of God to be spoken in the session; that may be conceived as directive or at least to a degree prescriptive. The basic ethical model for the Christian minister is that of *didache*.[2] This is teaching which has not so much to be obeyed as absorbed and appropriated by each Christian and individual and community. The customary balance lies between law (prescription) and grace (responsible living in the light of the gospel).

In every situation pastors will search for these marks of the theology that is both their distinctive skill and the business of the Church that they represent. As a result the outcome will always be in the fullest sense outlined above, worship. This is the foundation and connecting point on which all ministry is explored. This perception also allows us further to refine the concept of reflection. This, it will be recalled, was left for further consideration.

THEOLOGICAL REFLECTION IN ROLE

Reflection is ill-defined. The standard theory of theological reflection suggests that we know what we do when we reflect. One difficulty of the action/reflection model is that it has elevated the concept of reflection to something special. In practice, however, reflection is a natural and instinctive human activity. Indeed, it is a mark that distinguishes human beings from other animals that they can reflect on their experience and behaviour.

In thinking about theological reflection, however, an unfortunate divide may open up between experience and reflection. The standard model suggests that the pastor has some experience as a result of an encounter or an action upon which, by implication at later leisure, he or she reflects. Through that process new learning occurs. Since the Christian minister's reflection is theologically informed, the learning is in the realm of applied theology.

But there is a false assumption here, both philosophical and psychological, that experiencing and reflecting are discrete activities. This suggests that an experience has its own existence and can become the object of thought. But experience and reflection are not so separate. The experience, whatever we mean by that, is in part constituted by the process of holding it for reflection. Equally the reflecting person is not divorced from the experiencing person. These two aspects of the individual contribute to one another.

For practical purposes in pastoral ministry we may make a distinction between the two, though not a division. But we first need to recognize that in the cycle of pastoring the order of events is not experience – action – reflection. For the pastor reflection precedes action. For reflection is self-referential. The central question of ministry re-emerges: 'What is happening to me and why?' Much pastoral activity, especially when it has been partially informed through therapeutic models, tends to drift towards being diagnostic. The pastor, confronted by another person with some sort of need, is inclined to ask 'What is the matter with her?' or 'What does he want or need?' This superficially sounds Christian. It witnesses to concern. But the weakness of the questions is that they are diagnostic. The minister enquires about others and seems interested in them – indeed, he or she is interested. But in the unstructured nature of pastoral encounters such an enquiry puts the minister at risk of projecting into that person. The need that is being presented will then, maybe after a time, appear to fit the pastor's presuppositions. But from the client's perspective such an encounter will feel alien and alienating. For the pastor will be dealing with his or her own agenda under the guise of ministry. The question 'What is happening to me and why?' initially sounds selfish. Where is concern for the other? The answer is that by using such a question as a test for the critical evaluation of what may be happening, which is reflection, ministers both use themselves and allow others to use them. This question, therefore, lies at the heart of any act of ministry.

We can elaborate this. The self-reference ('to me') draws attention to the need for empathy. Empathy contrasts with sympathy. To sympathize with someone, which is not necessarily an inappropriate reaction in some pastoral circumstances, is to use categories from one's own experience and invite the other to use them to orient themselves. Sympathy, for instance, is being used when someone says to a bereaved person 'I know how you feel. When my husband died, I found. . .'. This remark may in some circumstances be unhelpful, not least because no one can ever be sure (know) how another feels. Yet in a straightforward bereavement, to use a shorthand, the thought that the other person might have had a similar experience can be enough to provide suitable support.

Empathy is different. It refers to the way that the pastor might seek to understand someone on their terms rather than on his or her own. The language sometimes used speaks of being able 'to get inside and live in the other'. Empathy is what a mother does in the early stages of a child's development. Before the child can articulate what it wants, mother and baby create a way of mutual non-verbal communication. The mother learns how to respond to her child without its having to speak. Sometimes she gets it right; sometimes she gets it wrong. But the quality of attention is as if the mother were under the skin of her child, knowing what it feels and needs. By doing this she both affirms the child and encourages its growth as an individual. Such empathy is the pattern for the relationship between pastor and client. This dimension is also prominent in counselling. But empathy is more than just a way of feeling. One of the pioneers of this understanding of the empathy between mother and baby, Donald Winnicott†, recognized that such relationships were never perfect. He coined the phrase 'the good enough mother'. She does not have to get everything always right. But she has always to be present to the child, even when wrong (Winnicott 1965; Shapiro 1982).

This is a useful model for the idea of empathy in a pastoral relationship. For it allows us again to use a contemporary concept derived from research into human behaviour without, however, requiring the pastor to become a counsellor. He or she only has to be in regard to empathy 'good enough', that is, to have some awareness of what is going on in any encounter. Theologically we might invoke the doctrine of the Holy Spirit, not as a catch-all but as a way of thinking about the empathetic aspect of 'What is happening to me?' For there is no such isolable entity as 'me'. Pastors, like any other human beings and in their particular role, exist in relationship. The Spirit is often discerned in interstices and spaces, working between the persons of the Trinity, between God and his world and in the theme of fellowship between one person and another (Taylor 1972).

One mark of psychological thinking in the late twentieth century has been greater awareness that individuals do not operate in isolation. The idea of the *tabula rasa* which might be coloured by different encounters and experiences almost, as it were, without a contribution from the person most involved, is foreign to most thinking. The interpersonal dynamics of every relationship affect both parties. The language used to describe this is that of transference and counter-transference. This has long been recognized, although some have been suspicious of it. More recently, however, we have realized that countertransference does not have to be screened out of any encounter. On the contrary it can be acknowledged, identified and then employed in the interactive process of interpretation. It is an essential dynamic in theological reflection.

Countertransference describes those aspects of the person that are unconsciously mobilized in an encounter. For example, the vicar may be talking to a parishioner in his role as vicar. But the idea of 'father' may be implicit in this discussion, whether it is used or not. As a result the father part of the vicar is stirred up without his being aware of it. His experiences of his own father and as a father himself are not formally germane to the discussion between the vicar and parishioner. But the feelings unconsciously aroused will be having their impact on what is going on. In such a context, the self-referential question, 'What is happening to me?' is a good one. It encourages pastors to examine who at any moment is the 'me'. It will also not allow them to escape from the complexity of any human relationship, least of all by invoking for themselves or the other the role of vicar or minister as a protection. But the use of countertransference goes further. It is a sort of reverse empathy, by which the parishioner gets under the skin of the vicar. In other words, curious as it sounds, aspects of the parishioner, chiefly those which are not being expressed, can be found by the vicar in himself.

THEOLOGICAL REFLECTION IN ROLE PRACTISED: AN ILLUSTRATION

Alan Bishop, a new vicar, tried to be gracious to parishioners who persisted for a long time in comparing what he was doing with what his predecessor had done. He knew, as no doubt did many of the congregation, that the previous vicar had not been incompetent. Neither, however, had he been outstanding. He had retired to the country in Dorset. There were many things in the church that needed to be changed.

Alan went about the task with care and sensitivity, carrying most of the congregation with him. One or two persisted in making negative comparisons between the old and the new regimes. But he bore it with fortitude. One woman, however, always criticized everything and, while people did not seem to agree with her, they gave her their attention and this disturbed the working of the church. The vicar was gentle with her, though firm in not giving way on the programme. Being a pastor, too, he was concerned for her own well-being, and wondered why she persisted in her carping.

About two years after Alan had arrived a meeting was held to plan the next five years work of the church. It went positively. But afterwards the woman again approached him to extol the virtues of his predecessor. After she had finished speaking, there was a pause. The vicar had to decide how to act and what was the pastoral response. He was aware that the woman had got under his skin and that he was feeling angry. That was not new. He was also sorry for the woman, but did not know how to express that without being patronizing. However, he also on this occasion found a new feeling in himself. 'What is happening to me?' was his reference. The answer was that he found a feeling not of wistfulness (in her case perhaps for the past, in his for a quieter life) but of powerful desire to be the former vicar. He felt in himself a strong sense that the former vicar should be hearing this. Risking that this was an empathic feeling, he interpreted this to mean that the woman was not going on about the past but about her own attachment to the person of the old vicar and her desire to keep him near her, whatever the cost to others.

A number of options were possibly available. But taking this hypothesis (that the woman wished to be with the former vicar, not to keep his policies alive as such) and speaking to it, the vicar took out his wallet, removed a £5 note, offered it to the woman, and said, 'Here's the fare to Dorset. If you need more, please ask me.' He did not have to expound what he was saying: both he and the woman knew what the interpretation was. She, not surprisingly, refused the money and walked away apparently angry. But a few days later she was able to come and speak in detail and reflectively about her bereavement feelings and the connection that they had with his predecessor.

147

This story first illustrates the way in which countertransference is employed in pastoring. It also illuminates the way in which the stance of theological reflection relates to role.

1   There is rarely much time in a pastoral situation. So the reflection and response have to be virtually instinctive. The problem for most people is that in such situations they first refer back to themselves as persons rather than to the role that they feel is being assigned to them. This is often why theological reflection seems such a difficult concept to grasp. If it is not reflection on role, then it is bound to become personally idiosyncratic and uncritical. Ministers can learn skills through training. The stance proposed here becomes second nature. Reflection is not a special activity but a quality of living in role.

2   Using countertransference is always risky: there is no guarantee that the pastor will have got it right. Indeed quite often it will appear that he or she has been mistaken. The first reaction of the client is quite likely to be dismissive, largely because the pastor's interpretation has been more accurate than they can admit. Nevertheless, as with the idea of the good enough mother, provided there is integrity of intent it appears that the response is likely eventually to be felt and heard as 'good enough' - engaging and serious, even if not welcome. This, too, takes some learning, although the confidence is more likely to be acquired through experience. But this will only be the case if the pastor is using his or her role. Otherwise the voice is simply that of another person, not from the role that is being negotiated in the encounter. Unless ministers respond from their role, they will not be heard as representing the tradition or even God. In that case the stance of theological reflection will have been lost and the work of ministry will not be performed.

3   Lastly, the interaction in this story was interesting. The vicar did not address the woman's desires head on, saying 'You want to go and see the old vicar'. He spoke at a slant by offering the fare. In this way he drew attention to what underlay the woman's wishes, as he perceived them. At the same time he invited her to become responsible for her own desires. The offer of the fare made her face herself: would she go or not? It is a mark of good pastoral work, especially when using countertransference empathetically, that it faces

people with themselves, the pastor doing so by using his or her own self.

INTERPRETING THE REFLECTION

This discussion leads to the final two words in the question: 'What is happening to me *and why?*' This helps to clarify the central distinction between role and person, which is essential for theological reflection. If the question becomes only 'What is happening to me?', it can encourage narcissism and even drift to being merely descriptive. This is one reason why sociological study on its own feels inadequate for pastoral ministry. The words 'and why' remind the minister that he or she is involved in a situation for a reason.

After reflection comes action. There is little need here to amplify what this might be, since it will obviously depend on specific contexts. It could, for instance, be a piece of pastoral advice or counsel, a ritual or even a sermon. There is usually little doubt which is appropriate and when. There is, however, one point in common to all of these actions from the perspective of pastoral theology. This is the mode of intervention. In every case it is interpretative.

An interpretation draws together three complexities, which are themselves interrelated. These are the individual or group involved; the context in which they find themselves; and the connections between them.

THE INDIVIDUAL OR GROUP

The pastor obviously deals with individuals and groups. This may be a penitent or someone addressed or a group being ministered to, such as a family in bereavement. Reflection as described here reminds ministers of the richness of people's lives. They can never expose all that they are. Even the most intimate of consultation touches a fraction of the variety.

THE CONTEXT

We have already discussed this. The key point to which ministers have to hold is that they are part of that context and by their presence they are contributing to it. For instance, in the case of a ritual, such as a funeral, the context is an amalgam of awareness of life and death generally, the many feelings about the deceased and the corresponding interplay of beliefs, guilt and hopes between members of the family and friends. But the minister is also part of this context, which is why he or she has been approached in the first place. For the minister represents something, possibly the ability to cope with the unmanageable – death and the unknown.

THE CONNECTIONS

The links between these various complexities are multifarious. They also constitute a factor in the interpretation.

THE GOSPEL AND PASTORAL INTERPRETATION

Some might think that interpretation is too passive or acqui-escing a concept for Christian ministry. The Church has its gospel to proclaim. Its concern is with the divine dimension to all human life, especially as an agent for change in both individuals and groups. But these beliefs are not denied by the interpretative stance. Indeed the reason why ministers are involved in any pastoral interaction is because they are Christian and represent something of the divine. Even the most secularized minister, who might, for example, be acting as a counsellor, still carries residual overtones of his or her being something different. The Christian gospel is a factor in the context which the minister brings. The presence of God in every human situation is part of the context which the minister represents and which is confirmed, however mini-mally, by the approach of someone or some people to the Church. Pastoral interpretation must involve the gospel.

Rather than taking an instance from ministry to individuals, we may consider preaching as an example of the interpreta-tive stance in action. Most ministers are familiar with the idea of categorizing sermons by type. They may, for instance, be classified according to subject matter, structural type or psychological method. Subjects may include apologetic, social concern, evangelistic, ethical and devotional themes or doc-trinal and biblical exposition. The structure devised should match the subject matter. The psychological method will also be apposite, whether authoritative, persuasive, co-operative or subversive (Sangster 1954; Buttrick 1987).

From a pastoral perspective a sermon is interpretative. It will take a specific point of intersection between the congregation's experience and the preacher, who represents the gospel. The sermon then interprets that nodal point. The listening congregation need not be a regular church congregation. At a funeral, for instance, the congregation will probably include many people with little, if any, direct connection with the Church. Several will be in emotional disarray through being bereaved. Special occasions present a similar mix. Whatever the moment, the preacher in facing this congregation will have to offer some sort of interpretation in the following series of steps:

1   Take seriously into account what he or she may know or hypothesize about the congregation.

2   From personal experience seek some points of empathy; then explore in himself or herself the resources of the gospel: – both those personally owned in the preacher's current state of belief and those which the preacher is expected to hold – Scripture and tradition.

3   Finally, find one point of intersection from which to interpret the corporate feelings of the congregation, their beliefs and unbelief, in the light of God's concern for and presence with them.

CONCLUSION

Theological reflection issues in review. This has a number of facets, but issues in three discernible areas.

1   There is the review of what happens to the person or group with whom the pastor has engaged. This is often called 'follow-up'. But as ministers usually explain, it is very difficult. Excuses are sometimes rationalized in terms of lack of time or the movement of people. In fact, however, the problem of follow-up is not just a managerial one: it is a component in the complex interchange between people and the minister which is the stuff of pastoral ministry. It is not so much that ministers lack time or people disappear, although both are true. It is also that people, having engaged with the minister,

are in most cases likely to distance themselves and get on with their own lives again without the apparent need for the minister or the gospel resource. This is a function of that dependent culture that is described in Chapter 10.

2   Review is also related to the minister. His or her own growth and acquired experience is a critical factor in the future of the Church's ministry. We have already referred to the idea of being 'good enough'. That does not mean that ministers should not improve their skills, any more than a mother may not learn lessons from the first child which can be implemented with the second.

3   But there is a third area, which we may describe as the sum of theological learning. If ministers are working with the applied theology of the Christian Church, they will necessarily learn new things about the concerns of Christian theology. Ministry is not a matter only of skills: there is a learning to be increased. This will add to the accumulation of wisdom that is the hallmark of theology.

The dynamic of this process is diagrammatically presented in Figure 3.

This process may be compared and contrasted with that of theological reflection, as described in the previous chapter. Its strength for the minister is that it roots all the material on which to think in the pastor and his or her interaction with others, this being always accessible and interpretable when role is kept in mind. Although this, and the formative question for ministers that has been expounded, might at first sight seem too self-regarding for the Christian, they need not necessarily be so. The safeguard is a strong sense of role. Once that is acknowledged, self-referential reflection as a mode of ministry becomes both theologically demanding (and illuminating) and ministerially rewarding.

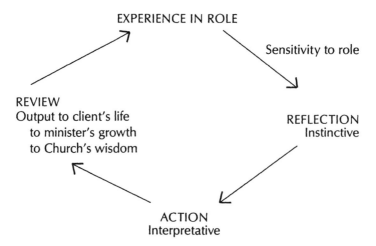

Figure 3: Theological reflection based on role

PART THREE

Church and Ministry

The final four chapters deal with aspects of Christian ministry in the light of the foregoing. Chapters 8 and 9 address the question of the relation between understandings of the Church and the forms of ministry that follow. They conclude by offering a model for thinking about and practising Christian ministry that can be employed by pastors of any denomination. The final two chapters explore specific dimensions to this ministry. Chapter 10 looks at 'common religion', which is a social phenomenon. Chapter 11 draws the distinction between ministry and therapy, which concerns the way that the pastor relates to individuals.

CHAPTER EIGHT

Understandings of the Local Church

Pastoral theology cannot be done without a strong ecclesiology. For pastoral theology always directs the Church's attention to people. These are not necessarily members of a congregation, but all, whatever their attachment. The Church in the mind of the pastoral theologian, therefore, has to be identifiable by such individuals or groups.

'CHURCH' IN PASTORAL STUDIES

The grand ecclesiologies of the universal Church are for the pastor always specific questions about ordinary people. Full ecclesiological exploration is foreign to pastoral theology. But in the continuing tension between universal and local, it will tend towards the local. This is because in dealing with people ministers are more likely to be handling some sense of the transcendent (or even of the divine) than of a greater or universal Church. Many people assume that the church which they encounter – a real, local church – is an access point to the divine. 'Church' takes on specific and local dimensions.

Industrial chaplains, for example, often report that when they first enter a factory or office they are asked which church they are from. The answer might be given in terms of denomination. But behind the question lies something more mundane. It is a question about the tower down the road or the spire across the green: from which *recognizable* church does the chaplain come? The local church, literally in its concrete manifestation, is the latching on point for further engagement.

A second point to note is the nature of a local church: it is a voluntary association. Whatever compelling reasons for belief or membership the congregation may testify to, no one is forced to believe or belong. Indeed, the motivations for anyone's belief are always hidden. It is salutary for ministers and church leaders to recall that, however intimately they may think that they know members of the congregation, the reasons why anyone believes or attends remain secret. Testimony rarely reveals much. And most people when asked why they believe will often respond that they do not know: they just do.

Churches, like all institutions, exist in people's minds. They are 'institutions-in-the-mind' (Obholzer and Roberts 1994). This does not mean that they are not also the all too real buildings and ministers, finances and people. But as an idea that people work with they are composed of the mixed, and often diverse, images that people have, together with what they are projecting onto one another and onto the organization concerned. Everyone associated with a church, for example, has their own mental image of what it is, what it is for and how it works. Discussion at a synod or a church council soon exposes this. It is not so much that people disagree, though obviously that sometimes happens. In debate people discover that they are working with different images or mental pictures and so have correspondingly different assumptions. In most organizations for much of the time there is sufficient congruence between these various notions 'in-the-mind' for decisions to be made. But every so often the variation becomes acute and is exposed. Conflict follows, to everyone's surprise.

> Though these diverse ideas are not often consciously negotiated or agreed upon among the participants, they exist. In this sense, all institutions exist in the mind, and it is in interaction with these in-the-mind entities that we live. Of course, all organizations also consist of certain real factors, such as other people, profits, buildings, resources, and products. But the meaning of these factors derives from the context established by the institution-in-the-mind. These mental images are not static: they are the products of dynamic interchanges, chiefly projections and transference. (Shapiro and Carr 1992, 70)

This way of viewing institutions is not peculiar to any one group, such as the congregation. 'Church' is a complex notion held in many individual and group minds, all of which affect one another. While the pastor has to be aware of the distinctive ecclesiology that informs his or her church (and, of course, also sensitive to the degree to which his or her personal valency may affect and be affected by that choice), the concept of 'church' is richer and more dynamically complicated. This understanding is more difficult to conceptualize than to experience. The way in which, for instance, people who have no direct connection with a church affect its life and existence is familiar to most ministers, whatever their denomination. 'Church' is always being created by a complex of feelings and associations, belief and unbelief. This is why the pastor needs a theological understanding of the local church, and an institutional one at that. It is, for instance, not much use having a fine theory of the Church catholic or of the body of Christ unless this is worked out in detail and in practice. Hence for the pastor the institutional dimension to the Church will always be paramount. This statement probably feels uncomfortable for most Christian people, ministers and students alike, unless they grasp what 'institutional' means in this context. It will also feel false, unless the other models of the Church are brought to bear upon this institutional understanding. In this chapter, therefore, we shall consider the Church as an institution and see how such an understanding is both informed and judged by other images.

THE INSTITUTION OF THE CHURCH

When we refer casually to 'the Church' we shift in one bound from what is grandly theological to what is awfully everyday. The Church of God is that familiar amalgam of building and minister, collection of history and hope, focus of beliefs and unbelief, love and hate. The institutional nature of the Church, therefore, is not to be confused with the process of institutionalizing. This occurs when the Church defines itself in terms of its structures and powers. It is sometimes claimed that institutionalization occurs when the model of the Church as institution is treated as primary (Dulles 1976, 32). This is obviously correct: the parade of believed power is one of the least attractive aspects of some Christianity, or indeed of any religious system. But the pastor's skill is to allow the institutional aspect of the Church, those realities to which people turn for whatever reason, to become primary in certain situations without their being allowed to dominate the Church's self-understanding.

For instance, a building may often be more important as an expression of faith than pastors realize. We noted earlier the importance of the church building in allowing people at work to place and so accept the ministry of a chaplain. Stewardship advisers know how in some places people, not necessarily those with close connection with the Church, will give generously for the fabric but be unwilling to support the activity of a church. Cathedrals offer another instance. They exercise a fascination that encourages pastoral ministry to people who seek the anonymity of the space and clergy who do not know them (Lewis 1995). Yet within the institution of the Church a cathedral is a major player in any power struggle.

The difference between the process of institutionalizing and taking the institutional nature of the Church seriously lies in the pastor's perspective. If, for example, a person with whom the pastor is dealing employs a simplistic idea of the church building, the minister might carefully and usefully assist them to re-evaluate the significance that they assign to their building. What they are using it for can be to some extent clarified and the underlying search be interpreted. This would be an excellent instance of proper pastoring. If, however, the building seems to be becoming an object of veneration in itself, and is encouraged to be, rather than a transitional one to be used in the pursuit of faith, then the institution has begun to institutionalize people's faith.

The key point to grasp about the Church as an institution is that 'church' (any church) is a negotiated concept. No church defines itself, although its language tends to imply that it does. In many modern churches this is reinforced liturgically in the Eucharist at the Peace: '*We are* the Body of Christ', say that worshippers to one another. In fact the Church is created through constant negotiation. This can be shown diagrammatically.

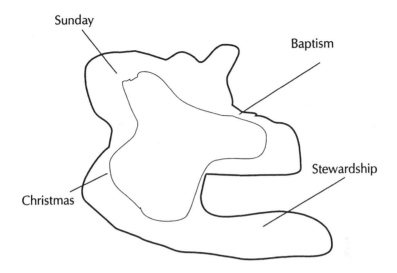

Figure 4: Dynamic diagram of a church

This picture may look awkward and strange. And, like any fixed image of something dynamic, it is too solid and therefore can be misleading. Nevertheless, it shows a local church as it is experienced.[1] There are two lines – an 'inline' and 'outline' (Miller 1977, 61). The inline represents the way that the church authorities and members perceive the Church. It is oddly shaped to represent the fact that there is no agreed view of any church. The associations of those connected with the Church both combine and separate to create a fluid outline. At some times of the year there may be a different overall view than at others. In the Methodist Church, for instance, self-awareness is probably strongest at the beginning of the year when the Covenant Service is held. The same intensity of commitment and awareness is not likely on the third Sunday in August. The outline represents a similarly fluid world of feeling. It is composed of the expectations, hopes and fears that people repose in the Church, whether they are members or not. The Church itself is continuously being constituted in the minds and feelings of all concerned through negotiation between the inline and the outline.

Like all diagrams, this one is unsatisfactory. It is fixed but represents continual movement, for people are never static. But this way of conceiving the Church draws attention to the way in which belief and unbelief are always changing, in flux. There is also in this drawing no way of showing that people themselves are not fixed either 'in' or 'out'. The diagram is dangerous: it might be taken merely to imply that there are two groups – the congregation (in) and others (out). But where ministers place people is not necessarily where they put themselves. Sometimes, for instance, the keenest member of a church might feel outside. At other times, as for instance over the occasional offices in the Church of England, the outsider may claim membership (to be 'in') and be surprised if this is not acknowledged. And, as with intercession, the members of the congregation themselves represent those who are not present. A worshipping mother, for example, remains also one of the group of other mothers in a community; the solicitor in church carries in some sense his or her legal colleagues with them. But given these caveats, this diagram discloses what it means to say that the Church (especially the local church) is a negotiated institution.

NEGOTIATING THE CHURCH

There follows a brief exploration of activities or events in the life of the Church by which its shape is negotiated.

SUNDAYS

The space between the inline and outline here is average. This represents the sort of expectations around which the Church is regularly negotiated. Those outside expect the church to be open, worship to happen and some people to attend. It is no surprise if the bells ring. Church people also expect that there will be a service and that worship will happen. This is, we might say, the norm of the Church: Sunday, worship, some people attending, some not.

CHRISTMAS

This is an intensified version of the norm. Here many, if not most people, whatever their association expect certain specific things of a church. For instance, more might attend, not necessarily for the Christmas Day worship, but for school carol services or concerts. They anticipate carols and Christmas readings, maybe a crib and the feeling of warmth and welcome that they associate with Christmas. Most years the press has the odd story of how this expectation is disappointed and people feel affronted. But so far as the negotiation is concerned, the two lines draw very close, almost into identity. The congregation largely holds similar expectations: carols, readings and bonhomie. The inline and the outline almost coincide.

BAPTISM

The distance here is again different. I have chosen an Anglican example, in the sense that this baptism is an everyday one of a child from the parish rather than one from a strongly church family. Infant baptism causes difficulty for some, but it remains a public point of negotiation about what the Church is. The expectations of those who come for the ritual and those of the congregation rarely coincide. But they are flexible: they could be wide apart or they could come close. For instance, a church which requires people to become worshipping attenders or even members before it will consider baptism would display a wide gap between the inline and the outline. A more traditionally Anglican view that, under certain conditions, a child brought to church will be baptized would narrow the gap, although never remove it. Indeed the focus of ministry at such times is the negotiation of what is expected on both sides. We have a drawing together without identity (see Chapter 10).

STEWARDSHIP

The final example, again not perfect but illustrative, shows what may have to be negotiated in a widely-ranging stewardship campaign. In many churches this will include an attempt to extend the giving basis. In a rural setting the whole village might be involved. In urban and suburban places people talk of the gradations of the fringe and how far to approach it. The gap between the inline and the outline now often becomes large. Those who understand the Church as an association (emphasizing the inline) seek to enlarge the membership or attract more support. The theme frequently is that the Church benefits or serves these people. They, therefore, might legitimately be asked to contribute money, time and talents to it. The unspoken word is 'membership': the hope is that many may join the Church. But to those outside, the concept of membership is often quite different. Instead of something involving regular commitment of time, talents and money, it is a facet of life which may or may not be mobilized from time to time. The Church in asking for money conforms to their expectations. But they have a powerful capacity to resist. The inline and the outline are so far apart that negotiation becomes difficult and almost impossible. The Church remains a negotiated concept. But the negotiation is more distant for both parties. The difference between how each group perceives what the other is saying is usually great. Stewardship campaigns often generate widespread anxiety in all involved.

The local church is a negotiated institution and the pastor's role in the process of creating it is significant. If, for instance, we take the four instances selected, in only one of them is the role of the public minister minimal. That is Christmas, when the expectations of all concerned are more general than at other times of the year. For example, the carols and crib may be more important for Christmas than anything that the minister does. By contrast the negotiation at baptism is likely to demand an authorized minister at some stage. Although all churches acknowledge theologically that a lay person may baptize, that permission is usually for extreme circumstances. In everyday life the people who bring a child for baptism expect someone who officially stands for God to be available and to perform the rite. Whatever the particular theology of sacraments of any church, an authorized minister is expected to preside. Here the negotiation of what the Church is for people at that moment often occurs chiefly around the minister.

Sundays are becoming interesting. Historically, in all but some free churches, the customary expectation of all, both those drawing the inline and those providing the outline, has been that worship will be conducted by an authorized minister. In most traditions, too, it has been assumed that this minister will also be the pastor who works with the congregation and community during the week. The congruence of pastoral ministry, teaching and leading worship has been a profound dimension to understandings of ministry, both catholic and Reformed. Now, however, this connection is breaking up as in many churches the Sunday ministers, lay and ordained, are no longer the weekday pastors. Whether this is a desirable development or one which the churches can even sustain remains to be discovered. But in terms of the negotiation which produces the Church in the mind, this is a trend towards separating the church's worship from its public pastoral ministry.

The fourth theme, stewardship, is complicated. Experience suggests that where the minister is willing to take responsibility for giving, then the church's finances are usually reasonable. Where he or she is not prepared to lead in raising money, there is often a problem. The stewardship movements in most churches, however, have emphasized the role of the laity. They have often been lay led and directed first at lay people. It is not impossible – though it would be difficult to know how to test this – that the distance between the inline and the outline on this topic may in part be due to this factor. For at all the other points in the scheme, a major factor in the negotiation as perceived both by the congregation and by others is the minister. He or she, as it were, belongs to both and constitutes one, but an important one, area of interaction which generates the idea of the Church.

When the Church is understood as institution in this sense, the range of other models of the Church can be brought to bear coherently. For this approach, taking seriously those points at which both it and others define it, makes a primary statement about every model of the Church – it does not, and cannot, exist for itself. The Church only exists for a series of tasks that it believes are assigned to it by God. Churches may debate the relative weight to be put upon each. And no church is likely to be able to perform them all. But the basic value of the Church, by which all other values are tested, is established in this institutional model. In this way this primary model of the Church proclaims its core values and embodies the essence of the gospel. If, however, the institutional model is not held as the focus, the others become alternatives and the choice between them eclectic. This creates further problems, since any model of ministry depends upon ecclesiology and not the other way round. If the ecclesiology is eclectic, then the models of ministry adopted will also be random or dependent on the psychopathology of the individual minister. In that case, what occurs will not be ministry – concern for and service of others – but personal gratification. By contrast, however, a firm sense of role, which itself must be related to the task of the Church, acts as a referent and control. In addition it makes ministry more accessible to those to whom it is offered. If nothing else, it acknowledges that they make a major contribution to creating the Church with which they are engaging.

The other models which fill out dimensions of this primary one are conveniently listed by Avery Dulles (1976). They are: herald, servant, sacrament and mystical communion. Each is a symbolic model; but each also tends to come to embody a specific ecclesiology and its associated theological tendencies. We shall briefly consider each, in relation to the primacy for the pastor of the institutional model.

THE CHURCH AS HERALD

This motif has become increasingly popular. It is part of the call for a 'Kingdom' not 'Church' theology. There is a pervasive sense that the era of the Church may be over and that within a plural world the cutting edge of the gospel must drive Christian living. In the United Kingdom the Decade of Evangelism (1990–2000) is a major institutionalized example of this theme. It calls the churches to proclaim their message anew to people. A similar debate about the relation between mission and evangelism preceded it. The calls, often through ecumenical agreements, were for the Church to become prophetic. The herald's work is to proclaim the word of God. The image draws heavily on St Paul, Luther, Karl Barth and theologians of the Word. A clear boundary is discerned between the Church and the Kingdom. But the Church always points to the Kingdom: it never embodies it. This model is a useful corrective to any sense of complacency that the institutional image generates.

The Church as herald puts considerable emphasis on the local church and the congregation.

> Local theology, as with many contextual theologies, is an attempt to develop an approach that looks forward. There is nothing particularly radical about this as Christianity has the symbol of the Kingdom of God to keep our eyes firmly fixed on the future. (Reader 1994, 135)

Although councils, popes and bishops make pronouncements, the local church has to work them out in practice. The Roman Catholic Church, for instance (at least in the west), has experienced this with the 1968 encyclical *Humanae Vitae*. The statements on birth control which came from the Vatican have to be lived with in local churches. A casuistry was generated which enabled believers to remain within the Church while at the same time reinterpreting papal pronouncements. This is an obvious case. But other churches have the same dilemma. The call, for instance, of the General Synod of the Church of England in the 1990s to boycott Nestlé's products had no meaning unless local churches adopted the stance. The model of Church as herald confirms the primacy of the local church.

The herald (Greek: *kērux*) in the Christian context proclaims the message (Greek: *kērygma*). This both addresses the inner life of the preacher by grasping him or her and speaks to the outside world with the challenge of the gospel. The model holds together the inline and the outline of the Church. One aspect of this is the prophetic ministry, speaking out the word of the Lord that has so grasped the inner world of the prophet that he or she cannot keep silence. Prophetic ministry is sometimes contrasted with pastoral activity. There has probably always been a divide between the proclaimers and the pastors. One of the historical debates, for example, in the churches' work in industry has been whether the minister is a chaplain or a missioner. Behind these two descriptions lie different assumptions. 'Chaplain' emphasizes that the minister is there to be alongside those among whom he or she moves, bringing a gospel insight to their lives as best they may. Such chaplains may, for instance, find themselves recruited by the personnel department to deal with human problems of the workers which are beyond their capability. Sometimes, as when redundancies are being declared, the firm may invite the chaplain to assist in counselling. A 'missioner' might do much the same. But those who claim this title talk more of influencing structures and changing conditions. Missioners have occasionally been drawn into one side or the other of disputes, usually that of the workers and their unions. The former ministry is characterized as 'pastoral'; the latter as 'prophetic'. There is a tension between the two, but private care and public struggle – the sub-title of Peter Selby's *Liberating God* – are connected:

> The private and the public world of each of us are connected like the strands of a rope and we cannot grow or be cared for in isolation from the world around us. That is not to say that the connection between our inner and outer worlds is simple and direct, or that it is always possible to be clear which is to have the priority. It is simplistic and a gross insult to the world's suffering to speak as though poverty and war will be eliminated by means of the progressive conversion of the hearts of individuals; it is also simplistic, and no less insulting, to suggest that personal maturity and inner resourcefulness are dependent on, or follow automatically from, better living conditions. The connection is more complex than that, but it is there nonetheless. We may have to make a judgement at any particular moment whether our best contribution to a situation is to attend to the environment or the inner world of a person. (Selby 1983, 5)

But how are we to make the connection? Selby rightly says that it has to be done situationally. But more can be said when we consider the idea of prophecy.

The image of the prophet popularly associated with the phrase 'prophetic ministry' is that of an Old Testament prophet such as Elijah, Amos or Isaiah. These are powerful anti-establishment figures, who denounce social injustice and religious laxity with the conviction, 'This is the word of the Lord'. They are remarkable for their integrity in the face of indifference and hostility. This picture is not false, but neither is it wholly true. The denouncing prophet in the Old Testament prophets was offering an alternative interpretation.

The work of the prophets was to extricate Israel from its certainty in the old saving actions of God into a new one rooted in what God would do in the future (von Rad 1962). This perception provides the continuum of prophecy between the old Israel and the new Israel in Christ and the link between pastoring and a prophetic ministry.

Jesus himself stands in the prophetic tradition. Yet, it appears from the gospels, he has little time for denunciation. His most severe castigation is reserved for those who are hypocrites within the covenant of Israel. Others are offered an alternative interpretation of those parts of their lives that they bring to him. Prophets in the earliest Christian communities continue this tradition. This is probably because they are believed to contribute 'a word of the Lord', which is now a word of the risen Christ. Their prophecies, therefore, are similar to those of Jesus, not so much denunciatory as interpretative.

The theme of interpretation brings the prophetic and the pastoral together. As interpreter the pastor or the congregation, like the prophet or herald, makes public use of himself or itself. If we follow Selby in relating these twin themes to the outer world, the environment, and the inner world of people, we can see that this is a means by which the two are brought together. It becomes clear that the 'environment' is that against which and within which a person's or a group's life are interpreted. That environment is not only a social and political reality but also the distinctive perception of the world that the Christian faith and some awareness of God generate. This world is linked with whoever is in need, more through the pastor's person or the congregation's experience than through anything the one or the other says or does.

THE CHURCH AS SERVANT

The servant Church has become a cliché. It is an overworked image. Originally it emerged against triumphalist tendencies in the churches. But now it is in danger of becoming an excuse for *laissez-faire*. Much of its appeal in the twentieth century has been because it can be appropriated by all and every church without inducing competition between them.

169

Which church is not 'a servant church'? The theme has served the ecumenical movement well (see p. 188). It has been especially useful in the growing rapprochement between the Roman Catholic Church and others following the Second Vatican Council. The theme has largely escaped serious criticism. As Jesus came to serve, so should the Church as the body of Christ in the world. Bonhoeffer's words have become a motto: 'The Church is the Church only when it exists for others . . . The Church must share in the secular problems of ordinary human life, not dominating, but helping and serving' (Bonhoeffer 1967, 203).

In principle the theme of the servant Church should give priority to the world in determining what the Church should be and do. But 'servant' is unclear. In passing we might also note that it is not applied to the Church in the New Testament. One result of this is that the idea of the Church as servant is filled out with assumptions about what a servant is without the moderating input of the Scripture. 'Servant' contains at least three different emphases:

1 working for the good of others – 'service';
2 working under orders – 'serving';
3 doing menial things – 'servile'.

Of these, the first has a key place in the Christian tradition. It emerges in the ministry of the deacon – *diakonia* (Collins 1990). But this ministry is notably directed not to the world but within the community of the faithful. As Dulles points out:

It would be surprising to find in the Bible any statement that the Church as such is called upon to perform *diakonia* toward the world. It would not have entered the mind of any New Testament writer to imagine that the Church has a mandate to transform the existing social institutions, such as slavery, war or the Roman rule over Palestine. (Dulles 1976, 93)

When servanthood and obedience are brought together, a weakness in the model becomes clearer. The Church is never invited to be obedient to the world. Its obedience is, and can be, owed only to God in Christ. Even when obedience to rulers is enjoined, this is because of their place in God's structures and not for their own sake. It might be that the command to love one's neighbour could be construed as a command to be that neighbour's servant. But it does not seem to mean working under the neighbour's orders or being servile. One effect of such a view is curiously to reverse the thrust of the image. The idea of the servant Church is supposed to give priority to the world and to others over any self-concern of the Church. For example, the sort of Church activity that follows from this model tends not to be concerned with making new disciples or enlarging the Church. The Church's continuing existence lies in the hands of God, who will ensure its survival so long as he has a purpose for it. Such a belief has led to conflict between the evangelistically minded and those who see service as the prescribed form of Christian behaviour. Yet in practice the theme of the servant Church constantly directs attention back to the Church and its existence. For instance, the high ideal of losing the Church's life in order to save it – a favourite theme of the servant Church – emerges as a preoccupation with precisely what sort of life should be lived in order for it to be lost.

The key issues in the servant model for the pastor are those of authority and obedience. Service in the New Testament picks up that remarkable notion in Second Isaiah that God can use anyone, even an enemy of God's own people, to serve his purposes. In Isaiah 44.28, after some passages about Jacob as God's chosen servant and a section on the vanity of the idols, Cyrus, the king of Persia, is appointed as God's agent (a shepherd or ruler) to 'fulfil all my purpose'. In 45.1 the prophet goes further: 'Thus says the Lord to his anointed, to Cyrus'. While the term 'Messiah' (anointed) in this period does not carry the overtones associated in Christianity and later Judaism, it is remarkable that this is its only occurrence in Second Isaiah and the sole occasion when it is applied to anyone beyond the covenant. 'Anointed' describes one who is authorized to act in God's name. The reference, therefore, is more than casual: it links God, task and authority to the extent, albeit unusually bold, of saying that God can and does authorize a pagan ruler to act on his behalf.

Christians make the connection between 'messiah' and 'servant' because they are joined in Jesus of Nazareth. The connection also illuminates the theme of servanthood, especially the servant Church. For the Church, like Cyrus, may be thought of as chosen by God with his task in mind and authorized to act on his behalf. This points away from preoccupation with questions of what precise service is required to the more profound issues of authority and authorization. The servant Church is authorized by God with a delegated function to further his task, however that is perceived. Such authority raises the issue of delegation. God chooses Cyrus and delegates to him a function. The same is true of Jesus. He is delegated a function which only becomes finally and painfully clear in the Garden of Gethsemane. The same model of task and delegation became true for the disciples and hence for the Church. The servant model of the Church directs attention less to action in the first instance than to the issue of delegated authority. When this is seen, the danger of the model pointing inadvertently inwards is lessened.

THE CHURCH AS SACRAMENT

The idea of the Church as sacrament has been mainly, but not exclusively, developed by the Roman Catholic and the Orthodox Churches.[2] A sacrament is both outward and inward, 'the outward and visible sign of an inward and spiritual grace' as the Catechism in the Book of Common Prayer puts it. The Church as a sign is not a difficult concept. The Church is supposed to embody the grace of God for all humankind to which it witnesses. That it is a witness to God, even if unworthily, is widely agreed by most churches. But the notion of sacrament enriches this theme. For a sacrament not only points to God's grace; it is also a sign that grace is present. It is for this reason that the idea of the Church as sacrament becomes problematic for many in the Protestant churches.

But the idea is worth pursuing. Since for pastoral ministry the institutional aspect of the local church is primary, it is important to hold to alternative images which can moderate any tendency towards institutionalizing. The Church as herald may sometimes be used to confirm the institutional model, especially in the Protestant tradition. The theme of the Church as servant may appear to endorse an introspection that makes it inadequate as a critical reference. Sacrament, however, brings two major questions to bear on the Church from the pastor's and the Church's perspective.

1 What about integrity?
2 What priority do we give to the individual within community?

1 In any pastoral activity the question of the minister's integrity inevitably arises. At one level it might be a simple matter of confidentiality and who may be trusted. At another, projective behaviour may dominate. A person, for instance, who feels guilty will probably be sensitive to their own lack of integrity. In such a frame of mind, a first response is likely to be defensively projective. Those parts of themselves that they cannot endure will be projected into the pastor, the Church or God. As a result, the minster's capacity to sustain integrity in the face of such projection is vital. Without this, the person being pastored will not be engaged at a level of any significance. Personal integrity is important. But believable institutional integrity is also required. This is the test of to what extent the Church embodies its witness and to what extent the pastor does so on behalf of the Church.

For example, institutional churches seem unable to avoid appearing to hold double standards. In the Roman Catholic tradition *Humanae Vitae* created problems for Christians in the west. The shock of the decision to ban artificial contraception still reverberates. The underlying issue was of authority and double standards. These have been resurrected by *Veritatis Splendor* (1994). The Church of England and the Methodist Church have both found themselves in similar difficulties over homosexual behaviour, especially with regard to ordination. As an institution, the churches could solve these dilemmas quite easily by having leaders take decisions in the authorized fashion. But the Church as sacrament is a modifying influence on any such simplistic approach to complex problems and holds the churches to the human reality with which they deal and of which they are composed.

2 A sacrament is never an individual transaction. The Eucharist, for instance, cannot be celebrated alone. Even the apparently private celebrant is held to be joined with the angelic host, even if for some that seems specious. Other traditions formally require a minimum attendance of three

people. Nor can there be a Eucharist without intercession. Such prayer brings others, both those known and many unknown, into the heart of the sacramental activity of the Church, where it is formed and affirmed. Through intercession the local activity of a church is kept 'other-aware'. The Christian sacraments cannot be administered to oneself. In this they proclaim the basic truth that everyone is born into some sort of community – a family, a race or a nation. The Church as sacrament embodies a central reality about the world which God has made and about God himself: there can be no private salvation. People are bound together.

This theme takes us back to the link between inner and outer world, the individual and the environment which is crucial for all pastoral theology. Whatever church tradition pastors represent, they need to be aware of these two aspects to the Church as sacrament – integrity and community. These themes also link the twin themes of ministry as being and doing. Ministers with their primarily institutional sense of the local church need the pressure all the time to be doing to be moderated by the sense of sacrament, which brings to bear a wider vision for reflection or being. This image also indicates that pastors, whether they so choose or not, embody for others an integrity which they expect to find, even if rationally they know that it is not available. That integrity will be something to which they will turn for forgiveness and absolution. Michael Bowering's story about the new minister, the churchwarden and the pedestals illuminates how the Church as sacrament works in practice (see p. 140). There the Church, as represented by the vicar, was also claimed by the parishioners. It stood for aspiration – the pedestal – which was not worshipped but was, like a sacrament, an effective sign. The vicar's pedestal effectively enabled other people to structure their lives on whatever for them were their pedestals.

THE CHURCH AS THE BODY OF CHRIST

In all traditions 'body of Christ'[2] is today one of the most prevalent models of the Church. It puts the emphasis upon the Church as a community of believers, the people of God, or, in words familiar now both from Scripture and the liturgy, 'the body of Christ'.

> The two models of the Body of Christ and people of God both illuminate from different angles the notion of the Church as communion or community. The Church, from this point of view, is not in the first instance an institution or a visibly organised society. Rather it is a community of men (*sic*), primarily interior but also expressed by external bonds of creed, worship, and ecclesiastical fellowship. (Dulles 1976, 51)

This theme suffers from two major weaknesses.

1 It may overemphasize the divine nature of the Church, implying that because people are together they constitute the mystical and divine body of Christ. That could, and sometimes does, lead to an inappropriate arrogance. It also ignores the extent to which Christian communities are as much subject to human dynamics as any other.

2 More significantly, the ease with which the phrase 'body of Christ' is used, usually without critical reflection, may lead Christians to forget how strange that metaphor is. In the New Testament there are two traditions connected with it. One, found principally in Romans and 1 Corinthians, stresses the mutual relationship between the members of the Church and their reliance on one another. The actual phrase 'body of Christ' refers to something to which Christians belong. The other tradition, as found explicitly in Ephesians and Colossians, refers to the headship of Christ over the body – the Church.[3] But for present purposes the difference is immaterial and less contrasted than it has sometimes seemed. The image, however exploited, draws attention to the unity of the various parts, to the congruence of different activities and responsibilities, and to the fact that the whole is held together not by its own efforts but by its divine vocation. Both images have in common their strangeness. Excessive familiarity and use has dulled this. But the writers' intention is to hold together the natural and supernatural dimensions of the Church. It is a strange collection of people; but it is also a strange product of divine grace, with a supernatural reference and tasks, the strangest and most important of which is worship.

A MODEL FOR PASTORS

The institutional model is primary for thinking about the Church in terms of its pastoral ministry, whether this is conceived as the work of the congregation or of representative pastors. The danger of institutionalizing is ever present. But if the concept of an 'institution-in-the-mind' is firmly grasped, the risk is less likely. This core model, however, is essentially modified in the following ways:

HERALD

Herald, prophet or preacher draws our attention to the Church's interpretative function. This is never to confirm the situation presented to it, whatever that may be. It will always, therefore, be standing at a slant, looking for the unexpected connection or hitherto unexamined question. Interpretation requires interaction between people's experience as well as reference to the transcendent. In the Christian tradition Christians are to seek God's work in his world as best as they can. This apperception (the mind's perception of itself as a conscious agent) is to be risked in interpretation, regardless of its fragmentary nature or the fact that it feels insufficient. The pastoral function which this emphasizes is the interpretative model of ministry.

SERVANT

The Church as servant points to the issue of authority which any claim to knowledge of the divine raises. It reminds Christians, especially pastors, that authority is both received and assigned. For example, the publicly authorized minister of the Church is in a distinctive position to be approached with expectations. That authority is a given. It responds to and generates expectations. But that authority is inadequate or even unreal until it is tested by being acknowledged and assigned by the person approaching the minister. The servant image sustains the theme of authority at the heart of pastoral ministry.

SACRAMENT

As sacrament the Church exposes its own expectations of itself. If the Church is not merely a sign, pointing to God, but an effective sign, a (not 'the') means by which God makes his graciousness available in his world, then the Church must stand under constant self-criticism. This was rediscovered by the Reformers when they realized that the Church must always be capable of being reformed anew – *ecclesia reformata semper reformanda*. The Roman Catholic Church seems to be discovering the same truth for itself as it follows up the 'new reformation' begun in Vatican II. Such a process can never be concluded. For every church the grace that it bears judges the way in which it functions. The judgement theme lies at the heart of sacraments. For the Church's ministers this is a reminder that everyone with whom they deal, whether individual or congregation, is never simply a client. These people are penitents to whom the ultimate ministry of the Church is absolution.

BODY OF CHRIST

Finally, the theme of the body of Christ, especially when elaborated into mystical communion, reminds all concerned with the Church of its strangeness. It is strange as an institution and is equally strange to those approaching it for whatever reason. Indeed, they probably feel strange too in so doing. It is curious that this model, in many ways the most 'churchy', points to religion and its irrational dimensions (see below Appendix 3). For pastors, if they ever feel comfortable in that role, it constantly prompts them to be aware of the strangeness of their vocation and how awesome are the expectations that are held of them.

CONCLUSION

Once the primacy of ecclesiology has been established, we can then turn to the model of ministry that most suitably today informs the work of the pastor. By now it should be clear that this is not just a matter of providing care. The complexity of the demands on the public minister, whatever the detailed differences deriving from the denomination, mean that without some way of interpreting these – a model of ministry – pastors will simply become increasingly confused. When that happens, as sometimes is evidenced in

CHAPTER NINE

A Model of Ministry

In recent years the phrase 'a model of ministry' has become prominent in discussions about the Church's ministry. But it is used in a variety of ways. In part this is because the concept of a model is itself unclear. Students, therefore, always need to check in which sense the phrase is being used.

THE IDEA OF 'A MODEL OF MINISTRY'

Three main meanings can be discerned:

1 Often it merely means 'modelled on' or 'copied', whether consciously or unconsciously. This view is usually based on history. Models of the Church's ministry always depend to some degree upon patterns of social life and of authority that prevail at different moments in history. Melinsky, for instance, lists five such models. He sees an imperial model emerging as the early church came to terms with its setting within the Roman empire. Similar, but more aggressive, is the military model, which encourages obedience, fight and instant response. More recently the industrial model, which emphasizes management, and the professional model, by which the minister is seen as an expert in godly things on a par with doctors or lawyers, have emerged. Finally there is the family model, with its stress on fellowship and brotherhood (Melinsky 1992).

This list is obviously incomplete. But it reminds us that the Church and its ministries do not emerge in a sanitized setting. The social contexts in which the Church finds itself, and to which it also contributes, affect the models of ministry which emerge. Melinsky indicates some points of contact. More important, however, for thinking about ministry are the unconscious emulations which occur. For instance, the house church movement, which claims to derive directly from the form of the Church presented in the New Testament, may be less a conscious return to a past than an unconscious joining with the present. To meet informally in houses, hold discussions and enjoy food and wine is the classic middle-class behaviour of the late twentieth century in the west.

2   A second sense of 'model' is more technical. This is a major discussion point in the philosophy of science. Such models order patterns of observed or hypothesized activity into coherent theories. How this occurs is much debated. The same is true of models of theological thinking about which there is also argument. These have two main facets and an outcome. The two facets are attention to experience, especially patterns in it, and awareness that religious models are analogical. Apart from some fundamentalists, most Christians recognize that all talk of God is analogical. Barbour has pointed out that

> the prohibition of graven images 'or any likeness' (Ex. 20.4) is both a rejection of idolatry and an acknowledgement that God cannot be adequately represented in visual imagery ... The creative theologian, like the creative scientist, realizes that his models are not exhaustive descriptions. Neither God nor a gas molecule can be pictured. (Barbour 1974, 50)

Models are not ends in themselves. They become heuristic tools, the test being whether they successfully lead to new insights, new theories and even new models being developed. They provide a systematic way of looking at disparate evidence. But there is more to the use of a model than just observing. Some theological writing seems to suggest that observation is enough. For instance, John Hick refines Wittgenstein's theory of 'seeing as' into his theme of 'experiencing as'. Wittgenstein† pointed out that we never simply see something; we always see it in a context. Context and observation together suggest that to perceive is to see according to a pattern. His well-known example is the duck/rabbit: the same image is interpreted differently according to some sort of disposition in the observer. The picture itself is neither duck nor rabbit: it becomes one or the other when *seen as* a duck or rabbit (Wittgenstein 1953, 194e). Hick has suggested that religious faith is similar. We experience life, but also experience it *as* – in this case as an encounter with God (Hick 1967).

The idea of a model takes such thinking a stage further. As we assemble a range of experiences which we consider to have been of God, we create a systematic way of looking. Believers, as they pursue their pilgrimage, gradually come to consider every part of life instinctively from this perspective of 'experiencing as'. This is especially true for pastors, because they experience many things as divine not on the basis of their personal faith alone but also because of their ministerial roles. A model of ministry is a way of interpreting life and its experiences as moments of the divine.

3   The third use of 'model' is probably the most familiar. It refers to a standard by which to evaluate something. For example, a model bridge may be built or computer-generated by engineers to test their theories before they erect the actual structure. This meaning is a more concrete version of the technical sense in 2 above. But it is worth mentioning. For one mark of a model of ministry is that it is able to harness more than the religious experiences and analogies of the Church alone. The work of the pastor has a gritty reality to it. In a sense, therefore, pastors, as they progressively construct a model of ministry against which to evaluate their work, will be not just theorizing but creating an almost concrete picture of what the pastor is. A major component of such a picture will be people with whom the pastor has worked. A vicar, for instance, who has trained a curate will be built into the curate's own model of ministry. He is likely to be invoked, initially consciously and as time passes with less awareness, as a paradigm for activity in a pastoral situation. 'What would X have done?', is not necessarily a flight question: it can be a way of using a working model of ministerial action. There is something parallel to the role of parents in the way in which those whom the pastor has respected and from whom he or she has learned continue to contribute to the minister's model.

Any working model of ministry will not be pure. It will be a mix of these three dimensions. Undoubtedly it will include an element of copying, whether conscious or unconscious.

But primarily the model of ministry will be a means by which pastors hold in as coherent a fashion as possible three main areas of their world:

1 the range of experiences to which they are exposed;
2 the undergirding concept of the Church, particularly the local church;
3 the more systematic theological insights with which the pastor works.

1 The range of experience to which the pastor is exposed is enormous and mostly incoherent. The aspects of people's lives that are presented are very varied. Most of them are fragments of everyday human experience which have for whatever reason become problematic. They may be specifically religious. Much is superstitious. Little (or at least less than the pastor might hope) is likely to derive from obviously Christian faith. Without a model of ministry, the pastor is likely to have any sense of role knocked around. He or she then either selects input, so as to control the boundaries of his or her life, or takes on board everything, regardless of its potential meaning and collapses in the attempt. This breakdown may be physical, involving alcohol, drugs or sexual adventure, or psychological.

2 The second area is the understanding of the Church with which the pastor works. Pastors occupy a range of roles. But their function as pastor derives from the prior understanding of the Church. There is probably some sort of correlation between the reason why ministers belong to a particular church and their personal psychopathology. But that does not explain everything. The understanding of the Church with which they and those with whom they deal come together affects the nature of the role that they occupy. And since the role is related to the prevailing model of ministry, it is essential that this model includes a reference to the underlying ecclesiology.

3 Finally there is the pastor's own theological undergirding. This is an important area which is often overlooked. Because the pastor's activity is practical, the theology which informs it is often left as an aspect of the Church or as a set of large and vague ideas. So, for instance, in the Church of England the minister's role is reinforced by an ecclesiological

assumption and a major theological motif. The assumption is that the Church of England ministers to everyone. This is sometimes argued as the basis of the parochial system, although on reflection it is clear that there is a difference between ministering to everyone and being accessible to everyone. The theological motif is that such ministry is incarnational. It is, so the argument runs, about being alongside more than about addressing people. But this theology may substitute for the critical relation between people's experiences and the pastor's interpretation which is the essence of ministry. The minister forgets that the doctrine of the incarnation is more about difference and negotiation than sameness (Carr 1989).

MODELS OF MINISTRY AND MODELS OF CHURCH

Potentially there are several models of ministry. Since analogy plays a major role in their creation, the number of analogies is large. In a recent workbook for those training for ordination, for instance, the pictures of sheepdog and lighthouse were put alongside more familiar ones of team leader or father/mother figure (Redfern 1994). We need, however, to distinguish the idea of a working model from analogies or pictures. Without a model to work with, pictures merely endorse the range of expectations and ideas associated with ministry. We are then thrust back upon incoherent approaches which the original idea of a model was meant to combat. By contrast, however, there is sometimes also a sense that any unifying model will become a straight-jacket imposed on variegated experience and perceptions of God to produce a false coherence.

In order, therefore, to sustain some consistency in ministry and at the same time not impose this constraint, the model of ministry needs to have two main characteristics:

1 It must relate congruently to the image of the Church with which we are working. As we have seen, this may vary from denomination and place. The same will be true of the minister's role.

2 Second, it must have built into it self-criticism or a critique which allows for and encourages change.

To achieve this the model of ministry must begin with the question of the Church and what it is for. The answer given will determine the shape of the ministry (Greenwood 1994). The Church's task may often be discerned from the way that its authorized ministers are treated. This is not a subtle form of clericalism. It is a recognition that the public minister carries a public role. He or she works inevitably at the edges of the Church where it and people meet. This meeting may be conscious, but the unconscious sense of the Church should not be overlooked.

The following figure is a heavily stylized diagram of a church in its environment. It picks up from the figure in Chapter 8, where the fluidity of the relationships was emphasized.

Environment

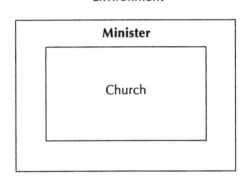

Figure 5: The boundary minister

It again presents the themes of an outline and an inline of the church. These are both, as we saw in Chapter 8, dynamic and the diagram is, therefore, misleading. But it clarifies the place where the public minister operates. He or she is always, when in role, on the boundary between the outline and inline; represents the church to those who seek something from it; and also stands as a sign to the church that its primary task is to work with people, not to indulge in internal activities. Seen like this authorized ministers have a crucial function: they both work for (on behalf of), with (collaborating) and to (addressing or challenging), the church.

The minister, as he goes about his job as a representative of the church on the boundary with the rest of society, has a great deal of hope invested in him. He is asked to show dependability and reassurance, while recognising at times that within the church and within himself there is much uncertainty and confusion ... This means that there is inevitably an element of childlike dependency in the relationship to the church, and thus to its representatives, in that to some extent they are asked to solve the insoluble, cure the incurable, and make reality go away. Ministers of the church then have to receive this dependency. Sometimes they get stuck into a paternalistic posture; sometimes they are able to help their parishioners both to recognise dependency and to discover their own resources and capabilities. (Miller 1993, 106)

Two objections are commonly made to this view.

1   It does not apply to all churches, but is peculiarly Anglican;

2   Current religious behaviour in Great Britain gives the lie to this concept of interaction at the boundary, so the model is false.

The first criticism has some justification. The quotation occurs in a study of an Anglican diocese. That church's specific form is distinctive, especially around the question of membership and belonging. Nevertheless, the basic argument applies to any church that is interacting with its setting. The style of that activity will vary, but the behavioural patterns underlying it are similar. For any dealings with religion and with a church are presumed to be dealings with God. And however God is conceived, the pattern of that perception will be in some fashion dependent. However close he is believed to be, God will always also be beyond (transcendent) and greater (almighty) and in a particular relation to us (for example, father/child). The argument, therefore, may be derived from an Anglican investigation, but it is generally applicable.

The second point raises questions about how to assess an interaction that is unexpressed. Social surveys regularly demonstrate greater public concern with religion than appears from the numbers attending churches (Davie 1994; Moses 1995). Proof is impossible. But the evidence that can be gathered supports the idea that the role of the minister and function of the churches remains more significant than measurable. But – and this is an important qualification – this can only be true in so far as authorized ministers deliberately put themselves in the way of working on the boundary between church and society, not limiting their role to a function within the church (Carr 1992 – especially the contributions of R. P. Reiss, D. Conner and J. S. Cox).

Images of ministry have a long pedigree in the Christian Church. The familiar pictures are of the minister as prophet, as servant, as representative (specifically *alter Christus*), as priest and as pastor. But any such model must connect with a model of the church. So each of these links with the models of the church that have been discussed: herald, servant, sacrament, body of Christ and institution.

THE CHURCH AS HERALD: THE MINISTER AS PROPHET

There is little to add to what has already been said on this subject. A church is only prophetic when there are actual prophets. The Church's proclaimed word needs witnesses. The elaboration in terms of pastoral ministry is the way in which witnesses are also martyrs – those who in their life and, if required, death witness to the truth. The minister's prophetic role is always to enlarge the question with which he or she is confronted; to interpret it in that larger context; and to draw out a mode of action with and for the client.

It is a common experience in pastoral work, as of counselling and indeed most approaches to interpersonal relations, that what someone first talks about is unlikely to be the subject that they wish to raise. Most people are familiar with the hour's meeting that only in the last five minutes gets to the matter in hand. However much the minister tries to direct the conversation it seems to make no difference. But there is a further dimension to this enlarging. The person who comes to a minister is not merely approaching someone who might be able to help but someone with a powerful representative role. The language used will probably not reflect this. But behind every encounter with a Christian minister lies something to do with God, since that is what they are known to stand for. The minister, therefore, should normally

186

during the conversation or ritual that results refer explicitly to God. The minister's feelings about this may be ambivalent. He or she may think that mentioning God is to confirm a false stereotype of the limited extent of the minister's concerns. Such a reference may even be regarded as opting out of the 'real' problem of the other person. The client, however, is meanwhile expecting the minister to mention God, although ambivalent about it. If the minister does, it feels stereotypical and can be dismissed. Yet, if the minister does not, why, asks the client, am I talking with a minister in the first place? Pastoral encounters sometimes reach such a stand-off. The answer is simple: the minister, as representative – herald – of God, needs carefully to draw specific attention to the source of a minister's authority. This is different from bringing in God as a solution or answer to the problem. But God is the context of the encounter and therefore is to be named.

This approach will also qualify the sort of advice that is given. Non-directive counselling has no place in the herald's ministry. This does not imply that such ministry is aggressive or authoritarian. But the authority of the Gospel is always brought to bear, even though, as will be the case, the decision whether or not to acknowledge it in their life belongs ultimately with the client not the minister.

One further point remains to be noted. As witnesses prophets are especially on guard against projecting into others. They bear something for the other. The image of martyr firmly indicates that pastors are willing to be used rather than protected in their ministry. Pastors use themselves as a reference point for interpreting what is going on. The theme of the Church as herald and of the minister as prophet emphasizes that the Church is also self-using, even to the extent of being willing to lose itself on behalf of others.

THE CHURCH AS SERVANT: THE MINISTER AS SERVANT

These two models are more congruent than the last, even to the extent of sharing a predicate. The model of servant both for the Church's ministry and for that of the minister is widely held. It has generated a model of ministry that opposes any authoritarian tendencies. Why has this model gained such a high profile?

The answer partly lies in the extensive ecumenical discussions about ministry that have occurred over the past century. The difficulties that the notions of 'bishop' and 'priest' raise do not seem to occur with 'deacon'. *Diakonia*, servanthood or service, is the easiest aspect of ministry on which to agree. In addition the theme of the serving Church discounts the triumphalism, actual and presumed, of earlier eras. Because service and the role of deacon go hand in hand, churches can discuss ministry on this model without much conflict. And the whole field is rooted in Scripture through the theme of servant in the Old Testament, especially in Second Isaiah, and its elaboration in the New Testament. This model also minimizes pressure to separate ministry *to* the people of God from ministry *by* the people of God (Cooke 1976). For *diakonia* has a wide application and links both service to the secular world with the idea of spiritual ministries for the body of Christ. But the key theme is that of how authority is received and how it is exercised (Collins 1990).

The servant stands amid a complex set of authorities. House servants, for instance, are responsible to the master who employs them and for whom they work. But they will be asked also to wait upon guests. They are thus accountable to those guests. How they behave reflects on the master and the house, as well as upon themselves. The servant is, therefore, both chosen – appointed by the master – and available for use at the whim of the guests. St Paul explores this in Philippians 2.5–9: Christ's servanthood is manifest not simply because he is appointed by God but in so far as he is willing to serve that appointment, whatever the cost.

Although it has often been used in a casual fashion, this model of ministry confronts the pastor with profound questions of authority. In today's churches anxiety often seems to be heightened when this topic is mentioned. This is partly because authority is frequently confused with authoritarian behaviour and partly because power is misconstrued as authority. The servant model illuminates these issues, since it draws attention to the minister's authority not from the perspective of one with power but of one under orders. What this says about the pastor's ministry is best seen when we consider delegation. Not only in the story of Jesus Christ but also in human experience generally the exercise of authority is less about using power than about being able to accept and make delegations.

Every pastor is in a position of authority. It is assigned by their church which has acknowledged their vocation and authorized them for ministry. The nature of that authority will depend to some degree on the particular church. But in all cases appointment carries authority. But this does not enable pastors to do anything. They cannot, for instance, usefully parade around the streets claiming their authority. A response which corresponds to this assigned authority is necessary. What is assigned is not for the minister's benefit; it is there to be used. The minister's authority announces that the Church (and therefore God) is present in a situation and therefore, in some way as yet to be explored, accessible. In a different way the same is true of lay Christians. But their authority from the Church is minimal. Their 'personal authority' is confirmed by their connection with the Church but does not derive from it.[1]

Assigned authority, therefore, has to be complemented by a validating authority which others give. The public minister may be authorized to act on behalf of the Church and hence also of God. But such authorization does not compel anyone to approach a pastor. The authority becomes real only when someone risks using it. Use does not imply that it is formally accepted or consciously acknowledged. But people may question the minister's authority and so locate themselves more clearly in whatever predicament or confusion their life is in. In the New Testament to be able to be a servant is a qualification for leadership. But this is designed not to give leaders authority (and even less, power), but to show them how that authority only has meaning when it serves others.

In Second Isaiah God delegates to the servant aspects of his own authority. Servanthood implies delegated authority, which is given not for its own sake but to further God's task – the Kingdom. Jesus is himself a paradigm of this. Argument continues about the extent to which he may have applied the title of servant to himself. But others perceived this aspect of his ministry, if only in retrospect. It seems clear that he believed that he carried divine authorization. His ability to accept that delegation was confirmed by the way in which the disciples associated with him and explored the issue of authority in him, ultimately in the cross. Disciples, therefore, might be described as those who both perceive the authority of their Lord and accept his delegation of it. By recognizing the authority of another person, their leader, disciples begin to grasp their own authority and learn to exercise it. This is servanthood.

Ministers are servants who are confident enough in their own authority to risk it being examined and used by others as a means to recover or discover their own. Their basic authority is that of being a human being; it might develop into becoming that of a servant of God. But in every case servant models of ministry are not about doing things for or with people but about exposing, clarifying and using the theme of authority. Grasp of this would enable many ministers to work more effectively and with less exhaustion.

THE CHURCH AS SACRAMENT: THE MINISTER AS REPRESENTATIVE (*ALTER CHRISTUS*)[3]

When the Church is thought of as a sacrament, an effective sign of God's presence, the role of the public minister changes. The images of herald or servant are concrete. There are actual people who are prophets (heralds) and servants. Thinking about sacraments takes us into a realm of more ethereal and less tangible images. For example, although at the heart of the Eucharist there are bread and wine the core of the sacrament lies in how they signify something other than themselves. If, as we have noted, the idea of the Church as sacrament is dangerous but can be used, is the same true when this model is applied to the pastor's ministry?

There are dangers of delusion if we identify the public minister either with the Church or as a sacramental adjunct. The theme of the minister (historically the priest) as *alter Christus* could be taken by Protestants as a Catholic aberration which is not worth further exploration. This argument has considerable force, but only if we define the Church from within. If, however, as has been argued, the Church cannot be defined that way but is always being created through transactions with the world, then this model has scope. For the negotiation is not between two fixed entities – the Church and the world – but between groups of people with their feelings and beliefs. The Church is a voluntary association of people who offer to use their beliefs, and hence their feelings, with all that vulnerability, to work with other people at the level of their expectations and feelings and beliefs. Such a description looks like a recipe for chaos. But that is the Church, whatever the denomination.

Since the idea of the Church as sacrament directs attention to its boundary with the world or society, then the model of ministry that derives from it will especially raise the question of the public minister's role in managing that boundary. Anyone in that role needs a strong sense of the Church which he or she represents. On this basis the theme of the Church as sacrament arises. It is linked with that of the authorized minister as representative.

But representative of what or whom? The answer is both of the Church (the source of immediate authorization) and of God (the one behind the Church who lurks in people's semiconscious when they encounter a minister). The first point is illustrated by the phrase which may still be heard about an ordinand: 'He's going into the Church'.[3] This popular view aligns the Church and the ordained minister. The phrase has been rightly criticized, but it contains a sound point. For there is a connection between the institution (the Church) and those who are charged with boundary roles (its ministers). The phrase correctly indicates where the minister is located and where his or her authority is assigned and confirmed – namely, to what extent ministers are boundary keepers. Leaders experience in themselves the ambiguities and ambivalences of their boundary position. But these feelings are not peculiar to the leader. They run through the whole institution, although they focus in its leadership. By using these and interpreting them the minister is able to lead, that is, to work with others at keeping (or putting) the institution in touch with its task. All leaders have this responsibility, whether they are authorized to lead or whether for whatever reason they find themselves in a leadership position.

The ministers' boundary function makes them both of the Church and given to it. The Church of England, for example, ritualizes this by generally appointing its vicars from outside the congregation. In the Free Churches the congregational involvement is more obvious. In the Roman tradition it features hardly at all. There are ecclesiological reasons for these differences. But whatever the mode of appointment, similar expectations are focused in the minister. He or she is expected both to represent the Church (including the local one in which they minister) to the world around and God to that Church – that is, to stand beyond it and address it.

Representation in the context of sacraments, however, possesses a distinctive dimension – the theme of judgement. This appears, for instance, in St Paul's specific warnings about receiving the body and blood of Christ unworthily (1 Cor. 11.27–34). But there is also a more general sense of caution associated with the sacraments. They provide sustenance for the Christian, either as a non-repeatable reference point for faith (baptism) or as a regular reintegration with the life of Christ (Eucharist). But at the moment they sustain the sacraments also judge. Baptism, for instance, represents a moment of decision for or against Christ. The profession of faith and the grace of God constantly judge the quality of Christian living by the baptized. With the Eucharist the test is to what extent the believer continues to discern the Lord's body or fails to do so. The Church as sacrament, therefore, is less a support than a judgement on believers about where they stand at a particular moment in relation to the one who first calls the Church into being.

The three massive themes of leadership, representation and judgement coincide in the model of the Church as sacrament. The model of ministry which derives from it proposes that the minister also leads, represents and judges. Unlike the other models of ministry, this is essentially related to that of the individual pastor and his or her authorization. It is instructive to note, however, that few, if any, churches manage to survive without some such ministerial structure. And while *alter Christus* sounds more Catholic than Protestant, the three themes are common to the ministries of all churches.

LEADERSHIP

Leadership is widely discussed. It is difficult to discover what form it should take in today's world and how it should be exercised. People are naturally nervous of charismatic leaders or those who too explicitly demand followership. The prevailing sense of individual autonomy makes followership a difficult concept. People are sceptical and only willing to follow anyone within limits. Yet there is also a longing for some sort of leadership to which to give allegiance. The notion of a boundary usefully illuminates this dilemma. For instance, the work of the Church is that of interacting at a series of boundaries. Among the most obvious are those between God and the world or between the Church and society or between the individual and the Church. At each of these there is an interaction. It does not have to be generated: it happens. Any idea, therefore, that the leader creates these opportunities is unnecessary. But such boundaries constantly need to be clarified or even pointed out again. That is the task of leadership. Any leader is expected to discern where a boundary lies and draw attention to what needs to be done about it.

Worship is an example. There the primary boundary that is consciously addressed lies between God and the congregation or God and the individual worshipper. Most of that interaction is the responsibility of the worshippers themselves. The minister or leader cannot intrude. Much of the time he or she has no idea what people are believing or thinking during worship. But the minister is expected to assist, even lead, in creating the conditions in which such interaction can take place. So the minister will speak *for* the people in prayers as well as speak *to* them in the sermon. He or she may ensure that a liturgical framework is followed and may also direct the time and the pace of the worship. In so doing the minister seeks to hold for people the crucial boundary on which they are working at that moment, namely the link between them and God. Wherever the mind of the congregation may go, it is the minister's role as leader to hold firmly to the boundary with God on which they are for the moment set and make sure it is not lost.

REPRESENTATION

The idea of the minister representing God to people or the people to God may suggest that the minister is here being thought of as mediator. Christians hold differing views on this topic. If any still hold that the minister – here perhaps specifically 'priest' – is the mediator between Christ and the Christian community, as if he held a power which could be exercised independently of the people, they are likely to be a declining minority (Schillebeeckx 1980). This view of ministry is no longer sustainable on either historical or theological grounds. Yet representation retains a place in ministry. If the minister becomes preoccupied with what they represent, they are bound to run into trouble. If, however, they always realize that they are probably being used by those among whom they are ministering to represent something for them, then they have an access point to that critical question of ministry: 'What is happening to me, and why?'

The essence of representation, therefore, lies not in the minister's conscious self-awareness but in the way that they allow themselves to be used to enable some sort of interaction to occur. Again, therefore, such leadership has a boundary function aspect to it. It is not a question of doing something and being followed because of that. The minister as leader or representative is used by others as a means by which to find their sense of direction or place in a confusing world.

The classic expression of this ministry is intercession. All ministers are expected to pray for their people. The ordination service in the Anglican *Alternative Service Book 1980* includes words which would be widely endorsed by various churches: '(Ministers) are to lead their people in prayer and worship, *to intercede for them*, to bless them in the name of the Lord.' This is an example of representation as a boundary function. When praying for people ministers do not mediate between them and God. They stand for them before God, holding them up in prayer. They do not pray instead of the people. Indeed it is their duty to encourage them to pray themselves. But they do pray on the people's behalf. Intercession is a further example of the key difference in all ministry and pastoral work between doing something *on behalf* of others and doing something *instead* of others.

JUDGEMENT

This theme inevitably follows. The minister is not a judge set over the congregation or people, although again that aspect to ministry should not be wholly discounted. Ministers all the time make judgements on people and some should be relayed to them. But in the sacraments the minister is the agent of the theme of judgement. In the biblical tradition two things become clear about divine judgement:

1   It often seems to come from unexpected sources. God may use those outside the Church or the religious community as his vehicle for his judgement.

2   The Church or religious community always stands first under God's judgement. So any lively church will expect to hear the voice of God coming not from the core tradition or activity but from its boundary with the world. There what it is about will be questioned or put under judgement.

For such judgement to be heard a leader must function on the boundary itself. It is sometimes said that the laity are more in touch with the world than the clergy or other public ministers. This is a strange and false assumption. Each group is in touch, but differently. But the minister will usually receive more of the judgement of the Church than the lay person. That is not surprising since he or she publicly represents the Church and cannot disown it. The minister is, therefore, often more in touch with the world at this level and consequently better able to articulate the judgement of God under which the Church stands.

The phrase which best describes this model of ministry is *alter Christus*. Although the image has been tarnished in the Church's history, in the light of the above discussion it can be seen to point to a vital dimension of public pastoral ministry. For the minister the theme draws attention to the great responsibility of such a position and not to any privilege. The way to preserve that perspective is twofold:

1   Always to hold to the fact that ministerial leadership is a boundary function. The moment that ministers feel themselves being pulled into the Church is the time to become wary. The theme of *alter Christus* can be useful here, for it indicates what it means to embody Christ. That is not to choose, but to be chosen, not to lord it over but to suffer, not to stand at the heart of the religious world but to seek at all times the tangential boundary moments or stances.

2   To remember that ministers have a distinctive spirituality. In many traditions ministers are formally expected to follow a special spiritual discipline. In the Roman and

Anglican churches, for instance, they are required to say the offices. But all churches expect their ministers to practise a different, not better, spiritual discipline from that of Christians in general. If ministers do not pray, who will? To be *alter Christus* reminds ministers of this duty and connects their praying to the Church and its task.

> In himself, therefore, he seeks to embody the Church's spirituality. He also connects it to his role by consistently relating that spirituality to the Church's task. He does not allow it to become an end in itself; he tries to interpret what this experience says about the task at any given moment and how it may be a resource for performing that task. In doing so he potentially exposes himself to pain and suffering, which, it might legitimately be claimed, he experiences both on behalf of the Church and on behalf of the world in which it is ministering. In this limited sense the notion of *alter Christus* might usefully be revalued. (Carr 1985, 51)

THE CHURCH AS THE BODY OF CHRIST: THE MINISTER AS STRANGER

If the idea of the Church as sacrament and the minister as *alter Christus* creates ecumenical problems, that of the Church as the mystical body of Christ and the minister as stranger might seem to pose even more. There is, however, a key aspect to a model of ministry that this description of the Church brings to the fore. This is the dimension of strangeness.

Contemporary thinking about ministry often runs into a problem about the way in which today's managerial and organizational approaches seem to squeeze out eccentricity. One mark of the Church's ministry through the ages has been the strangeness of some of its ministers (Hinton 1994). This might be dignified as holiness: they were too good for this world. Sometimes, beginning with St Paul, it might seem like canonized awkwardness. At other moments it is sheer eccentricity. Every tradition contains those who did not quite fit the Church but who achieved much for God. There is, it appears, a necessary strangeness, which may be heightened in a few but which is to be found in some facet of most public ministers. Today it is usually hidden as not quite reputable. But in spite of all current trends towards social accessibility, ministers remain strange or different. A new vicar in a village for instance, will soon discover how far one can be one of the people in the pub and how soon one is expected not to be quite like them. The same is true in urban and suburban setting, *mutatis mutandis*. One of the professional skills of ministry is to discern this boundary and then live and work with it.

Ministers are criticized because they are too busy doing things and have not enough time to be (Peterson 1993). There is some truth in this, although in a world in which 'being' is a leisure activity for most, the idea of professionally 'being' is difficult. Nevertheless, this demand signifies a search for someone to embody depth or meaning which cannot otherwise be found, just to be: action will follow. Others take a more active view, regarding the minister as a functionary. In the Church of England, for example, this distinction is worked out around such issues as the freehold and stipends. Does the vicar of a parish have tenure in order to be able to serve the parish without outside forces ordering him or her around? And should the clergy receive a stipend – that is, their keep – and not a salary, which would imply that they are employed? The questions are posed differently in the various churches, but underneath all lies this topic for consideration: is the minister to live in relation to the Church and the world with a different freedom from that which is expected of lay people and other church officers? The minister's skill is to represent the strangeness (the otherness) of God and be a place where that strangeness can be encountered. The busy-ness of doing, therefore, is the place where the otherness of being is worked out.

R. P. Reiss, writing from his experience as Team Rector of Grantham, has expressed this clearly. Although he writes explicitly from an Anglican perspective, the argument is applicable to the role of any minister whenever the Church is thought of as the body of Christ. For theologically he gets away from the dangerous triumphalism associated with that image and shows how the ministry that follows is rooted in creation. The description, as worked out here, accurately describes the ministry of the strange one in and through the mystical body of Christ. He discusses the life of an imaginary vicar called Richard. At the end he offers this argument for what he has done and been:

> [Richard] was challenged to defend his emphasis on pastoral involvement with the community. 'Where does it lead?' he was asked. 'How many more people have been brought to Christ through this world?' 'How is the congregation encouraged by it?'

> 'Well, I suppose it starts from a doctrine of creation', he replied. "God saw all that he had made, and it was very good." I know sin has disrupted that original goodness, but I don't believe that it has completely obliterated it. The world that I am involved in, the whole world of the community including its institutions, is, I believe, of God. And if God be God then my responsibility is not to imagine I am taking God to the community, but to find him there. Sometimes, when the opportunity is right, I can then point him out to others, but it is not because I possess God as a gift to give. He is the gift which sometimes I find. My task is then to interpret what has happened so that others can see him as well. And what I find is that God is present, not just through the goodness of creation but through redemption as well. God's way of working was focused in Christ, and he continues to work in that way. So when I see good coming out of evil, love transforming bitterness, forgiveness healing injury, I believe that is of God.

> 'Occasionally I can serve that process. I never know in advance what is going to happen. The situations are often messy and ambiguous. But by praying, and by trying to love, I can sometimes be an instrument of God's peace ... When I am invited into some secular organisation I am not quite sure what they want. But they know I am a priest, a "walking sacrament" as Austin Farrer once put it. They know that in some way I stand for God and his presence in the world, and I suppose in some curious way my being there shows that God is there as well. T. S. Eliot once talked about "the still point in the turning world". Well, maybe that is what I point to by being in the place, and that might

just make some people there reflect on the values and purposes of the institution as part of God's world.' (Reiss, in Redfern 1994)

THE CHURCH AS INSTITUTION: THE MINISTER AS PRIEST

By now the total model of ministry is beginning to build up. And, as will be becoming clear, the particular titles are not confined to their associated model of the Church. In the final section we return to the model of the Church which combines all and consequently the model of ministry that brings together most of the influences outlined. The term 'priest' is invoked with hesitation. For it has been, and for many remains, one of the most divisive points among Christians. However, as with all the language in this chapter, it, too, is open to being revalued.

We have already seen that the pastor's basic model is that of the Church as institution. Their role in this context clarifies the idea of priest. The essential point about the priest is that he or she acts on behalf of others. Indeed, it is because of the way that such ideas have evolved that many churches have rejected the term and its associations. It is frequently pointed out that in the New Testament the term is only applied to Jesus Christ and never to any other individual, although priesthood is found as a collective description of the Church. In the light of history and the use of power that has been wrongly connected with priesthood, the objection carries genuine weight. On the other hand, for the pastor to lose the priestly dimensions of pastoring diminishes that role. It is not, after all, as though 'pastor' is without its own problems (Moody 1992). There are three main reasons for elaborating the image of priest here:

1 The theme of priesthood brings together the ministry of the whole Church while acknowledging the specific ministry of those who are authorized. All that follows in this section, while largely about authorized ministers, can be applied to the ministering congregation.

2 Priesthood connects pastoral ministry to the significant dimension of liturgy.

3 This theme pays proper attention to the assumptions

with which many people seem to approach any minister, whatever his or her self-understanding.

THE PRIESTLIKE PASTOR

The notion of boundary has been prominent throughout this chapter. Sometimes it is largely in the mind; sometimes such boundaries become almost as fixed as lines on a map. Among the boundaries with which the minister is concerned are those between life and death, between God and this world, and boundaries between the Church's task (what it is here to do) and the feelings and beliefs of its members and of others. The minister is essentially asked to work on these and other boundaries. This theme traditionally became associated with mediation: the priest mediates between God and this world. One example is intercession. A bishop after retirement was discussing his sense of lostness. He did not especially miss the power to decide or the public recognition that he had received as a bishop, although possibly there would have been some of that around. But he put it this way:

As a curate I learned to pray for some people, and as a vicar I prayed for my parish. While teaching at a college, I prayed for my students. When I became a bishop I prayed for my clergy and their parishes. Now I am retired, I have no one formally to pray for.

He did not mean that he had ceased praying. He prayed but without a sense of any clear role in which to do so. There is always a mediatory function to the work of any minister, whatever his or her tradition.

The theme of intercessory ministry is elaborated into that of the pastor through a quotation from Keats, from the sonnet *Bright Star* (see Carr 1985). To describe this he coined the word 'priestlike', which better describes the role of pastor than the more familiar 'priestly':

The moving waters, at their priestlike task,
Of pure ablution round earth's human shores.

This phrase brings together the traditional idea of mediation and the idea of boundary activity. It also conveys that sense of permanent flux that pastors experience. Ministers, as it were, wash around the edges of people's everyday worlds, working to cleanse some of the detritus that inhibits people's lives as children of God. Pattison offers something similar with his definition of pastoral care: 'Pastoral care is that activity, undertaken especially by representative Christian persons, directed toward the elimination and relief of sin and sorrow and the presentation of all people perfect in Christ' (Pattison 1988, 13).[4]

The quotation from Keats also directs attention to the form that such ministry takes: it is one of 'ablution', a term with overtones of washing (baptism) and forgiveness (absolution). Such ministry is that of the Church, which we may conceive as the priestly people of God. But it becomes focused in those who carry a representative function for that Church and for the people with whom they are ministering.

In thinking on ministry the focus of attention has today tended to shift to what the priest or pastor can distinctively do. This leads to discussions about presidency at the Eucharist, sacramental acts and leadership in general. Such reductions unsurprisingly leave nothing distinctive for the authorized minister. But the location of the Church's ministry is at the boundaries of human life – 'earth's human shores'. It follows that the Church's essential focus is on its activity 'on behalf of'. The question of what ministers can or cannot distinctively do is not necessary. The limits of their authority to act do not have to be delineated. The focal point of the pastor's ministry within the priestlike task is that *he or she is expected and authorized to stand on behalf of others for a moment at a point where, for whatever reason, they are (or feel) unable to stand for themselves.* This sentence is a definition of the pastor's ministry, with all its essential components:

1 *expected and authorized.* The authority of the minister is to be used and explored as a means by which people may rediscover their own authority in a situation.

2 *to stand on behalf of others.* Ministry is to bear something. Frequently this will have an explicitly spiritual dimension.

3 *for a moment.* Ministerial skill includes being able to discern the fragment of life which is being handled, to minister in that moment, and then to leave. Letting go is an essential component of pastoring.

4 *at a point.* Ministry tends to be concerned with a moment or fragment of people's lives. The minister, even

when well-known by a family or individual, is allowed by people to touch points or parts of their lives, never the whole.

5 *where, for whatever reason, they are (or feel) unable to stand for themselves.* The qualifications in this phrase are all significant. The reason why people feel in need of some ministering is unimportant in itself. Looked at by the pastor there may be good reason for his or her presence. Equally it may seem trivial or irrelevant. But when engaged with a minister, people often themselves do not know precisely why they seek assistance. Sometimes they genuinely need the minister: they cannot develop spiritually without help. An obvious example would be someone who comes for confession or formal counsel. They are looking for the authoritative speaker for God. More often, however, the approach is diffident and based on feelings which cannot be expounded: 'I know you are very busy, and I don't know why I am here, but I felt I had to talk to you.'

A distinctive example of such ministry still occurs in funerals. Here the minister is used to manage part of a process (bereavement and mourning) which many people cannot handle without such help. The pastor stands for them in one facet of the process, that of the ultimate boundary of life and death, God and this world (see Chapter 10).

LITURGY AND PASTORING

There is always a liturgical dimension to pastoral ministry. Since the pastor is being asked to hold onto some sort of reality which the person whom he or she is pastoring cannot for that moment sustain, then one way is likely to be that the pastor does something ritually to enable that reality to be held. For instance, pronouncing formal absolution for confessed sins is a key part of the pastor's activity. Whether in the Catholic tradition of formal confession and absolution or not, the authorized minister sustains this ritual function. Although the penitent may, indeed often will, not overtly express the need for confession, the characteristics of many pastoral encounters are confessional. But the parallel between the liturgical and the pastoral function is more important than the actual liturgical acts which the pastor may be called upon to perform (Ramshaw 1987).

We have also noted that pastoring is not necessarily one-to-one. The preacher's function is systemically similar to that of the pastor only in the setting of a large group – the congregation. The same is true of leading worship. Whether rehearsing a regular liturgy or an occasional office, the pastor holds certain realities on behalf of the worshippers. For instance, they manage the time, to some extent the space through movement, and the process. Leadership here is performed on behalf of the congregation so that they, freed from these demands, can engage with God in worship. In practice this may mean for them a sense of the suspension of the usual constraints of time and space in the process which carries them through the experience of worshipping God. The minister does not suspend time and space, or remove reality, whatever people might wish. The pastor holds to these realities in such a way that the worshippers can find for themselves the space and opportunity to change.

POPULAR ASSUMPTIONS

The third reason for connecting priesthood with pastoring is that this reference matches popular assumptions. These are not all about priests. Indeed many outside the churches may be as suspicious of the word as those within. But we are considering function. It seems that whatever the church background – and especially if there is none – people believe that the minister somehow stands in for them and genuinely does things which they cannot do. For instance, people seem to need a minister to articulate the unsayable. This becomes obvious in two ways.

1   The pastor is expected to be able to pray, even if people are uncomfortable with praying. It is 'proper' or expected. And at moments of ministry, few if any ministers are insensitive enough to launch into a theoretical discussion about why these people do not need a minister but could pray for themselves.

2   When communities grieve or rejoice people turn to the Church to mark in a distinctive way a significant moment. The association of the Church with disaster is not fortuitous. It is noticeable, for instance, that even after over twenty-five years of trouble in Northern Ireland, the voice of the local

minister, sometimes priest, sometimes pastor, occasionally archbishop, was the one which was turned to by both people and the media when yet another atrocity occurred.

In such circumstances the local vicar ['Vicar' here can be replaced by 'minister'.] is often the person who is invited to articulate the grief or heroism of the people. For a moment his is a trusted and significant voice. Because he is provided to be and to pray there, when the media come he is the person whom they find. (Tilby, in Carr 1992, 83)

THE MARKS OF MINISTRY

What distinctive form will such ministry take? The priestlike ministry of the pastor in the institutional model of the Church is essentially interpretative. No word is completely satisfactory to describe the richness of this ministry. But 'interpretative' best describes both the stance and the activity.[5] We need, however, to be clear about the sense in which this term is used in this context. There are three marks to such a ministry: the use of the self; the use of vulnerability; and confidence in the minister's authority. They obviously interrelate.

USING ONESELF

Anyone who interprets uses themselves. Translators, for instance, do not mechanically replace words or sentences with different words or sentences in another language. They take what they hear, process it within themselves to an understanding, and give it back interpreted. The skill lies in using themselves. A consultant in a group acts similarly. They not only look at what they observe; they also examine what is happening to them, their own feelings, and using both offer an interpretation of the group. Interpreters, therefore, use themselves. The difference in interpretations lies in which transcendent reference that is adopted. As the interpreter takes and uses the feelings engendered in them, he or she has also to relate this to something that transcends the here-and-now of the encounter. That is usually something like the task for which people have met.

But even this is inadequate as a definition. For when the

interpreter is a religious figure, he or she also represents God, the one who provides the ultimate or truly transcending context. That is why it is the mark of Christian interpreters that they will usually mention God.

Ministers offer interpretation based on what is happening to them and why. This is always with reference beyond what is immediate. For instance, an Anglican parochial church council might in the heat of debate forget that it represents both the congregation and the parishioners. In such setting this sort of pastoral ministry still applies. The minister has to interpret what is going on by reference to his or her own feelings. These the minister puts in the context of the transcendent reference of the task of the council, which is something to do with managing the affairs of the church. He relates his or her feelings to this task and so may come up with an intervention which enables the body to get back on course with its work.

USING VULNERABILITY

The theme of vulnerability is over-emphasized in the contemporary Church, whether it is the vulnerability of the individual or of God. However, there is a proper vulnerability of ministers. They find themselves dealing with whatever may be happening to them. But since they are prominent objects for people's projections, what happens to them is often emotionally powerful and debilitating. Nevertheless, it is out of this use of themselves that the ministers interpret. They aim to be able to articulate something useful about what is happening so that the individual or the group concerned may make something their own and get on with their work.

USING AUTHORITY

The third, and often most vexed, question is that of authority. We have already considered the potential confusion between authority and authoritarianism. But the authority of the pastor as minister in relation to the institutional Church is vitally important. Indeed it is one reason why the institutional model does not find immediate favour with many. Nevertheless, for the minister, awareness of the nature of authority, especially his or her own, is central to ministry.

Failure here confuses people, who, whatever they may eventually say, look to the minister to act on the authority that they have assigned to them.

One experienced organizational consultant – not a Christian minister – was sometimes asked what authority he had for making an observation or offering an interpretation. His reply was invariably, 'My authority is that I am right'.[6] The instinctive response, which frequently came, was that this was an arrogant and authoritarian response. But after a little thought we can see that it is not and that it is true. What he was saying, unabridged, was:

> I have listened and observed what is going on, as I see it; I have examined my own feelings while I have been involved in this activity, as I experience it; I have considered how this relates to the task of the enterprise as that has been told me and as I perceive it; and putting all these things together I suggest this interpretation. If you can point out where I have misunderstood what I observe, or have failed to grasp my own feelings, or where I have got the wrong view of the task, then please say so. If I am wrong, then we can move on again; if I am right, then we can do something about it. My only authority for saying what I have just offered is that I am right and therefore you can join me in further exploration because we are in the same context and dealing with the same issues.

Had he, of course, said all that, his clients would have been put off for good. His succinct and challenging interpretation – 'My authority is that I am right' – was more useful and usable. Likewise, ministers who speak on the authority that they are right invite scrutiny and further exploration. They are not being dogmatic and they are not being authoritarian.

Such exercise of authority marks the model of ministry of the pastor in relation to the Church as institution. It will be informed by the other pictures that we have discussed. But as the holding picture, the one to which to relate all others, it offers down to earth realism, theological justification and historical undergirding for ministry at the end of the twentieth century.

CHAPTER TEN

Ministry and Common Religion

The phrase 'common religion' describes the cultural form that Christianity takes as a religion in a society. Christianity has dominated the religious scene in Europe for nearly two thousand years. This is not to say that the people of Europe have been or are all Christian. Such a claim is nonsense at whatever level it is made (Wessels 1994). In the USA such religion takes a different but still recognizable form. Religion in America may no longer 'properly be understood only as an integral part of a larger European society' (Hudson 1965, 3). But the pervasiveness of the Christian churches as the bearers of religion is notable (Edwards 1987). In Latin America Roman Catholic and Pentecostal churches find themselves dealing with the same phenomenon. No doubt with the Christianizing of much of Africa the same will eventually be true there. In the United Kingdom for most people, especially those with minimal religious affiliation, any religious expression of either individual or social life is almost bound to be through the agency of a Christian church. It is, therefore, inevitable that ministers of most Christian churches will find themselves expected also to be religious functionaries. The level of demand will vary according to which church and which nation. But most ministers in their pastoral activity will find themselves at some time treated as ministers of religion, not just Christian.

NAMES FOR COMMON RELIGION

A number of names describe such religion. Among the most usual are 'folk', 'common', 'implicit', 'popular', 'residual' and 'customary'. To some extent these terms are themselves church-dependent. For instance, 'folk religion' is usually associated with the Lutheran and Reformed tradition, while 'customary religion' is preferred by Roman Catholic writers. All, however, refer to the same underlying phenomenon: the manifestations seem to determine which word is used.

FOLK RELIGION

This phrase is widely used in English writings. But its main association is with the German word *Volk* and with the German and Scandinavian churches. The emphasis is on corporate, often national, expressions of religion. In Great Britain examples would be Remembrance Sunday services, occasions of civic rejoicing or, more often, mourning, and possibly above all a coronation.[1] But the sort of religion being discussed here tends to take a more individual or family form. Classic moments of folk religion, such as a baptism or wedding, are not usually times when there is public expression of religious activity other than on the part of the family. In Great Britain and the USA religion tends to be a more private matter. Hence the term folk religion when used carries different overtones. 'Folk' in English is attached to such ideas as a 'folk museum', a 'folk song' or a 'folk dance'. So 'folk religion' sounds pejorative. The religious activity is regarded as quaint. As a result ministers may find it difficult to recognize that it contains genuine feelings and belief.

IMPLICIT RELIGION

The roots of this term lie in religious education. It refers primarily to the idea that people may have religious experiences which, for some reason, neither they nor others publicly acknowledge (Hay 1987). The stress is upon religious experience, which may be highly individual. But it has also been a phrase around which people in various disciplines – historians, social scientists and theologians – have come together:

> For them it refers not only to those self-conscious, momentary experiences of vision or ecstasy that suddenly come upon the individual. It can also refer to continuous commitments. They may be deliberately chosen, or imbibed

with one's culture – and that 'one' can be individual or corporate. (Bailey 1986)

CUSTOMARY RELIGION

The sight of footballers crossing themselves before a match has become familiar. For many it stirs a twinge of concern: what precisely did it mean? How superstitious was it? This form of behaviour is mostly associated with the Catholic tradition and is known as 'customary religion' (Hornsby-Smith 1992). It is a mix of personal and public, but it is crucially an expression of official religion. The practices of the Church – such as crossing oneself – are trivialized and occasionally removed from their usual context. But they remain recognizably Christian – and necessarily so. Nothing else would seem to do. One of the reasons that such religion causes anxiety, however, is that it is a point where outward expressions of official Christianity intersect with other religion, especially old paganism. That is why this phenomenon is also sometimes called 'residual religion'. The origin of the residuum is not obvious, but seems to come out of some highly primitive religion.

COMMON RELIGION

This phrase seems the most useful, although even this is not value-free. The three points that this term holds together are:

1 What is believed is not the paramount question. Creed and theology are not prominent considerations, although there may be more than is superficially obvious to the minister. The belief matters, even if it takes the form of popular everyday beliefs, many of which concern fate and destiny. So, for example, when a couple comes for a wedding they may not have much understanding of beliefs about marriage. Discussion with the pastor may become stilted as he or she tries to expound a view of marriage. 'So why do you want to be married in church?' the pastor eventually asks. 'Because it's right,' they reply. This is the answer beyond which the couple cannot go. They hold an unarticulated belief, but the content of it is not central in this expression of religion.

2 Ritual is always sought. It may even be that this is where the continuance of common religion most clearly lies. New

rituals can be created. For instance, within the last few years the custom of placing flowers at the place where someone has been killed has become widespread. Originally it seems to have been associated with violent death, for example in Northern Ireland. But the custom, possibly through the influence of television, has spread to any death, accidental or deliberate. Common religion accrues such rituals. But at the same time, even in a society in which the individual or family seem possibly more adept than their predecessors at creating their own rituals, there remains a wish for 'rooted rituals'. These are those that are recognizably social and which therefore have to be performed by someone outside the family unit. For historical reasons the churches have become the holders of these – the rituals of entry (baptism), transition (marriage) and ending (funeral) are the most obvious.

3   Finally all such religion retains some connection with the community, even if this is minimized as much as possible. For example, a wedding rite may today be considered almost a private transaction, even the sealing of a contract. Few other than immediate friends and family may be invited. But the fact of the rite itself includes, however minimally, some public acknowledgement that the marriage retains a public dimension. It affects and is affected by the community in which it is taking place.

THE CHURCH AND COMMON RELIGION

Ministers and others sometimes assume that common religion is either debased Christianity or semi-Christianized paganism. This leads them to assume that common religion lies outside, even over against, the Church. Such a view is heard, for example, in the pejorative language which is sometimes used to describe those who approach the churches' ministers for a ritual. But such a simple division is not an appropriate way to regard common religion. The confusion of religious beliefs which are semi-articulated by someone who approaches the minister for a rite are unlikely to be so very different from the similar amalgam of belief which is held by the most committed church member. Ministers are dealing with the same phenomena of religion in different contexts of ministry. Because someone says a creed it does not mean that they either understand or believe what they are saying. When, therefore, ministers put heavy demands for understanding on those who approach them for, say, baptism, they need to reflect carefully on what they are doing.

It may also be thought that this phenomenon is confined to certain churches and is therefore not everyone's concern. In England, for example, it is obvious and likely that the Church of England will have to handle this more than, say, the Unitarians. People with no obvious religious affiliation are likely to revert to that of their dimly remembered past. Often this will be to school experience or a parish church. Because the Church of England through its parochial system puts itself in the way of such ministries, it inevitably picks up a great deal of residual religion. But other churches find the same, not least the Roman Catholic and, depending on the area of the country, some Free Churches. Most ministers are likely to encounter this phenomenon to a greater or lesser extent.

Common religion throws ecclesiology into confusion. A couple, for instance, summon up the courage to approach the minister about having their baby christened. They attend church rarely, probably not at all. But for whatever reason – and they will not be able to articulate it clearly – they feel that they should mark this moment in their and the child's life. They may be nervous, silent and difficult to talk with. But underneath, especially if the pastor refuses or appears to refuse, they are quite determined. This is because, however odd this may seem to the church members, they feel that this is 'their' church. They come as members in their minds and not as clients seeking a service. Unless ministers grasp this basic point, they are almost bound to offend. For when common religion is expressed it is always about some sort of joining, whether to a tradition, or through a ritual to others past, or in some fashion to ancestors. 'Grandma would have wished it', is not an uncommon response. Again, lest church people think this primitive, it might be worth reflecting on the implicit ancestor worship that marks both Protestant and Catholic traditions. The influence of the great men and women of the past, both ancient saint and more recent member, is powerful in churches.

The most obvious points of such ministry are birth, marriage and death – baptisms, weddings and funerals (see further Carr, 1994). In all three rites changes are occurring. In the west ministers are performing fewer marriages. But this is a general social issue and not peculiar to the Church. The churches are trapped between their wish to uphold the sanctity of marriage and the pastoral exigencies of modern life. The recent relaxation of regulations over where marriages can be solemnized may have a further impact.

Baptisms are more difficult. So far as common religion is concerned this a rite performed on babies: adult baptism is not an issue. In Great Britain the number has declined. But in relation to the current levels of church attendance it is still remarkably high. This suggests that this field of common religion remains complex. Part of the difficulty in evaluating what may be happening lies in the churches themselves. Through ecumenical debate and because of internal uncertainties and the long public arguments, it is unclear whether the churches appear to people less willing to engage in this ministry than they are expected to.[2] There may be, therefore, a mismatch between the churches' idea of their own identity and the social changes around such rites. Even a difference in attitude between lay and ordained people has been noted (Astley and Pickering 1986). This makes detailed evaluation difficult. However, it would seem that baptisms will continue to be an issue for some time.

Funerals have generally been regarded as religious occasions. Recently there has been some anxiety expressed in some churches as to whether it is appropriate to conduct funerals for those who are not obviously associated with the Church. This is matched by a growing interest in secular funerals (Walter 1989; 1990). However, the widespread expectation is that the Church is a proper body to handle some of the ritual of death, although this may be being surrendered to doctors and death is treated increasingly as a medical condition and a private affair of the individual (Walter 1994). It may be doubted whether this position can be sustained for long. What happens will depend as much on the attitude that the churches convey as much as the disarray in personal belief that is today manifest.

In pastoral ministry to common religion understanding

helps. But it does not relieve the emotional and theological pressures that are generated. There are six reasons for this. And these also explain why for much pastoral ministry dealing with common religion is often an acid test of the minister and the Church. Each reason is equally important: they are not listed in any order.

'RAW' DEPENDENCE

We have already considered the underlying dependency that marks all religious behaviour. Common religion presents that dependence in an unsophisticated form. This is expressed in the explanations that people offer for their apparently becoming suddenly religious. It is a question of doing what is 'right' or 'proper', having no choice but feeling that they ought to behave in this way. They also have high expectations of the Church and its ministers which can rarely be met. That is not because of inadequacy in the minister. It is because irrational expectations are so unconfined that no one could possibly meet them. Ministry to moments of common religious expectation are important for minsters, since they expose them powerfully to the dependent attitude that underlies all ministry but which is often obscured. These moments are not deficient occasions for ministry. They are the paradigm on which all pastoral ministry is based.

ACCESS TO THE MINISTER

Such raw dependency means that these encounters also test the minister's own sense of ministry. At a conference ministers are sometimes invited to define the distinctive quality of their ministry. They often reply that it lies in their availability. When the leader points out that they are not available, since they are away at the conference and so far as is known the world has not fallen in, discomfort ensues. Ministers tend, in line with the undergirding stance of the faith that they profess, to be (or think that they should be) available for people. That is what ministry is.

Such declarations of belief are necessary. Those who emulate Christ's ministry will hopefully find in themselves that living for (on behalf of) others that marked his life. But the test comes when this being available goes outside the minister's control. This is less a question of time than of feeling. To what extent can the minister endure having his or her cherished beliefs questioned and challenged by the religious demands of those who come for the occasional offices? The pressure to defend God, or the faith, is such that the minister can fall into a split frame of reference. On the one hand the gospel is about free access to the grace of God. The minister will wish to embody that welcoming side of his faith. On the other hand there is apparently little or no response to the gospel message from those who seek this ministry. Curiously, therefore, whatever the emotional energy generated by them when they summon up the courage to come, it appears to be less than that required by the minister to sustain the split in himself between welcome and resistance. There is nothing unfamiliar in this. It is an aspect of the dichotomy between law and grace. But there is a profound difference between such a dichotomy in the textbook and that felt when facing a moment of such ministry.

RITUAL

The focal point for this ministry is ritual: people want something done. It may be the baby christened, the marriage solemnized, the body buried, the house blessed, a prayer said. But in general content matters less than what is done and how it is done. This creates new problems for the minister, who is concerned with understanding and the meaning of words. In the Church of England, for example, the language of *The Alternative Service Book 1980* rite for funerals is more explicitly Christian than that of the Book of Common Prayer. Use of the new rite has encouraged some clergy to reconsider whether they should bury anyone who was not an active member of the congregation. They feel that the words must have clear reference. No minister can discount meaning. Christians are not in the business of gobbledegook. But the notion of meaning is not solely a matter of the words spoken. Communication includes a range of other signals, of which the words are one set. The sensed attitude of the minister, the environment, the seriousness or otherwise with which the occasion is treated, all these are as much part of the meaning that people construct. The key for the minister in such occasions is to realize that what is done is more significant than what is said.

People's sensitivity should not be underestimated. A vicar in an urban parish decided no longer to baptize any children. From time to time the Church of England becomes anxious about baptizing babies, especially when the parties have little or no obvious link with the Church. This was one such period. Instead of baptism the vicar offered a service of blessing and made it as much a community affair as he could. For a while people, including regular worshippers, were mystified. Some were offended and disconsolate. However, a short while later two women were overheard in the street:

'Our girl's baby was christened this week.'
'Oh, I heard that the vicar didn't do that any more. We had to go somewhere else, but it wasn't the same. We'd have liked to go to our church, but he wouldn't do it.'
'He does, dear. It's just that he doesn't use water now.'

The need for ritual and the fact that the vicar offered it, albeit a deficient form for many, was the communication. The vicar may have thought that he had defended the Christian tradition, taught the significance of baptism, and offered a welcome to those in some pastoral need – all desirable activities. But the construction of the people remained that they got roughly what they wanted – a ritual. Incidentally, the vicar reverted to baptisms: he felt that the loss of encounter and potential ministry was too great a sacrifice. But there are people in that area of London who presumably still think they were baptized but without water.

RITUAL AND RITE

It is important to distinguish these two words. The ritual that the minister performs is needed by those who come. But the rite is something greater. Much of it may be little or nothing to do with the minister. For example, in a funeral the rite involves acknowledging the death, meeting the undertaker, dealing with the family and friends, coping with mourning, arranging the tea or reception afterwards, fitting a monument to the grave, and so on. Within that sequence the ritual of the funeral occupies a significant but small part.

John Taylor gives an excellent example of the difference in a story he tells from his time as Bishop of Winchester. His gardener's son was baptized in a local church. The bishop and his wife were invited. They enjoyed the service but afterwards they did not go to the party, thinking that they might have been intruding on a family occasion. Next day the bishop met the gardener who was obviously hurt that the bishop and his wife had not attended the party.

> That made me go back and think. For him the drinking of the champagne and the cutting of the cake were just as much part of the ritual [I would use the word 'rite' here: the champagne was another 'ritual'] as the sprinkling of the water. That was for him a rather strange part, he could understand the rest. The point was that the Church has always assumed that Baptism is *its* ritual which it can dispense to those who seem to qualify for it, but which it certainly has to explain. I came to see that what we are asked to perform is *their* ritual, and if we are prepared to do that as one of the still surviving rituals of our society, then we can claim the right to say, 'Can we tell you what we see in this?' and to explain the deeper Christian understanding of that ritual. (Taylor, in Ecclestone 1988, 134)

If 'ritual' and 'rite' are confused, the minister will expect the occasion of ministry to bear more than is the expectation of those asking for ministry. In such cases the room for misunderstanding and generating hostility is considerable. A minister alone might be able to bear this or even justify it as the cost of ministry. But to do this is to overlook the network effect of such ministry. Because remembered rites are significant in the lives of individuals and families, what one minister did on one occasion creates the preconceptions of what others might do at different times. It is a mark of ministry through such offices that the minister becomes responsible not just for what he or she does but also for what successors and colleagues elsewhere might be able to do.

CHRISTIANITY AND RELIGION

The last two points are more overtly theological. In this ministry primitive feelings and beliefs predominate. As a result ministers, even when dealing with committed members of the Church, are handling the phenomenon of religion rather more than their more familiar – and cosy – Christian assumptions. It is as though this ministry strips specific religious belief and practice, whatever they may be, down to the submerged aspects of belief and behaviour which are usually unspoken or unaddressed. Such ministry, therefore, is always problematical, although the difficulties and demands are not where the minister often believes them to be. They often slide into a blaming mode, in which those asking for such ministry become the focus of resentment or anger. 'Why should I deal with these people who only want what they want, do not want my gospel, and will have nothing to do with the Church and God afterwards?' No minister will have exercised pastoral ministry without such emotions lurking somewhere.

But the sensitive minister will also realize that what these people by their requests are doing is exposing the fragility of his or her own faith. It is probably not by chance that those churches and ministers that are the most dogmatic about belief and conformity are those which have the most difficulty in addressing the issues raised by this ministry. The likelihood is that they are not accustomed to having their belief challenged other than by recognized challenges, which can be rationalized. These challenges would include those from the Bible, the tradition or the doctrine and practice of a church. The occasional offices present a deeper test of belief. Yet however much the minister may resent the approach, the challenge lies in the nature of the gospel rather than in the clients. There is a saying of Jesus that to save their souls people need to surrender even that which they hold most dear (Mark 8.35). If faith in Christ is that which ministers hold most dear, their willingness to compromise or risk even that (as is often demanded by such ministry) is under trial.

THEOLOGICAL PROBLEMS

The last point follows from the preceding one. Whatever the pastor may decide to do when faced with such ministry, a theological question is attached. For it raises the question of God and his dealings with the world, as well as such issues as sacraments, blessing, religious behaviour and worship. All that needs to be said here is that the theological questions which arise from outside the Church through such ministry, are more powerful and challenging, and usually more important than those which are generated in the Church. It is sometimes claimed that the churches need a new apologetic for today.[3] But any such apology has to be rooted where people think it might matter. And the transitional points in their lives, which still occasionally demand religious expression, are as good as (if not better than) most for the attempt.

THE PROCESS OF MINISTRY

Much ministry to common religion is unstructured. People approach the pastor for whatever reason that occurs to them. Ministers are at the whim of inarticulate feeling and chaotic belief. They will, therefore, be better able to orient themselves if they can grasp the underlying dynamic process that is involved. There is, however one caveat: a structure in the mind by which to try and ascertain what *may be* going on cannot be imposed on those seeking ministry as if it represented what is *actually* happening.

The encounter has four phases: the approach, interpretation, ritual and feedback.

THE APPROACH

This is almost always to rather than by the minister. Consequently what happens at this point is important, since it will probably determine how the rest of the encounter may go. However the approach is managed, the key point is the need for an authoritative figure. Because the minister will eventually conduct the ritual people reasonably wish to come into contact with that authority early on. Two points follow:

1 It is not possible casually to devolve responsibility at this point. So, for instance, in a busy city church or in a village where there is no resident minister lay people are likely to play key functions in being the access point for people as they make their approach. But this role cannot be casually assumed. And if a system to employ them is in place, the question of how such a person is seen to be authorized needs to be carefully sorted out.

2 Whoever the 'minister' is at this point – whether lay or ordained – that person needs to be confident of being in role rather than just a welcoming person. For somewhere already in the action of coming is a sense, however minimal, of

approaching the unapproachable – God or the divine. The person met must be able to be perceived as having authority to represent that dimension of life.

INTERPRETATION

The second phase is where the Christian message and the life of those seeking the ministry come together. But since the client will be presenting only part of their life, the response of the pastor will also be to use a fragment of the gospel and not attempt to invoke the whole. The ministerial skill here is to be able to find the latching-on point to use. The minister embodies the gospel and perhaps even God himself. It is, therefore, not a time to point away from oneself by using too much written material, the Bible or the Church's teaching. All these resources are at this moment embodied in the minister. He or she must use them as best as they can. This is why churches need learned ministers. They are to be those who can be believed to know enough to be able to speak with authority about the faith.

Interpretation, as has been extensively discussed earlier, is the heart of this ministry. In a pastoral encounter of common religion, the parable is given. In preaching, the preacher will seek a parable, an instance or an illustration and bring it to bear on what he or she is trying to communicate. In a pastoral encounter of this type, however, the parable is already given: it is that bit of the people's story that the pastor can hear resonating with the gospel. So, for instance, in a newborn baby lies an acted parable of almost anything. It might speak of love, affection, demand or disturbance. In discussion no doubt all of these will be around. The pastor's intuitive skill will be to discern which of these to take and elaborate as the interpretative point about the couple's life and the Kingdom of God.

The interpretation will also provide a useful bridge to the next phase. Some consistency between what happens in this meeting and what will occur in the ritual itself will assist people in making connections between the fragments of their experience and the wholeness of life to which the minister is pointing. The second phase of the process, therefore, is crucial in several ways. It shows that the people's experience is valued for its own sake. It indicates the depth of what they are seeking, their raw experience and sensed temerity in approaching the Church for the ritual that may eventually be performed. Here, too, the minister is tested about his or her capacity to be what they are believed to be – representative of God, the Church or meaning.

THE RITUAL

This is the core of the process. People seek it and for it they will often go through complicated demands set by the churches. There are two key facets to performing a ritual:

1　It is a series of formalized acts. Ritual cannot be extemporized. A number of steps move people from one point in their lives to another. Obviously, for instance, in a wedding the couple come unmarried, go through a series of formal acts – inquiry, promises, vows, rings and declaration – and leave in the different state of being married.

2　These acts 'work' because of their symbolic quality. It is less what the words apparently mean than what their use signifies that conveys the message. The Church has some rituals that are available for people. But common religion also surrounds this core with other rituals, the importance of which should also be noted. Some of these may be local, what has always been done in a place. Others seem to have become more widespread. It may be a point of interest at a baptism whether baby cries and 'expels the devil'. There are many additions to funeral rituals, depending on the social background of the bereaved. A familiar example comes from weddings. When the couple's hands are joined and they are declared to be man and wife a custom has developed that is not in a rubric: the minister wraps their hands in the stole. This has become 'a popular action in the sense that at this point the congregation leans forward to watch, then relaxes with an audible sigh' (Barker 1978, 73).

FEEDBACK

The fourth phase can be dealt with briefly. Pastors often discuss how to follow up the contacts that they make through these offices. But the problems prove largely insuperable: people move away, the minister has little time, and most strangely those who were so eager to associate for the ritual often seem to wish to have nothing further to do with minister or Church. By now it will be clear why this is so: the primitive nature of the religious urge involved is such that its needs are in most cases fulfilled when the ritual is performed. That is why the pastor's interpretative opportunity lies before this, not after. However, there are two points of feedback that the pastor should hold in mind:

1   As has been mentioned, how the minister acted at this moment in a person's or family's life is a crucial part of the interpretative experience. The pastor becomes the 'notion-in-the-mind' of 'minister' which is carried in the memory of those involved. To that extent, therefore, feedback will usually be indirect and some other minister will probably experience it unwittingly.

2   Within the geographical area of a church itself, however, it is surprising how often as a result of contact through a moment of occasional conformity the minister finds himself called up by the same family or a branch of it for further ministry. Popular superstition claims that problems or tragedies come in threes. No minister could endorse that. But it is noticeable how often a minister who has been pastorally involved with a family finds himself caught up with them again or with others who are known to them.

WILL THESE RITUALS CONTINUE?

Debate, sometimes heated, continues in the churches about dealing with common religion. Christians generally seem less comfortable with it today, especially in those churches such as the Church of England where it has historically played a major part. To what extent the churches' public agonizing has contributed to a decline in the expression of such religion is difficult to assess. Nevertheless, it is clear that at the moment such ministry is at best holding its own and may be declining. But that does not mean that residual religion is disappearing.

On 22 August 1994 two women announced on the radio the formation of a society to promote 'secular baptism' (*sic*). Their argument was simple: the birth of a baby is a moment for affirming values, both for the infant, the family and for the society in which the child will grow up. The only place

221

where this can at present be done is a church. But fewer people wish to make the churches' religious claims, even conditionally. So a secular baptismal rite is needed. The speakers seemed oblivious to the religious nature of their discussion, largely because they confused 'Christian' with 'religious'.

However, there can be no guarantee that the Church's rituals will continue to be invoked for these rites. Common religion expresses itself mainly in occasional encounters with the Church – 'occasional conformity'. One, for instance, which has become difficult for some churches is confirmation or its equivalent. Apart from the Roman Catholic Church, most churches have held to this rite as a puberty transition. It marked the shift from childhood to adolescence and potential adulthood. This was symbolized by the contrast with baptism, in that the confirmands answered for themselves. There may be several reasons why this rite has declined in significance. In part there has been the theological argument about the completeness or otherwise of baptism (Thornton 1954; Lampe 1967). This has come to the fore during ecumenical discussions as some agreement on a common basis for Christian recognition has been explored. Another factor may be the affirmation of family life in the Church today. The emphasis, for instance, on children coming to (and in some instances receiving) communion makes the significance of confirmation as the gateway to that experience doubtful. But another consideration may be the progressive loss of a clear transition point of puberty in the contemporary world. As the period of adolescence has been increasingly acknowledged and examined, so its definition has declined. When does a child become an adolescent? Few, if any, seem to know. As a result any religious marking of transition at this point declines.

But in conclusion three points may be noted:

1 Religion as a phenomenon always needs to be distinguished from specific instances. In common religion, whether it takes Christian form or not, there seems to be something that is fundamentally human. Indeed the period in which religion is discounted may be ending. If so, there will be a need for an apologetic which argues for the Christian interpretation of the religious feelings that people may be able more easily to acknowledge. The theological challenge of these

occasions, therefore, is profound. They are not just an inconvenient residue from a now lost Christian era.

2 Even though the number of contacts seems to be declining they represent a level of contact between the churches and people which is statistically more significant than Sunday attendance. It would be a curiously unevangelistic church that rejected such encounters, especially in uncertain times.

3 Whatever happens and whatever policies churches may adopt about such religion, pastors have to hold to the fact that uncertainty, disarray, emotional disturbance and even unbelief, as these are represented by those coming for such ministry, is more disturbing to the pastor than he or she probably realizes. If this is understood, at least ministers may not fall too easily into the trap of projecting this disarray into the vulnerable and dealing with it there. The pains of such ministry are borne by the minister.

CHAPTER ELEVEN

Ministry and Therapy

In the history of Christian ministry the late twentieth century will be noted for the distinctions that have to be drawn between the pastor's theologically based ministry and the therapeutically oriented thinking which dominates the caring professions (Jacobs 1993). However much ministers may resist being put into this group, caring describes an aspect of their work. Concern with psychology is not a new dimension to the Church's ministry. Nevertheless, tension is still felt between pastoring and therapy. Harry Guntrip mentions the remark of a medical psychologist: 'Shun the psychologicallyminded parson'. But he also noted that there may be two sides to this argument:

> Perhaps it was intended as a salutary protest against the enthusiastic amateur who reads a few books and thinks he can embark forthwith on psychoanalytic treatment. Maybe, on the other hand, it expressed a rather jealous desire to fence round the field of psychological science as a monopoly of the medical profession. (Guntrip 1971, 19)

THERAPISTS AND PASTORS

It is even more true now than when Guntrip wrote that the agreed overlap between the work of therapists and pastors is broader. Movement is not all one way from therapy to pastoring. Some therapy, since it works with the whole life of the person, is recognized as also touching the 'spiritual' dimension. This may be specifically observed in two developments.

1 Some analysts and therapists have become interested in religious phenomena for their own sake. In an earlier age these were often treated reductively. Indeed some regarded anything religious as pathological. In part this might have been due to Freud's own predispositions. But studies by among others Eric Fromm (1950), Anna-Marie Rizzuto (1979), William Meissner (1984) and Neville Symington (1994) have carried this debate forward. This approach at least gives possible legitimacy to the notion of spiritual experience which has its own validity (Carr 1989).

A change has also come about in the context in which therapy has developed. Freud and some other earliest analysts were largely hostile to religion. They shared the methodological atheism or agnosticism of most explorers of human behaviour at the time as they tried to establish new sciences. These contributed significantly to the secularizing process which was once expected to have a more profound impact than it has. Religion and religious experience looked like the residue of a past which would disappear. This has not happened. And while there is no overwhelming turning to the Christian churches, there is an increasing interest in a wide range of things which are loosely called 'spiritual'.

Some emerge under the heading of the New Age. This collection of esotericism represents for some the way in which to be in touch with the numinous and hold to a sense of spiritual experience. Without dogma or doctrine freedom exists to legitimize any experience. Christians will have questions. But in today's culture this phenomenon provides one way to give legitimacy to a religious dimension to living and to experience which may be claimed as 'spiritual'. At the heart of the New Age lies the longing for transformative experience. One among the legion of sources for this is psychotherapy (Carr 1991; Perry 1992). Both the theory and application of psychology, therefore, are coming together to acknowledge at least the possibility of religion and of a distinct spiritual dimension to human experience.

2 At the same time the churches and their ministers may be recovering a stronger sense of their identity and becoming less worried about being supplanted by the 'new priests' of psychotherapy. The various 'ologies', especially sociology, anthropology and psychology, seemed once to be conspiring

to destroy the churches' ministry. Browning's warning from the nineteenth century seemed to be coming true in the twentieth:

> Greek endings, each the little passing-bell
> That signifies some faith's about to die.
> *Bishop Blougram's Apology*

They either posed questions that pastors could not answer, so that they felt undervalued. Or these disciplines became so attractive that pastors abandoned the search for their distinctive theological role and took up different jobs. Some became academics, others counsellors or social workers, in order to feel that their contribution to human well-being was genuine. In this climate the pastor seemed to be becoming obsolete. There are signs, however, that this tide is also turning and that the distinctive role of the minister is being rediscovered, although numbers offering in most churches in the United Kingdom remain small.

There is, therefore, today less sense of a conflict between psychology and theology and between counselling and pastoring. The pastor's basic discipline is theology. But since the material with which ministers deal is human they will take advantage of the human disciplines in thinking through their theological basis. It is helpful to remember, too, that many therapists are also now reflecting on the possible limits to their discipline and where it may overlap with religious teachings. And both will be aware of the religious dimension, whether to the more occasional encounter of the pastor or the more in-depth sessions of the counsellor. The work of the latter has been well described as 'an undogmatic religion of personal attention' (North 1972).

COUNSELLING AND PASTORING

There are five main points of comparison between counselling and therapy on the one hand and pastoring and theology on the other.[1]

INDIVIDUAL FULFILMENT CONTRASTED WITH FREEDOM AND SOCIAL BENEFIT

This is a crude differentiation but remains important as a

basic orientation. The theme of *shalom* that was discussed in Chapter One lies at its root.

> Seldom do we find in the Old Testament a word which to the same degree as *shalom* can bear a common use and yet can be filled with a concentrated religious context far above the level of the average conception ... We constrict the term if we equate it strictly with 'peace'. At root it means 'well-being', with a strong emphasis on the material side ... When we consider the rich possibilities of *shalom* in the Old Testament we are struck by the negative fact that there is no specific text in which it denotes the specifically spiritual attitude of inward peace ... We are forced to say that in its most common use *shalom* is an empathically social concept. (von Rad 1964, 404)

In the Jewish-Christian tradition ideas of healing, integration or even inner peace are coupled with some sense of the social benefit that results. This might be seen, for instance, in the greater wealth of the individual. But that wealth is then to be used for the benefit of others. Personal integration alone is an alien concept.

When considering counselling and individual fulfilment, the contexts tend to be those which the individual determines. Most presenting problems are eventually linked with relations with parents, family history and problems of authority that have consequently arisen. This factor indicates the limitations of counselling by contrast with pastoring. Pastors will not deny or even ignore those contexts. But they cannot be satisfied with them alone. For the pastor represents a distinctive context to the client which is implicit in every encounter. This is the transcendent reference which is mostly called 'God'. This is what the pastor works with.

Some Christian ministry is offered as if God were a (or the) resource in a situation. Then the pastor sees himself or herself as mobilizing God to help the person in need. In so doing, however, the pastor is likely to ride casually over those dimensions which a counsellor would address – relationships, family, parents and feelings in general. Yet to pay too great attention to these is to be in danger of becoming merely another counsellor and denying the pastor's public role as person of God. If, however, God is seen as the determining context of any pastoral encounter, suffusing all parts of it, both present and past and the various roles that the parties also hold, it becomes possible to recognize this transcendent reference. Thus the pastor will remain in touch with the pastoral role and the client will have the benefit of the belief that his or her assumption about the pastor has some basis in truth: the pastor is a God person and represents God in that context. In practice, when this happens, the past is often exposed for interpretation.

A man came to a pastor after being bereaved. It was one of those instances when follow-up to a funeral happened, though at the instigation of the man himself. He was an occasional church attender, but not specially devout. He talked about many things, but it was clear to the pastor that he was avoiding something crucial. The discussions (there were three before the issue was reached) pursued their course. They felt to the pastor desultory. Whenever he was offered even a mild interpretation the man stood up, walked round the room in an agitated fashion and looked away from the pastor and out of the window, complaining that he did not want 'all this psychological stuff'. Eventually he came to the point. During his wife's final illness he had become close to a family friend. He had slept with her, as he put it, not out of any grand passion but 'for comfort'. He now felt guilty, partly for having done it, partly for having not told his wife and partly from a strong sense of having offended some sort of right – he would not at this point name this as 'God'.

The story is not unusual. But the last reference to 'what was right' was crucial. The pastor, feeling that he should tread gently, tried to allow the man to express his feelings, which he did. In the end the man turned angrily on the pastor and said, 'I don't want interpretation: I know what I did. I think I know myself enough to have some sense of why. I also know I'm deceiving myself by rationalizing what I did. You must tell me that I did wrong.' The pastor felt the ambiguity in himself. Was he to counsel further and take this last request as a attempt to put him in a judgemental role, with the chance that he would be dismissed as unsympathetic? Or was he simply to say, 'Yes. You did wrong'? In fact he refined it. He deliberately mentioned God: 'Yes. You did wrong in the eyes of God. Does that help?' Then he held his breath. The man sat aghast for a moment: he seemed not to have expected this. Then he crumpled, admitted to much more adultery, to feelings of offence far more against God than his wife, and began to acknowledge aspects of himself that he had rationalized away. The transcendent reference which he sought in the pastor, that of God, became a genuine context with which to work at sorting out his life.

A difficulty with the idea of transcendence is that it has been associated with magic and supernatural power as well as with impossible vision. It sometimes seems that the therapist is able to do 'more real' work with someone. There being no magic and no vision the therapist and client can direct attention to various levels of reality, testing them and exploring them together. The pastor has to admit that there may often be some truth in this implicit criticism. But when the possibility of an eternal dimension to life, the transcendent and the consequential religious belief, are not ruled out *a priori*, then a way of holding to them in any context is needed.

One way in which this has traditionally been done is through 'the cure of souls' (Oden 1984). The Latin word *cura* carries stronger overtones that the English words 'cure' or 'care' convey. It draws attention to a context and includes both care and concern and responsibility. In this case the *cura* is 'of souls'. It refers to the responsibility of the pastor to see the life of people wholly in the setting of eternity. The idea of 'souls' represents the eternal dimension of the person's life, both in quality and quantity. Pastors, therefore, are to see clients in their eternal context and their work as contributing to an individual's eternal destiny. This need not mean, as it may have sometimes in the past, discounting the present. Indeed much contemporary Christian thinking has elaborated the Johannine theme of eternal life as a quality of existence.

The work of the minister in any situation may have a material dimension. An example would be feeding the hungry. It may also have a therapeutic dimension, such as providing relief from an anxiety or stress. There is no distinction between therapy and pastoring in the quality of attention to the 'here and now' of the individual. Or it may have a more overtly theological dimension, consciously putting the life of the person concerned into the context of eternity. But by holding to the transcendent and the eternal in the here and now the pastor will hold in mind and bring to bear as judged appropriate two dimensions which are missing from the counselling meeting.

1   A pastor will not only relate the present to the past, but will also see this as best as may be in the context of the future. What has brought someone to their present crisis may have its roots somewhere in the past. These cannot be disregarded. But the aspirations of someone coming to the minister should not be discounted. To some extent they may be longing for magic and have to be resisted. But this approach also relates to hope and what may be looked forward to. The future is always a dimension of divine encounter, not least in a pastoral engagement.

2   The here and now is valued not merely as representing an outcome from the past. It has its own value for the individual and in terms of what that individual might represent and be useful for in a social context. The counsellor will address the individual; the pastor must address the individual in his or her actual or potential social context.

SPECIFIC TRANSFERENCE IN COUNSELLING IS CONTRASTED WITH GENERAL UNMANAGED TRANSFERENCE IN THE PASTORAL ENCOUNTER

The therapist's work is to encourage and interpret the client's transference. But transference is not peculiar to the patient/therapist pair; it is a phenomenon of everyday life. It is, therefore, something with which the pastor will be familiar, even if the language to describe it is new. But the pastor handles it in a social context outside the constraints of the therapist's contract with the patient.

Examples of specific transference in a pastoral relationship are common. The woman parishioner, for instance, who develops a fixation on the male minister may do so for many reasons. But one among them may be the search for a rewarding response that she was denied by her own father. To deal with this the wise minister needs some defence such as being unwilling to see her alone or having a way of referring her to a larger group. One of his tools in coping will also be awareness of his own countertransferential feelings.

But there is also a wider form of generalized transference with which the pastor as public minister has to deal. This is what might be called 'institutional transference' (Shapiro and Carr 1992). For example, a boarding school will have rules about who may and who may not visit the pupils. These will look like a series of restrictions, at least to the pupils. A teenage student, however, who also experiences her parents as restrictive to her freedom when she is at home, is likely to resist restrictions at school because she experiences the school as if it were her parents. They both seem to fail to acknowledge her needs. So as a pupil at the school she makes a transference of her attitude to her parents onto the school.

This dimension to generalized transference may be overlooked by pastors, unless they have a strong sense of the range of roles that they occupy. One of these is as representative of the Church. And however apparently to do with everyday human affairs a pastoral encounter may be, it will be suffused with expectations of this role. It is therefore more than likely that the pastor will experience transference on behalf of the institution (the Church) that he or she represents. That is difficult to manage, not least since it is virtually impossible to explore the origins of such transference.

So far as the pastor's theological approach is concerned this question will inform a doctrine of sin. There has been a tendency to consider this in terms of the individual and his or her behaviour. But sin is also social. Perhaps the most useful introduction – and it is interesting that it relates to Pauline psychology – is the statement: 'Therefore as sin came into the world through one man and death through sin, and so death spread to all men because (Greek *eph hōi*) all men sinned' (Rom. 5.12). This text is a notable problem. Six different explanations have been discerned (Cranfield 1975, 274). But overall Paul seems to be striving to hold together both individual responsibility and the idea that sin came into the world independently of the actions of contemporary individuals. For the latter he blames Adam. But although Adam – the one other than ourselves – is responsible for the presence of sin and death, all human beings are also individually responsible for their contribution to the continuing reign of sin and death. The social and individual aspects are held together.

JUST AS THE COUNSELLOR WORKS WITH SPECIFIC TRANSFERENCE AND THE PASTOR WITH MORE GENERALIZED CONTEXT, SO TOO WITH THE PROBLEMS

The counsellor tends to handle, at least in the initial encounter, a single issue that is presented or a connected set of problems. Much of the pastor's work is with general encounters, often those which have a social base. Pastoral ministry, for example, is usually concerned less with problems than with transitional crises. The request to bless a house or a ring is a call for help in managing a transition. More obvious are the requests for weddings, baptisms and funerals.

Ritual might be thought far from the work of the counsellor. But the counselling context is suffused with its own rituals – the length of time (the fifty-minute hour), the guaranteed uninterrupted period, the seating arrangement, including the idea of a couch and the payment. Few of these rituals are available to the pastor. But the different types convey their different messages. For the rituals of the counselling encounter affirm the role of the client in relation to the counsellor. They are widely known but they can only be experienced individually when a client seeks counsel. By contrast, however, the rituals of the pastoral encounter are public and social. There are no private rites except those of the confessional. But even then the priest is publicly available. All these rituals possess a social context.

The theological undergirding of this aspect of pastoral ministry may be the doctrine of the Trinity. This has returned to the forefront of systematic theology and prominent among recent emphases is the social dimension of persons in relationship. There seems to be a wish to link the whole with the parts through a formulation which stresses the creative relationship of the persons (Zizioulas 1985; Gunton 1993).

> The Trinitarian conception suggested by the two transcendentals we have examined ... is that of sociality ... its central concept is that of shared being: the persons do not simply enter into relations with one another, but are constituted by one another in relationship. Father, Son and Spirit are eternally what they are by virtue of what they are from and to one another. Being and relation can be separated in thought, but in no way separated ontologically:

they are rather part of the one ontological dynamic. The general point, to use the words of John Zizioulas, is that the being of God is not a blank unity, but a being in communion ... Personal beings are social beings, so that of both God and man it must be said that they have their being in their personal relatedness: their free relation-in-otherness. (Gunton 1993, 214, 229)

CONTACT BETWEEN A COUNSELLOR AND A CLIENT WILL BE CLIENT INITIATED

The last two points and this one hang together. Someone might go to a counsellor because it is recommended. But counsellors, even when they advertise their skills, do not initiate the meeting. By contrast encounters with the pastor are more informal and casual and are often initiated by the minister. For example, there is a long-standing tradition of pastoral visiting by ministers. It may be the minister calling on members of the congregation; it may be an industrial chaplain visiting a site; or it might be a vicar visiting parishioners who may not have any direct contact with the Church. In that fashion the minister often initiates the encounter which leads to the pastoral engagement. But there is also the less formal approach which occurs because the minister has a public role. Simply because he or she is there the minister constitutes an invitation to encounter: 'I don't want to bother you, vicar, but would you mind ... ?' It is part of the pastoral strategy of all churches, whatever their ecclesiology, that they have identifiable, usually ordained, ministers for this purpose. That is why pastoral ministry is not only itself theologically informed but also raises theological questions for the churches.

The issue over who initiates a contact and how it is done again exposes the question of authority. The counsellor has a different authority from that of the pastor. It is a perennial problem for mainstream therapists and their associations that it is impossible to define the way in which a counsellor could be formally authorized. He or she may have qualifications and the backing of such associations as the British Association of Psychotherapists. But these bodies do not authorize. Ultimately counsellors are self-accrediting. Their authority is assigned to them by those who come for help. This does not diminish their authority: it is a constituent part of what it means to be a counsellor.

In the Church's ministry the pastoring offered by a lay person is exactly the same. He or she is self-accrediting, basing their availability on their beliefs and their accreditation on their testimony. They are assigned such authority as anyone with whom they deal cares to give them. But publicly authorized ministers are in a different position. They carry the authority of the authorizing church which ordained them. This authority is to represent the Church and, because of the nature of the Church's belief, also God. This point should not be underestimated in a world in which the question of God and scrutiny of claims to access to him are the norm. The fact remains that the authorized minister is a 'Church and God person'. Indeed, because of that he or she is also to some extent deprived of the testimony which is the bulwark of the lay person's ministry. This is not a matter of qualifications, although most churches require some before a person is authorized. It is a question of being able to represent the Church and God.

That authority is, therefore, different from that of the counsellor. Yet both counsellor and pastor have also to be assigned authority by those with whom they deal. The minister who believes that his or her authority derives from God and that is enough has to learn about negotiated authority, not least where matters of belief and tentative approaches to the divine are concerned. But the quality of what is assigned will be different according to the authority which is believed to belong to the minister.

THE COUNSELLOR'S CONTRACTUAL RELATIONSHIP WITH THE CLIENT IS FIRM AND IS RELATED IN SOME WAY TO COMPETENCE AND EXPERTISE, WHETHER ACTUAL OR BELIEVED. BY CONTRAST THE WORK OF THE PASTOR IS BASED ON REPRESENTATION AND CONSEQUENTLY A DEGREE OF INCOMPETENCE

Counsellors and pastors naturally vary in their levels of competence. Each may be to a greater or lesser degree skilled. But this is not the point. The critical question is the form of relationship. Projective identification is used in different ways in therapy and pastoring. The pastor is always to some degree a substitute for God. As a result the projections which are put onto him or her have an extra distance to them which puts them beyond full interpretation. Not only is the pastor's encounter with someone likely to be briefer than that of the therapist; it will also have a dynamic end to it. Its incompleteness is an essential part of the meeting which is acknowledged, though not necessarily consciously, by both pastor and penitent.

The pastor's distinctive skill, therefore, will lie less in a different set of interpretative tools from the therapist than in the way that these are used. And the task will be theologically always informed by the question of God. For if the penitent has some however dim sense of God as represented by the pastor, it will be the pastor's responsibility in role to be both aware of that and able to respond. This frees the pastor from primitive ideas of God as either a resource or a bandage for problem situations. Nor can God be brought in, since both theologically and pastorally he is already in the situation both as far as the pastor and the penitent are concerned. Indeed it is curious but worth noting that possibly as the churches become less sure about God and questions of what that word means, there is less uncertainty in others. This point has been explored elsewhere and need not, therefore, be elaborated here.

CONCLUSION

The world in which today's pastor works is therapeutically saturated. The assumptions of most people, however unconsciously, are psychologically informed. There is, therefore, a need for the pastor to understand this as context and seek to work within it. The acids of psychologically informed criticism of religion, however, have at the same time done their work, leaving pastors unsure about the status of their belief and more importantly the beliefs of those with whom they deal. It is, therefore, essential that pastors are familiar with the nature of the therapeutic approach. They will also discover that they have to work out their pastoral theology within that world without surrender to it.

Appendices

The first appendix offers those beginning pastoral studies through placement some practical advice. The other two amplify themes that have been introduced but not elaborated in the text.

APPENDIX 1
DOING A PLACEMENT AS A PARADIGM OF MINISTRY

Placements are a central feature of modern pastoral training. This section explains how the work on a placement should model and become the basic stance for all ministerial life.

APPENDIX 2 AN ANALOGY OF EXPERIENCE

'Experience' has been mentioned throughout the book. This appendix offers a slightly more philosophical reflection on this difficult concept.

APPENDIX 3 IRRATIONALITY AND RELIGION

This article offers an extended theoretical discussion of the dynamic in which the Church and its ministers are caught up.

Doing a Placement as a Paradigm of Ministry[1]

Placements have become a core element in pastoral training. Theological students will be expected to do one or more during their course. They provide an opportunity to establish a way to approach a new situation. This serves the immediate learning process. But it is also intended to become so embedded in that when students later become public ministers they will instinctively adopt a similar stance.

THE AIMS OF A PLACEMENT

Among the aims that are normally listed in a syllabus we may note:

INCREASED SELF-UNDERSTANDING

Students, whatever their background, need during training to explore themselves. This is not a question of personal self-awareness. That, when required, can be achieved through counselling, therapy or spiritual direction, as appropriate. The self-understanding through a placement is designed to be related to the vocation to ministry and the role that follows.

The obvious difficulty is that a student may feel that this is a time to discover something about the role of a minister. But that is impossible. For however much authority may be ascribed to an ordinand, this cannot be compared with the authority of ordained ministers. It is important, therefore, that the analogical nature of learning through placement is grasped. Students cannot learn what it is to be a public

239

minister. But they can discover what it is to take up a role and to learn about how authority is assigned and earned. Such self-understanding in role relates directly to the fundamental learning which every minister undergoes in every new situation.

INTEGRATED LEARNING AND PRACTICE

Integration is a key theme in pastoral studies, although it often feels more easy to discuss than to discover. Nevertheless, the work of the minister must always be integrative. To learn about the process of integration is an essential aspect to theological training. It is, therefore, essential that questions of learning and practice are held together by a working hypothesis and that the relation is not merely assumed or left to the student to determine.

THEOLOGICAL REFLECTION

All syllabuses include reference to theological reflection as a mode of study. How this is described and the emphasis given to it vary. The aspect that it most difficult in a placement is the action outcome, with which the cycle starts anew. It is for that reason, if the experience of reflection is to be complete and relate to the ministry that will later be exercised, the work required of the student on placement needs to have the possibility of action both as an outcome and a test.

DOING THE PLACEMENT

RECORD FEELINGS

The ministerial question that has been extensively discussed earlier is 'What is happening to me and why?', recalling that the 'me' in this sentence is the person in role. While, therefore, careful attention to facts is essential, it is important that the student on entering a placement notes his or her feelings, even when (even more especially when) they are confused or out of sorts. If, for instance, the student feels that he or she does not wish to be on placement and would rather be somewhere else, that is a feeling that importantly requires to be noted. Later its significance may become clear. But unless it and its context are noted, it will be lost.

RECORD DATA

It is obvious that data are essential. This is partly to avoid excessive introspection and unchecked feelings. It is also important to remember that memory is deceitful. Data, therefore, will include such matters as time, place, people and even intention before the encounter. Important background data must also be assembled. For example, if the placement is in a church, the background will include something about the communities among which it is set, a profile of the church (building and people), as well as its connections with other groups and individuals.

RECORD REFLECTIONS

This is the point at which the student's theological understanding is explicitly involved. In the course of the study ideas and insights will be stirred up in the student's mind. These will be to do with Scripture, tradition and theological understanding. Again, unless these are recorded, they will in retrospect be re-ordered into a frame which the student will justify to himself. The possibility, therefore, of pastoral experience impinging on and changing the student's theological outlook will be minimized, but without that interchange between gospel and situation *as this is felt in the student* neither learning nor pastoral study will occur.

RISK INTERPRETATION TO ONESELF

It is clear that interpretation to others is, for the student, often going to appear, and even be, dangerously ignorant. But unless interpretation is risked, learning about a pastoral ministry will be lacking. Students will, therefore, interpret what is happening to themselves and keep a note of these interpretations. Many of them will, when reviewed, prove wrong and will be discarded. But unless they are risked, learning will not occur or be consolidated.

WRITE

Students are required to produce a report on their pastoral placement, usually written. But behind the final production there needs to be a proper record of all the above. There are a number of ways of doing this and students will determine their own. One is to keep a diary in a large book with the pages divided under the following headings: Date, Data (People, Place, Aim), Feeling, Reflection, Outcome, Notes. It does not matter how rough this is, so long as the student can draw comparisons and connections. If the information, whatever its initial quality, is on the pages, then later work can be done with it.

PLACEMENT DAY BOOK – SPECIMEN PAGE

DATE	DATA			FEELING	REFLECT	OUTCOME	NOTES
	People	Place	Aim				

An Analogy of Experience

A key theological problem which this approach raises is that of analogy. Since anyone who speaks of God (believer, pastor or theologian) speaks analogically, this is not surprising. It is, however, such well-trodden ground that a disquisition seemed inappropriate in the book. But a useful approach to the subject, which is directly related to this study, is offered by John E. Smith (1968).

When we talk at all about experience, the two domains of literal and symbolic language overlap to such a degree that they seem almost to elide. This is sometimes regarded as a distinctive problem for theological discourse, but is a phenomenon of every use of language, in particular when we are trying to compare and draw together sensible experience (the conscious world) and a transcendent one (the unconscious). This is a vital observation, since it means that there is no 'private' language, either for theology or for the human sciences. Both have to be accessible in the public arena, however much for their internal purposes they may develop a jargon. One consequence of all languages being in this public arena is that they can be used interchangeably. This is not a recipe for confusion, a new Tower of Babel, but a recognition that since languages from various disciplines are speaking about, at least at root, a common topic – human experience – then in principle it should be possible to find and examine connections between them which might illuminate the particular work of each discipline in its own field.

No analogical comparison is possible without asymmetry. If there is no imbalance between the terms being used, an analogy is merely a tautology. One way of appreciating this is to recognize that a distinction is presumed between what is to be understood and the means by which the understanding is to be achieved. Smith cites two well-known examples. Clerk Maxwell used the analogy of a swarm of bees to interpret the behaviour of molecules in a solid object like a table. Huygens described light waves by comparing them with the effects of a stone being thrown into a still pond. Obviously the bees were not the table nor the ripples the light waves. But the type of language makes what is not known comprehensible and so enables us to develop our understanding and thinking. Once we recognize this asymmetry we can see why no analogy is ever exhaustive. There is built-in room for refinement, either in the thing understood or in the means being used to achieve understanding. Drawing an analogy, therefore, is always an incomplete dynamic process between the object and the process or between two types of language – literal and symbolic.

Smith suggests that experience can be employed as a basis for analogy in theology. We appeal to specific human experiences (such as loving, pleasing, hating, judging) as a way of understanding religious ideas. The concept of experience acquires a distinctive role in theological reflection, which is just like that which it possesses in religious practice. It becomes the medium of interpretation between this finite world and its ultimate ground. But there is a problem:

> If religious insight is to be made intelligible, and if such insight into the meaning of existence as a whole for finite things cannot be a matter of immediate or intuitive apprehension, the question arises as to what feature of existence is able to perform the mediating function. (Smith 1968, 53)

Smith proposes that the feature is the fact of experience itself. But if notions derived from this are to be related to an understanding of God, and not merely restricted to the human sphere, a major condition must be fulfilled. In an analogy the nature of the thing characterized determines the mode in which the characteristic itself is manifested. So, for example, in the case of Clerk Maxwell's table, the characteristic of the table, which (as he wished to explain) is composed of many molecules, determined how applicable and effective the analogy of a swarm of bees was. When, however, the thing characterized is an object of faith or belief, as in the case of God, special attention has to be paid to this point. God necessarily transcends and includes all finite being, among which is numbered the person who is drawing the analogy. And since *human* experience is being used as the means of analogy, we may infer that 'the meaning of any terms or experience used to make intelligible an insight of faith about God, must *at least* be as rich as the meaning which the term or experience has for human beings' (Smith 1968, 55).

This reference to richness is important, since it reminds us to watch for the reductionist tendencies to which reflections in this field are prone.

An analogy, however, is not drawn for its own sake. It is made with an intention that points beyond itself. For example, a religious analogy about God is doing more than trying to suggest what God is like and to say something about him. Consequences are to be drawn both from the attempt to draw the analogy and the content of the analogy itself. We need to ask what is being confirmed or explored. Many religious analogies, for instance, could be said to be concerned with 'the way of discipleship'. No analogy can confirm that way, but it may indicate some of the linguistic peculiarities about our human quest for God and so encourage us to or dissuade us from pursuing this. Since we are dealing with an object, God, which transcends finite being, it follows that there will be no simple, direct support for the ideas that we generate when we think analogically. But it is legitimate to see whether there is any indirect support, and this is what Smith does. He suggests that this indirect support for our ideas of God is found in the concept of experience itself.

The first indirect support is that experience itself can be identified and classified as something which emerges in the evolutionary history of human beings and their consciousness. There is a biological foundation to our psychological and sociological interpretations of existence, which implies that experience is not a tissue of subjectivity or something sustained in the private domain of the individual. It can, therefore, be discussed and analysed. Indeed, we might go further and claim that because of this foundation to the fact of experience, study and analysis of it is essential to there being experience. It is something that we inherit but also create.

The second indirect support is more interesting and complicated. Smith argues that experience is pervasive and also assumes intersubjective form. This is demonstrated from three angles. First, there is the fact that we engage in experimental intervention and control. Things are not just assumed to happen to us. We try to understand and manage them as a matter of course. Second, in any historical community, all sorts of experience pervades the self-awareness that it develops and holds. Third, although it is difficult, we can make comparisons across cultural boundaries and differences. This last point is important, since it ensures that we can experiment with the nature, content and form of experience. But Smith rejects on commonsense grounds the idea that experience as a concept can be restricted to what may be tested by experiment. All phenomena in human experience simply cannot become the object of experimental enquiry.

This idea that experience itself can be employed as a means of analogy is useful. First, however, there is a further aspect to the use of analogy that should not be overlooked – it is also a heuristic method of argument. Discussions on analogy tend to focus on the logic of the reasoning and how we may move from particular premises to certain conclusions. The heuristic method, however, encourages the taking of logically unwarranted steps in order to achieve the solution of apparently insoluble problems. For instance, the mathematician Euler intuitively saw a solution to a problem but could not find the logical steps to it. The required answer obviously lay in a certain direction. So he hypothesized his conclusion and retrospectively eliminated any argument which proved unhelpful in creating the ordered solution. This heuristic method is significant in today's world, for instance in cybernetics and systems theory (Polya 1971). There are risks in combining heuristic and analogical thinking, but it can prove creative. To do this in our present discussion indicates that we need a process which has three parts.

1   We have to establish a dynamic model for interpreting experience. Without some such interpretation there can be no *usable* concept of experience. Such a model is noticeably absent from Smith's argument, and leads to some disappointment when he handles theological concepts. But I have proposed one using some contemporary psychoanalytic ideas

of both the individual and the human setting. It will inevitably be in some respects deficient, since no model is ever complete. But it offers a coherent way of interpreting the dynamics and realities of human experience without being *a priori* selective. We are thus also relieved of any tendency to slip into an atomistic stance in trying to handle evidence drawn from human experience. The essence of the interpretative model that has been offered is that it is always inclusive, moving between one dimension and another – for example, individual and group.

2   Any model which is used to interpret human experience must also be employed to interpret the dissimilar term in the theological analogy, namely the particular Christian doctrine under review.

3   This method may allow us to look for new light on the ultimate meaning that may be contained within finite experience. This is merely an assumption, but it may be that the psychological and sociological concepts, which are used for interpretations, point beyond those matters and concerns for which their users generally stand. In other words, analytic ideas in themselves, even though often employed to defend an anti-religious stance on the part of the user, may in fact indicate other areas of existence which the user cannot perceive, but which, if there is to be any communication between God and humankind, must be addressed. Anthropological, psychological and sociological theorists and pioneers have been unaware of some of the profounder religious and theological implications of their work (Bowker 1973). Another hint of this area may occur in the wistfulness which is often displayed by workers in fields of human behaviour. But at the same time we cannot underestimate contemporary disillusion with the capacity of the Christian Church and its theological themes to articulate these feelings. We may, however, be able once again to move back to being able to do this through a revalued appreciation of the Christian classics.

Smith's proposal to use experience in analogical thinking is strengthened as a result of this three-part process. The problem of analogy remains, because it is built into any use of analogical thinking, and especially when the second term is a transcendent object of faith or belief. But by employing the dynamic interpretative model of experience, we refine

247

and make graspable the other term, which had hitherto been elusive. A broad use of analogy is proposed, with due regard being paid to the heuristic component. We, therefore, have a means in principle of creatively linking contemporary insights and interpretation of common human experience and major Christian doctrines, or interpretations of God and his dealings with the world. Sound pastoral practice, informed by psychological and sociological ideas and views, can now be integrated with sound theological thinking, informed by Scripture and the Church's traditions.

Irrationality and Religion

This is a revised version of an article that first appeared in J. Krantz, ed., Irrationality in Social and Organizational Life, *proceedings of the eighth A. K. Rice Institute Scientific Meeting (Washington, A. K. Rice Institute, 1987). It is reproduced here, with permission, for those who wish to explore in more detail some of the theoretical issues of this book, particularly the application of psychodynamic thinking to religious questions.*

INTRODUCTION

For much of the twentieth century it has been suggested that religious belief is irrational. Behind this assumption often lurks the further thought that any irrationality is undesirable. There are many reasons why religion has lost much of its former status in public esteem. Yet the power of religion seems to remain strong. For example, the rise of Islam is raising serious political and economic issues for the world at large. At a more personal level the persistence of powerfully sectarian behaviour within dominantly secular societies defies reductionist explanations. The siege at Waco, Texas, in 1993 and the televangelists, however discredited their predecessors, are two obvious instances. Studies demonstrate two persistent points about religion: first, even when there is a decline in practice, the longing for some public religious activity persists; second, religious practices, especially prayer or occasional worship, are more widespread than the prevailing secularism of western culture would seem to imply (Bowker 1973; 1978; Reed 1978; Hay 1987; Meissner 1984). The question, therefore, of irrationality and religion is not a curiosity. It raises important questions for individual psychology and social understanding.

When we consider religious institutions from a socio-technical perspective, however, there is an obvious problem: What sort of system is a church? Miller and Rice regarded religious institutions as 'examples of enterprises with coincidence of task and sentient boundaries' (Miller and Rice 1967, 255).[1] This made their future in the modern world at least insecure. Subsequently, however, further work has interpreted churches as open systems (Reed 1976; 1978; Carr 1985; 1994; Ecclestone 1988; Shapiro and Carr 1991; Miller, 1993).

For many who participate in Tavistock-style group relations conferences it suddenly dawns that the unconscious life of a group is more than a theory. In a small study group at my second Leicester conference[2] one of the members was an elegant woman dressed in black with a distinctive scarab medallion. We used formal titles. She was a formidable 'Ms'. I was 'The Reverend Doctor'. In that group of highly intelligent and rational people, sudden anxiety developed. It was focused on the medallion. Eventually the woman was driven to remove it and lay it on the floor in the middle of the group. In turn my twin titles were used in an extended and powerful fantasy about the power of both religion (Reverend) and healing (Doctor). This was used to rescue the group from its irrational fears and work resumed.

The incident is not so unusual. It demonstrates what is well known: irrational behaviour inexplicably emerges, even in a group of sceptical, logical people. The way in which the members trusted my untested competence in two fields – religion and medicine (I am not medically trained) – also suggests that when dependence is being mobilized, irrationality is lurking somewhere. And the symbol of the scarab, together with the small ceremony of its removal, reminds us that symbols and ritual, major marks of religious activity, remain inordinately powerful, regardless of any specific belief that a person may have in or about them.

But there is a further point. This story derives from a group relations conference, where every action and experience, however insignificant, is noted and available to be interpreted. In that setting we are accustomed to making the adjustment from seeing the individual alone to considering the individual in the context of the group and the group in turn within its environment. 'The individual is a creature of a group; the group of the individual' (Miller and Rice 1967, 17). Individuals often function on behalf of one another. A person's irrational behaviour, therefore, may not be merely a manifestation of personal pathology. Groups can similarly function on behalf of one another as they interact with their environment.

There is, however, a further extrapolation – risky but necessary. This is to enlarge the concept of 'environment' and consider how organizations themselves may function on behalf of and within those vast, largely undefinable, but powerfully effective concepts like 'society' (Khaleelee and Miller 1985; Shapiro and Carr 1991). This is an exciting, but difficult, area to contemplate. When we become aware of the group our sense of the complexity of the individual increases. Intergroup behaviour heightens the level of confusions within a single group. When we add 'society' our range of awareness is further enlarged, until it becomes mind-boggling. Some trainee social workers once objected to learning a systems approach to their work, not because it was wrong or unhelpful, but on the grounds that it required them to do 'world therapy' before they could help any individual (Barnes 1984, 27). This sense of an even larger setting makes comprehension more difficult. But it is no less vital because it introduces another major variable into an already extensive set – culture.

In thinking about human behaviour and differences we may minimize the scale of the environments, assuming them, sometimes noting them, but not examining them or risking interpretation. It may be that we think this material is superficial by comparison with the universal and fundamental concept of 'the unconscious mind'. But any reflection on religious behaviour requires us to address questions of meaning which are not amenable to easy interpretation, because they arise in an ever enlarging series of contexts. The sort of issue, for example, that our present study might take us towards, whatever our interest in religion might be: Are primary dynamics, such as dependence, expressed in culturally determined ways? Or is there a qualitative difference in the nature of dependence because of the cultural context in which it is discerned? Or, to put this as a simple religious question: are two worshippers – say a British Christian and an American Jew – both exhibiting the same dynamic behaviour when they worship, or is there some qualitative difference in the dynamic itself? Reflection on the large-scale issues of, for example, religion and culture might cause us not merely to apply the interpretative tools of group dynamics but to reflect upon them and refine them. The topic of irrationality and religion, therefore, is important, whatever one's estimate of religion or personal belief.

RELIGION AND IRRATIONAL BEHAVIOUR

Irrational behaviour and religious belief are inseparable. The uses to which religious fervour are put sometimes defy credibility – Ireland, the Middle East, the Klu Klux Klan, televangelists and so on. But these are extreme instances of the way in which religion is a primary means by which the irrational parts of our existence are acknowledged. Mainstream religions tend to diminish the significance of disturbingly irrational Dionysiac experience – ecstasy, speaking in tongues, maenad dancing, and so forth. They marginalize it into sub-groups. Yet every religion seems to sustain a body of such people (Miskotte 1967; Gordon 1981; Clark 1986). One hypothesis may be that, receiving powerful projections from the more 'respectable' believers, they represent facets of the core of belief as significantly as the more orthodox. Mysticism offers more reflective people a similarly specific religious experience. Others become preoccupied with demons and devils. Within the Christian tradition Quakerism offers an interesting instance of this dilemma. It is found both as the Shakers, who continue the quaking tradition, and as the undogmatic, socially aware, quiet people. Serious thought about religious belief, experience and behaviour cannot be confined to the area of rationality alone.

Sometimes religious behaviour is treated as a primitive manifestation of human irrationality. Accordingly it is being, or at least will be, superseded by more rational styles of life. This view, however, looks increasingly mistaken as the twentieth century progresses. The search for a purely rational basis for living was an instance of nineteenth-century optimism (Lecky 1865). It contributed among other things to the originating of psychoanalysis, which in turn gave further credence to the search (Vitz 1993). Towards the end of the nineteenth century in Germany some scholars proposed to remove the Revelation of St John from the New Testament. This apocalyptic book, with its weird visions, bloody violence and lust for vengeance, was regarded as too unsophisticated. The Christian Church in civilized Europe had outgrown it. Within a few years, however, the symbolism revived during the First World War, and has remained powerful throughout our era. It was extensively quoted by Theodore Roszak (1970) in the counter-cultural protest against the tyranny of the fact. Bettelheim provides another instance. Reflecting on his experiences in Dachau and Buchenwald, he has described why we dare not ignore the irrational dimension of human life, if we are to escape the brutalizing pressures inherent in mass society (Bettelheim 1979).

We need, therefore, to examine another possibility. Religious behaviour may be a primary means by which people, both individuals and societies, address their inevitable and necessary but normal irrational aspects. Irrationality cannot be, and is not, discarded as human beings grow towards an enlightened rationality.

Irrationality is inseparable from religion. Many discussions, however, tend to restrict themselves to questions of individual behaviour and personal pathology. A more significant study is how and why irrationality is manifested in religious bodies. Such an investigation is obviously important for churches, their leaders and members. But it has wider significance. First, if among their tasks religious bodies specifically handle aspects of irrationality in everyday life, then the competence with which they do so will affect groups and individuals far beyond the confines of the churches. Second, if we can determine how and why a religious institution handles irrationality, we may have the beginnings of a paradigm which could be of use to other institutions for interpreting this side of human behaviour as it appears to them.

RELIGION AND NECESSARY DEPENDENCE

From his study of groups Wilfred Bion described three well-known dynamics which he called 'basic assumptions' (Bion

1961): dependence,[3] fight/flight and pairing. He also suggested that each seemed to be associated with particular institutions within his English cultural setting: fight/flight with the army; pairing with the aristocracy; and dependence with the Church. Within a society each major institution might hold one facet of basic assumption life so as to enable the rest to get on with their work. For example, if the Church acknowledges that it is being used to hold the dependence, this might free the army not to bother with it and get on with fighting.

This observation now seems simplistic and this summary makes it appear even more so. But it can be refined (Shapiro and Carr 1991). The specific function of churches in handling dependence has also been profitably explored (Reed 1978; Carr 1985). In pluralistic societies, whatever their religious history, it is unlikely that churches alone function in this area. All institutions may need to come to terms with the fact that they function with and on behalf of one another. Nor can religious bodies claim to be the only ones which handle dependence. But by their affirmation of belief in God they do explicitly acknowledge that they are in that field.

There is a link between dependence and irrational behaviour. In the case of religious institutions the connection is obvious: churches and similar bodies explicitly acknowledge dependence by calling for trust in God, by affirming appropriate dependence in acts of worship and by their free pastoral activity offered to all regardless of their affiliation. Religion is also a primary means of acknowledging the irrational facets of everyday human life.

> I doubt very much that religion is about to die out. The awareness out of which it grows is too widespread for that. More dangerous, because more likely, is that it may continue to be isolated from the mainstream of modern life. Human realities which are resolutely ignored tend, as Freud pointed out, to return in bizarre and fanatical forms. (Hay 1987, 212)

This comment, with its reference to 'the mainstream of modern life' and 'realities which return in bizarre forms', connects with some contemporary discussions of religious belief and experience. Rizzuto (1979) has argued that the idea of the living God may function as a transitional object which profoundly affects our sense of ourselves. Such an object 'comes from without from one point of view, but not so from the point of view of the baby. Neither does it come from within; it is not an hallucination' (Winnicott 1951, 238). Most transitional objects are ephemeral. The idea of God, however, remains alive but dormant. Like any transitional object God is beyond magic and ambiguous as regards control.

> Most of the time he shares the unpredictable life of the small child's teddy bear; when needed he is hurriedly pulled from his resting place, hugged or mistreated, and when the storm is over, neglectfully left wherever he may happen to be. (Rizzuto 1979, 203)

Two points are worth noting. First, that this area of transitional phenomena is where art and imagination are also located. These should not be disparagingly contrasted with so-called scientific thinking. They provide a means of holding in an examinable way the range of human experience. Second, this affirmation of the significance of illusion in normal development and everyday life is helpful in enabling us to hold to a distinction between illusion and delusion. Illusion becomes delusion when it shifts out of the intermediate area into either a person's inner or outer world alone (Carr 1989).

In discussions of religion and irrationality we enter that area between illusion and delusion. Here imagination, art and religion flourish. These are all dangerous, since they connect the 'normal' with the 'riskily marginal'. We might in the supposed interests of being rational try scientifically to explain them away. But in so doing we should lose much, if not most, of what makes us human and creates civilization. On the other hand, we might, by labelling this dimension of life 'irrational', make it one which no reasonable person would wish to consider. It is then abandoned to pathology alone.

Most studies of religious experience focus on individuals. But if we are to put that individual experience and its interpretation into its wider context, we also need to consider the institutional aspects of religious behaviour. Religious bodies sustain the notion of God and so make it available to be used by individuals and groups. But they also have other functions. Caught up in dynamic interrelation with other institutions in a society, they explicitly address the problematic world of necessary dependence.

Dependence is a difficult dynamic. It is often treated as if it were better avoided. To be described as dependent, even within the laboratory conditions of a group relations conference, can appear to impute weakness. When we are in touch with our own dependence, or its manifestation in groups or organizations, we become uncomfortable because we are then face to face with a primitive aspect of ourselves. The substance of most religious belief and practice, whatever form it takes, includes basic emotions such as fear, hope, love, anxiety and guilt. Each represents a significant emotional state and a possible opportunity for irrational behaviour. They are all double-edged: without such feelings we are not human; because of such feelings we may become less than human. Dependence, too, which prevails as an underlying dynamic to our existence, has a similar effect: to acknowledge our dependence and work with it is the mark of human maturity. But to be dependent destroys that autonomy which gives individuals their value.

We need, therefore, in thinking about irrationality to face two issues: first, dependence and how provision may be made for it to be handled; and second, how we are to interpret the precise form that irrational behaviour takes in individuals and groups, especially the difference between what may be diagnosed as delusion and what is based on illusion. These issues are common to all organizations and individuals, and on the larger scale to societies and cultures. Religious institutions distinctively, but not exclusively, function in these two areas. Any interpretation, therefore, has potential benefit for clarifying not only the churches' task but also that of other institutions. Nor, we should note, is irrational behaviour linked with dependence alone. But it may at least be identified in that context and explored.

The outcome of this discussion so far is that we should expect that churches will inevitably be repositories of irrationality, because their activities are largely involved with dependence. Because religious institutions specifically take seriously dependence and existence between delusion and illusion, they can also allow irrational behaviour to be acknowledged and even examined without it uncritically being labelled pathological.

To amplify this I offer three propositions. They are inevitably culturally conditioned. The illustrations are British and Christian. But the three propositions can also be discerned within other cultural and religious contexts.

PROPOSITION 1

Existence between illusion and delusion is common to all human beings and its corporate or social acknowledgement is primarily found in their religious institutions.

Religious institutions interact with their contexts more profoundly than they may recognize. The experience found within any particular group cannot be isolated from that of other groups. Even when there is no obvious connection between them they are related to one another. The idea of relatedness[4] is easy to acknowledge in theory but hard to face in practice. Leaders in any organization find it difficult to recognize, especially when the enterprise has as many built-in rationalizing positions as a religious body – tradition, Scripture, hierarchy, structured liturgy, and ultimately God. The internal dynamics can sometimes be appreciated, but 'the contextual dynamics' often seem either incredible or at best so bewildering as to be left aside.

Changes in a church's belief or practice may have repercussions which reach beyond its members. In 1980 the Church of England produced a new Prayer Book, the first since 1662, apart from a revision in 1928. People from all walks of life, many of them explicitly affirming their atheism, signed a major petition, questions were asked in Parliament, and the literati produced a book of essays on why the Church of England should not create new forms of liturgy, especially for those who did not attend. This national discontent was also expressed locally in parishes, as non-members as well as members of congregations behaved in the same way. At the level of their everyday work with people clergy frequently report irrational behaviour related to dependence on the part of those who have no wish, interest or apparent intention of joining the congregation. It seems as though at the unconscious level the production of a new Prayer Book affronted dependence and thus generated rage. But such fury was difficult to express, since it was in part self-directed because of the guilt felt at not believing or attending church. This was then projected not onto God, which would have been far too risky, but the Church and especially its public representatives – bishops, clergy and the synod. It may be that the English scene is more easily discussed because of its size and history, but similar stories are told from the USA. People wish to assert that they are not religious and wish to have nothing to do with the churches, but at the same time make claims upon them which are not polite interest but forceful, irrational demand.

Religious institutions provide others in addition to their members with a means of handling dependence. But they further seem to be used to affirm the irrational dimension to everyday human life. Behaviour, which is considered bizarre elsewhere, is taken to be legitimate in churches. People, for instance, may lose their wits. This can be a form of religious ecstasy. But more often it may be seen when, for instance, otherwise able business people make incompetent, even crazy, financial decisions in church councils. Churches do not have an explanation for irrational behaviour, although the dependence with which they are required to operate may lead people to expect this and religious groups to collude with that expectation. But they have a basic interpretative function, which can provide individuals and various groupings with a focus for projection of the irrational parts of themselves. Experience suggests that these irrational pieces of behaviour emerge from deep in people's selves, an area where the boundary between illusion and delusion is narrow and problematic.

Another, lighter illustration comes from the days when the Oxford and Cambridge colleges were male establishments. Three topics of conversation were by custom forbidden at social gatherings – politics, women and religion. These were instinctively banned because they roused passions of a deep, unmanageable and destructive kind. They took rational men into areas of their lives where rationality did not and could not hold sway. This story demonstrates the connection between irrationality and dependence, which leads to the continuance of religious institutions. They keep alive the ultimate illusion of God as transitional object, which may be used to contain destructive aggression. Churches are not themselves such an object; what they profess, God, has that function. We might also hypothesize that the scope for irrational behaviour here is doubly strong. On the one hand there is the profound psychological material in each individual. On the other stands today's social anxiety caused by the prevailing assumption that belief in God is delusive and thus a sign of madness. Many projections will merely be projected and abandoned. But by acknowledging the fact of such projections, religious institutions put themselves in the way of interpreting some, and in so doing make a useful statement about human beings and their life in the world.

There is also a corporate dimension to this topic. It is possible to think of projections between institutions and not just of institutions being used as a repository for those of individuals. When corporate madness appears in a nation, for instance, rational behaviour becomes scarce and the institutions which usually embody it (such as universities) may be the first to prove incapable of coherent response. This observation suggests that, if corporate irrationality is to be confronted, it has first to be acknowledged in a place which is felt to be secure. Religious institutions have a high profile in this field, since those who are unafraid of myth can demythologize most effectively. Nazi Germany offers the most recent instance on which we can now gain the perspective of distance. Maybe South Africa was another. This is not to suggest that religious people and churches possess a superior understanding – that, too, is merely a further manifestation of dependence. But they do by their stance towards another world – God, life after death, a spiritual dimension to existence – stand for a major area of human life which many feel to be non-rational (and some call, irrational). It wells up from individuals and societies in surprising fashion. If churches do not defensively deny this, they are, through their affirmation of this dimension to existence, usable by individuals, groups and institutions for constructively exploring their own irrationalities. In different terminology we might say that if any society is sinking into corporate delusion, the power of affirmed illusion, as offered by religious bodies, may become more effective.

PROPOSITION 2

The first requirement for working at everyday irrationality is a holding environment. This is created by interaction at the unconscious level between members of a society and its religious institutions.

It is now a commonplace that inspiration is not the preroga-tive of artists. People often find that they reach the solution to their problem by abandoning the struggle. Reed (1978) instances the mathematician Poincaré finding Fuschian functions or Wagner hearing in his half-sleep the opening of *The Ring*. Ernst Kris (1952) adopts Freud's concept of 'regres-sion in the service of the ego' (Freud 1908) to describe this process of revelation. For the artist or scientist the environ-ment which facilitates this process seems to be his own unconscious mind, to which the problem is surrendered. A parallel can be drawn with corporate behaviour. Religious institutions may facilitate regression for individuals and for larger groups. The activity of and unconscious use of religious institutions can be conceived as a social holding environment.

Three aspects of this function of religious institutions require consideration.

1 Religious institutions represent the management, or at least affirmation, of the ultimate boundaries to life. Obviously the notion of 'God' itself represents some such ultimate. This concept raises questions of truth which lie beyond us here. Most religions are invoked to manage entry into the world (initiation rites) and exit from it (funeral rites). Even where religious practice appears most residual, these two occasions when the two ultimate boundaries to existence are affirmed remain the most celebrated. Life is a series of transitions from one state to another (Erikson 1980). The major public ones – birth, adolescence, adult relationships, and death – are often ritualized. But there are correspondingly others which are freely and autonomously managed by people (Beattie 1970). Rituals, therefore, especially *rites de passage*, are not

260

simply manifestations of dependence. But if everyday transitions are to be confidently managed, then the effective ritualizing of the major transitions, which is a function of religion, even if not always conducted by religious institutions, is necessary. Whether such behaviour could continue in a world devoid of religious bodies seems doubtful, but there is no way of experimentally testing that.

Religious institutions do not only function for their adherents. There is an intergroup dimension to their practice, which from time to time becomes overt. The popular religiosity of christenings, weddings and funerals is problematic for churches precisely for this reason. Those who are not committed adherents still claim to be members and turn to 'their' church or religious association for such rituals. These provide a facilitating environment for constructive regression, which furthers the development both of the participants and of others. If not interpreted, however, such behaviour appears to be merely another instance of a rush to uncreative dependence. Some understanding of such apparently irrational behaviour, therefore, is crucial not only for the survival of the institution in which it is being focused, but also for the welfare of those holding these expectations.

2 The corporate aspects of this provision emerge in various public religious events which do not especially concern believers alone. As might be expected, these are largely to do with death: funerals and memorial services are important facets of the life of individuals and nations. A Christian funeral of an individual, for instance, may bring to the church mourners who do not particularly believe. Often they may be the first to comment afterwards on the value of the service in assisting them to come to terms with themselves and their sense of loss. An instance on a national scale occurred after the British had fought the Argentinians in the Falklands' campaign. The Dean of St Paul's Cathedral and the Archbishop of Canterbury devised a thanksgiving service in which they attempted to handle both the ambivalent feelings in the nation about having been involved in such a war at all and the emotions of the bereaved. Religious ritual was not solely the vehicle for expression of grief. It was able to be used as an interpretation which seemed then, and perhaps even more so with hindsight, to have been a classic

interpretation spoken by the only people who could be 'heard' and validated as authoritative because it was right.

A religious institution, therefore, holds for a wide clientele, certainly larger than it knows, the idea that profound and incomprehensible experience, which takes people into their unconscious selves, requires interpretation. Because such bodies also stand for the seriousness of ritual, not least because they perform it and live by it, they sanction ritual (some might call it 'irrational') behaviour and with their own idiosyncratic rituals offer space for people's emotions. And, as in the Falklands' story, from time to time such bodies may be used to articulate what others cannot express.

3   The holding environment in societies to which religious institutions contribute seems to have a double aspect to it. It functions as containment: the ritual seems to act as an interpretative medium through which projective identifications may be exposed and faced (Shapiro and Carr 1991, 23–6). At the same time it also facilitates constructive regression because religious institutions hold out in a complex world an affirmation of the one transitional object that does not decline to nothing as we grow to adulthood. The notion of God remains hidden until occasionally required or, to people's surprise, it emerges almost of its own volition.

One last point, however, needs to be clear. Religious institutions alone do not provide such holding environments. That would ignore two obvious points. First, many people have no immediate contact with religious bodies and it would be an extraordinary claim that they were nevertheless being directly influenced by them. Second, in our pluralist societies it is unlikely that any single institution handles any one dynamic. There appears to be a network of institutions which provide the holding environment for contemporary living. Perhaps because this has not yet been grasped, our institutions – and individuals, too – are at present in more than usual disarray and irrational behaviour is prominent in both.

PROPOSITION 3

While therapy diagnoses and treats extreme instances of human life between illusion and delusion, its 'normal' forms are usually handled competently by individuals themselves, possibly because of the way that all institutions, including the churches, function in a society.

The final proposition is unremarkable but runs counter to much of today's assumptive world: most people manage their lives competently. A major concern when we think of irrational behaviour should, therefore, be not so much with the disturbed individual personality as with the loss of role which results from institutional confusion. Whatever roles each individual has in a variety of settings – family, work, neighbourhood, nation, and so forth – underlying all are suppositions about value. The basic role assigned to each of us is that of being a human being, with its associated questions of responsibility. Many people are nervous with this question and uncomfortable when it is raised. But it will not go away.

There is a tendency for people to beware of acknowledging their interest in or belief in the transcendent because of a prevailing assumption in this secularized age that to do so is a sign of psychological disturbance, or at least of immaturity. But questions about God, death, value and ultimate meaning, the experience of worship, and the like, cannot be divorced from this dynamic interpretation of religious institutions and irrationality. These function best when they are at their most distinctively religious. This is an important observation for those with an interest in human behaviour and that of institutions in particular. The reason for this is that any religious institution is simultaneously dealing with three interconnected phenomena:

BELIEF

This is a distinctive aspect of the self and of groups. The precise interpretation of this dimension of human life remains obscure, but, as Michael Polanyi (1958), Liam Hudson (1972) and Gregory Bateson (1972) among others have demonstrated, it is not amenable to a reductionist solution, to which a post-analytical world is prone. Eliade (1957) makes a similar point about the 'sacred', when he argues that it is embedded in the structure of consciousness and is not a stage in the history of consciousness.

GROUP PHENOMENA

Churches work with these on a large scale. Most religious activity is not taken up with individuals, but occurs in largish groups, both actual and in the mind – extended families, the universal Church, Islam, Judaism, and so forth. The phenomena which large groups evidence are notoriously confusing and at times manic (Turquet 1975). We should, therefore, expect irrational behaviour to predominate in such bodies. Without it, they would not exist, and without living with the interpretative struggle, they lack *raison d'être*.

COMMITMENT

Finally, religious institutions operate in the area of commitment. This issue seems at present almost intolerable for contemporary people, at least in the west. It produces schizoid behaviour – intense moments of serious commitment to some one or some cause and oscillation into similarly intense dissociation. Here in personal lives we find the connection between irrational behaviour and the failure to be able to acknowledge dependence. Dominated as we are by powerful but largely unexamined assumptions about individual autonomy, this dimension to our existence is at present difficult to acknowledge and even more difficult, when recognized, to live with. But whether or not we engage with the beliefs and theological interpretations of life offered by religious bodies, there remain basic data to be dealt with – dependence and irrationality. The issues are not just theoretical – they go to the heart of our individual and social existence (Rycroft 1985).

First, unless dependence is acknowledged and affirmed, any sense of inalienable rights is at risk. We are all necessarily dependent in our origins: not one of us chose to exist, but we are each created. There is, therefore, a profound dynamic sense in which any rights by which we assert our autonomy are assigned to us rather than possessed by us.

Second, since the irrational parts of ourselves are integral to our normal, everyday existence, responsible behaviour means taking into account the whole range of ourselves – not just the sophisticated and rational, but also the irrational. One is not preferable to the other; they are complementary and if either is denied, loss and bizarre behaviour are likely to ensue.

Whatever else, therefore, religious institutions may or may not do, they persistently indicate through their incorporation of the fundamental transitional object that is 'God' the essential connection between necessary irrationality and inevitable dependence in individuals, institutions and above all society.

Notes

INTRODUCTION

1. It is, of course, also an activity of other religious groups, but I am not qualified to discuss these. See, for example, on Jewish pastoral care Katz (1984).

CHAPTER ONE

1. It is difficult to find a suitable term for 'the person with whom the pastor is dealing'. We might use 'penitent', but that would today only describe a few. Other possibilities include 'person being counselled'. Stone makes a useful point about the problem of language:

   > To identify the people involved, I make the following distinctions: *clergy* and *pastor* refer to ordained ministers, priests and rabbis. *Minister, pastoral carer, helper* and *caregiver* refer to laypersons as well as the ordained. The person in crisis is identified in a variety of ways, such as troubled person, person in distress, counselee, and parishioner. (I avoid the term 'client', traditional to psychotherapy, because it seems less appropriate in pastoral situations.) (Stone 1994, 10)

   In the rest of the book I have used, in as value-free way as possible, 'client'. It is not fully accurate, but may be good enough.
2. In the Church of England a priest is appointed to a parish as its vicar and assigned the cure of souls there. His or her primary responsibility is, therefore, to work with those who are not members of the congregation. What is more, the parishioners have a technical claim on that ministry. There is, of course, a continuing discussion as to whether such a form of church possesses theological legitimacy. An accessible introduction may be found in Carr (1992).

CHAPTER THREE

1. Marx wrote the comment in an obscure publication in 1843. Chadwick (1975, 49f) points out that Lenin changed the preposition to 'opium *for* the people' and that Marx's original phrase in context is more wistful than contemptuous.

CHAPTER FOUR

1. The work of Elliott Jaques over these years demonstrates the way in which this approach has developed and been modified in the work of one leading practitioner. For a technical discussion on the process of change see Jaques (1995).
2. This volume is a collection of working notes emerging from action research. They cover a wide range of organizations, including a diocese in the Church of England. I have contributed a postscript to that study.
3. A neurosis is a functional disorder in a person's medical condition. It is often quite mild, such as a depression. A psychosis is an abnormal or pathological state in which the patient loses contact with recognizable reality.
4. The phrase 'dynamic equilibrium' comes from the sociologist Talcott Parsons (1951). It refers to the way that social institutions create self-balancing systems. The theory is opposed by others, especially Marxist sociologists, on the grounds that it ignores the conflict that they believe to be inherent in society and that it fails to explain change. This might be a fair criticism, except that in the present context the interaction of an institution (for example, Church or family) with its social environment is the focus of study. That is always being negotiated and therefore is in a constant state of change. If so, then the internal life of the institution must also be changing. The critics have possibly underestimated the meaning of 'dynamic'.

CHAPTER FIVE

1. 'In *A Priest to the Temple* he [George Herbert] advanced the Anglican view that "the country parson hath read the Fathers also, and the Schoolmen, and the later writers, or a good proportion of all" (Ch. V '*The Parsons Accessory Knowledges*'). There are no grounds for thinking that Luther and Calvin and other Protestant authors would not have been included among the "later writers"' (Sykes 1995, 49). Similar expectations were held of Free Church ministers. But it is an ideal – see Hinton (1994).

CHAPTER SIX

1. I am indebted to the Revd Dr John Ponter, a former colleague at Chelmsford Cathedral and now Team Rector of the Ecumenical Parish of Stantonbury, for some ideas in this chapter and for a number of instances and illustrations.
2. The publication of John Robinson's *Honest to God* in 1963 remains a watershed in the popular acknowledgement of these and other issues (Bowden 1963).
3. In the accompanying footnote Gunton cites with approval Alasdair McIntyre (1988), p. 392: 'The contemporary debates within modern political systems are almost exclusively between conservative liberals, liberal liberals and radical liberals.'
4. This is a further instance of my indebtedness to Dr John Ponter who provided the basic story. He is not responsible for the use made of it here.

CHAPTER SEVEN

1. 'Vicar' has a technical meaning (see Chapter 1 note 2). But in the eyes of those outside the churches, it has also become a generic term for any ordained minister.
2. *Didache* is Greek for 'teaching' and is contrasted with *kerygma* (proclamation). The degree to which they should be differentiated is disputed, but the two categories remain useful. *Didache* is the Church-directed teaching of the faith in action. The word is also the title of an ancient treatise on morals and behaviour. The date of this is uncertain. Some put it in the late first century but this seems unlikely. It is, however, a product of early Christian history.

CHAPTER EIGHT

1. Here specificity is both necessary and a potential hindrance to engagement. What follows has an inevitably Anglican tinge to it, but the argument is not exclusive to the Church of England. It can be paralleled with some adjustment in most churches, especially those that set out to engage with people other than the members.
2. If strictly following Dulles, the phrase would be 'mystical communion'. But this is so peculiar to the Roman Catholic Church that I have substituted what is in fact the chief referent for that model, namely the metaphor of the body of Christ.
3. It is interesting that the phrase in this context may be even

grander in its reference. For example, in Col. 1.18 the reference to the Church may be an addition to an original understanding of the body as the whole created order.

CHAPTER NINE

1. See above Chapter 6. The following extract well describes the problem of the concept of 'personal authority':

   People spoke freely about their 'personal authority', but this seemed largely to disguise their perceived lack of place in the organizational structure. 'I acted on my personal authority' somehow sounded more legitimate than 'I did what I wanted', although it seemed to amount to the same thing. In effect, the need to exercise 'personal authority' suggested that staff members were feeling organizationally disconnected from the director and that they, therefore, could not speak with the authority derived from his having delegated certain responsibilities to them. (Shapiro and Carr 1992, 98-9)

2. *Alter Christus*, 'The other Christ'. The term is usually kept in Latin because translation makes it too harsh and firm. The word *alter* in this context does not imply equality or competition. The idea is that of representation or even embodiment.

3. I had thought that this phrase was peculiar to the Anglican and the Roman Catholic churches. But I learn from Free Church colleagues that it is also sometimes found among them.

4. Pattison seeks to avoid specific reference to ordination, but 'undertaken especially by representative Christian persons' is a good description of the concept of 'priest' as I am using it here.

5. In earlier publications I used the word 'consultancy' to describe this model of ministry. I have found, however, that in spite of trying to make clear the particular sense in which that word is used, the association of 'consultant' with 'expert' and 'senior' has made it difficult for people to grasp the essence of this ministry. For the relevant sense of 'consultant' see Miller and Gwynne (1972) and Carr (1985).

6. The consultant was A. Kenneth Rice. The phrase seems not to be written anywhere, but it is reported from conversation with his colleagues.

CHAPTER TEN

1. The last coronation was in 1953. When the next takes place, the impact of social and cultural change on a major occasion for common religion will be studied with special interest.

2. A major factor has been the widely acclaimed Lima Report, *Baptism, Eucharist and Ministry* (1982), which seems to recommend adult baptism as the churches' norm, but remains (as do many churches) almost agnostic on infant baptism, which is the phenomenon of common religion.

3. Apology, or apologetic theory, is that which argues the case for the Christian faith. It has customarily been offered on intellectual grounds, with an emphasis on three points: (1) it is more reasonable to be religious than not; (2) Christianity is the most reasonable of religions; (3) orthodoxy is more rational than heresy. But in today's world, where the intellectual climate is so suffused with the human sciences, the first two points (which matter most) are as likely to be argued experientially as intellectually. Hence the work of the pastor as theologian will be sustained by theological endeavour around ministry to common religion.

CHAPTER ELEVEN

1. A paper by Christopher Moody (1988) stimulated and shaped these thoughts.

APPENDIX 1

1. Placements are required in the Church of England and are customary in most other churches' training programmes. Behind this appendix lies a study of the pastoral studies' programmes of most of the colleges and courses of the Church of England.

APPENDIX 3

1. The distinction between task and sentient boundaries lies at the heart of the socio-technical approach to organizations. *Task* refers to what the organization is there to accomplish; *sentient* describes the belief system of the participants. The interrelationship of the two is the core of an organization's life.

2. The 'Leicester Conference' is an annual two-week Group Relations Conference sponsored by the Tavistock Institute of Human Relations and the Tavistock Foundation (Miller 1990).

3. Writers often use 'dependency'. Bion himself usually used the adjective 'dependent', but, if the noun, it was 'dependence'. It may only be a language difference, but *dependence* is more value-neutral than *dependency*, which tends to imply malignity.

4. '"Relatedness" describes that quality of connectedness that we have with notions that are *only in the mind*, in contrast with "relationship", which indicates at least some personal contact' (Shapiro and Carr 1991, 83).

Glossary of Names

Adler, Alfred (1870–1937). Austrian psychoanalyst. One of Freud's early collaborators. He gradually came to reject the theory of infantile sexuality and emphasized aggression and its part in stages of development. He was concerned with people in context, seeing the longing to belong as at the heart of human striving. He was also interested in group psychology and group therapy. His work was used by Jung and has had an impact on educational theory.

Aquinas, Thomas (c. 1225–74). The teacher whose doctrine has essentially become that of the Roman Catholic Church. Known as 'the angelic doctor'. He spent much of his life in Paris. He used Aristotle's thought, making a series of key distinctions, such as between faith and reason and matter and form. His 'five ways' are attempts to prove the existence of God. In addition to writing theology, he wrote a number of hymns which are still sung today.

Barth, Karl (1886–1968). Swiss theologian regarded as the founder of neo-orthodoxy. He stood against liberal Protestantism, especially its valuing of human reason. His thinking was biblically based, without falling into fundamentalism. He led the group of pastors and theologians who drew up the Barmen Declaration (1934) against Nazism. His *Church Dogmatics* was a vast enterprise which was incomplete when he died.

Berger, Peter L. (1929–). American sociologist of religion, who explicitly works on how religious belief may today be affirmed in the midst of a dominantly secular culture. He argues that religion in spite of appearances continues to function as a social legitimator. Collaborator with Thomas Luckmann (q.v.).

Bion, Wilfred R. (1906–81). British psychiatrist and psychoanalyst.

272

As a result of work with soldiers in the Second World War he developed a theory that group process reflected aspects of individual analysis. His seminal book was *Experiences in Groups* (1961). In this he applied ideas discovered in therapeutic groups to everyday group contexts, including ultimately speculation about the psychodynamics of society. He is widely regarded as a seminal thinker in several fields of human behaviour.

Comte, Auguste (1798-1857). French thinker, who is regarded as one of the founders of modern sociology. Having lost his Christian faith, he believed that human life required some religious foundation. He therefore tried to create a positivist (his word) system with humanity replacing God at its centre.

Dilthey, Wilhelm (1833-1911). German philosopher, who emphasized the difference between the new human sciences and the natural sciences. His religious studies focused on the cultural functioning of religion in society. He also argued for the importance of the psychological elements in the study of history. He wrote a life of Schleiermacher (q.v.), to whose original work he was indebted in the study of hermeneutics.

Durkheim, Emile (1858-1917). French sociologist, regarded with Weber (q.v.) as one of the founders of modern sociology. He believed that society as a concept precedes the individual and that consequently social explanations for behaviour are more necessary than psychological ones. This put the burgeoning attempts at psychological typing as a way of explanation of behaviour in context. He viewed society as an order bound by shared beliefs. One notable study was on suicide. Sociology as a discipline studied social integration and disintegration.

Engels, Friedrich (1820-95). Companion and colleague of Marx (q.v.). He was a philosopher who produced his own studies as well as completing and publishing some of Marx's after his lifetime, especially *Das Kapital*. Together they produced the seminal *Communist Manifesto* (1848). He complemented Marx's Jewishness with his Christian background from which he departed, probably after reading D. F. Strauss' *Life of Jesus*.

Erikson, Erik (1902-94). American psychoanalyst, best known for his theory of the stages of human development. He also attempted

273

to apply psychoanalytical insights to historical characters – psycho-biography – most notably Martin Luther and Mahatma Ghandi.

Freud, Sigmund (1856–1939). Founder of classical psychoanalysis. He explored and wrote extensively on such themes as transference, the unconscious, neurosis, repression and sexuality. His early theory concerned instinctual drives. He was a creative thinker, who continued to generate new ideas throughout his life. It is difficult to estimate the long-term impact of Freud. His way of thinking has changed western culture. Yet none of his theories have remained intact in subsequent study. He may in the end prove to have been wrong on many points, but right in discerning the sort of material (especially the unconscious) that he worked with.

Hardy, Alister Clavering (1896–1985). Zoologist and marine biologist. In addition to his distinguished academic career, Sir Alister Hardy had a lifetime's interest in religious experience. He worked by collecting data from various sources, a programme which has been continued by the Religious Experience Research Unit at Manchester College, Oxford (later the Sir Alister Hardy Research Centre). He believed that religious experience was both natural and more widespread than was allowed in most modern studies. The system of categorizing he adopted is becoming more sophisticated, although it remains a controversial enterprise.

James, William (1842–1910). American psychologist and philosopher (incidentally the brother of the novelist Henry James). He spent most of his life at Harvard. He oscillated between philosophy and psychology, being a professor of each at different times. His psychological studies pioneered both experimental psychology and phenomenological exploration. His philosophy was a mix of pragmatism and empiricism. He was a trenchant critic of idealism, but equally could not surrender to the logic of strictly empirical approaches. His 1901-2 Gifford lectures, *The Varieties of Religious Experience*, remain his most important work.

Jung, Carl Gustav (1875–1961). Swiss psychoanalyst who worked with Freud, although they finally parted company. He developed a theory of types, two of attitude and four functional. These became the basis of his Analytical Psychology. He argued for a collective unconscious and archetypal images, which appear in symbols. This led him to explore religion, myths and primitive history. He moved outside Europe with field trips to Africa and South America. His work pushed at the edge of things, including what was then considered appropriate for a psychologist. His studies still influence many other disciplines.

Kant, Immanuel (1724-1804). German philosopher who has had a profound influence on Protestant thinking. He 'had to remove knowledge to make room for faith'. He held that all knowledge requires a component from nature, so knowledge of the supernatural is impossible. But the inner voice of conscience could assure people of truths which cannot be established by reason alone. So the ideas of God, freedom and immortality can be supported, but based upon an innate sense of duty in each of us. Religion then becomes recognition of divine demands. Kant was less systematic than his successors, who created systems known as 'Kantian'.

Klein, Melanie (1882-1960). Austrian-born psychoanalyst, often regarded as having made the greatest contribution after Freud. She innovated analysis of children, exploring the earliest relationships between babies and objects. She also shifted thinking from Freud's theories of drives to one of developmental states. This had especial significance in the treatment of psychotic patients. Her work remains controversial but widely influential.

Lewin, Kurt (1890-1947). German/American. The founder of social psychology, who pioneered laboratory study of complex social behaviour. He coined the term 'group dynamics' and was also the creator of action research as a mode of consultancy.

Lombard, Peter (c. 1100-60). Teacher in Paris and later bishop. Most famous for a compilation of quotations from the Latin Fathers (*Sententiarum libri quatuor*). This became a standard theological textbook of the Middle Ages. He was also one of the first to argue for seven sacraments. His work was controversial but widely used, only being superseded by that of Thomas Aquinas (q.v.).

Luckmann, Thomas (1927-). American sociologist with a special interest in religion. He argues that individuals need something beyond their biological individuality through the mix of society, individual and religion. But in modern society formal religion is being irreversibly privatized. Although, therefore, people remain religious and not secularized, their religion will now be the sum of their choices from the range available rather than belonging to a church or other institutional body. Luckmann has written with Peter Berger (q.v.).

Luther, Martin (1483–1546). The leader of the German reformation. An Augustinian monk who spent most of his life at Wittenberg. His 95 Theses were the spark that burst into flame and led to the conflict with Rome. The break between Luther and Rome came about by 1520, in which year he wrote three major books. He also translated the Bible into German. Luther's character seems to have been complex, hence its attraction to Erikson (q.v.).

Marx, Karl (1818–83). German sociologist and philosopher. A prolific writer and revolutionary activist, his major work is *Das Kapital*, which was only partly published during his lifetime. He aimed to expose the way in which capitalist society worked, arguing that a classless and communist society could replace it. He was not well-known during his life. The practical application of his ideas in the Bolshevik revolution in 1917 and their exposition as an ideology have made him famous. He is still regarded by many as a significant social scientist.

Newman, John Henry (1801–90). A leader of the Catholic movement in the Church of England and later a Roman Catholic cardinal. Famous for his preaching in Oxford and the *Tracts for the Times*. He moved to Rome in 1845 and published his *Essay on the Development of Christian Doctrine*, a key theme in his thought. He is also known for his spiritual autobiography, devotional hymns and poetry.

Piaget, Jean (1896–1980). Swiss psychologist and philosopher. He was especially interested in the way that human infants, and later children, develop logical thinking. He believed that this skill was constructed rather than innate. His hypotheses about young children remain controversial. He argued for a series of developmental stages in each of which the child goes through a process of satisfaction, conflict as a result of apparent contradictions, and the new stage of another set of intellectual structures, which start the next stage. This theory has had wide influence among educationalists, including those concerned with religious education.

Schleiermacher, Friedrich D. A. (1768–1834). German theologian who emphasized feeling and dependence as the basis of religion in contrast to the prevailing rationalism of the time. His influence was considerable, although it was countered by the neo-orthodoxy of

Karl Barth (q.v.) and Emil Brunner. He held that monotheism is the highest form of religion and that Christianity is the finest among the diverse religions of the world. There is a renewed interest in his work, partly because it might lead to a reductionist position with regard to the reality of God and partly because of the recovery of the importance of feeling in religious behaviour.

Starbuck, Edwin Diller (1866-1947). American academic at Harvard, where he was a pupil of William James (q.v.). He was the first person who compiled a questionnaire about people's religious experience. The research was instrumental in more widely known work by James.

Troeltsch, Ernst (1865-1923). German theologian and philosopher. He applied the emerging sociological approaches of his time – especially those of Max Weber (q.v.) – to the study of history and theology. His most substantial work in this field is *The Social Teaching of the Christian Churches* (1908-11; ET 1931). His thinking has been studied afresh by theologians in recent years, largely because he addressed the issue of historicity and the truth claims of faith.

Vincent of Lérins (dates unknown, but died before 450). He was famous for a book which was a guide to the true Catholic faith (*Commonitorium*), which includes the Vincentian Canon.

Weber, Max (1864-1920). German sociologist, along with Durkheim (q.v.) one of the founders of modern sociology. He was fascinated by the study of power relations in societies. This led, for instance, to his notable study of the connection between Protestantism and capitalism. He argued that to understand people's actions the inquirer also had to understand the meaning that people assigned to them and how these meanings were expressed in and held by social structures.

Whitehead, Alfred North (1861-1947). Originally a mathematician, notably working with Bertrand Russell. In 1924 he moved to Harvard, where he became a professor of philosophy. He rejected the Newtonian concept of a world which can in principle be explained in terms of mathematical order. In its place he stressed the importance of organism and the processes which involve its development. This theme became the basis for subsequent work by process theologians.

Winnicott, Donald W. (1896–1971). Child psychiatrist and psycho-analyst who spent a lifetime working with children and parents. He particularly emphasized the connection between child and parents, especially mother, and focused on this interaction.

Wittgenstein, Ludwig (1889–1951). Austrian-born philosopher who did most of his work in Cambridge. His ideas are found mostly in aphoristic collections. His thought roughly falls into two periods. The early Wittgenstein studied how language worked and con-tributed to the positivist work of the time. Later he discussed the idea of 'language games', arguing that these are a collection of ways of communicating through publicly accessible data. It is the later work which has most been taken up by theologians.

References

Ahern, G., and Davie, G. (1987), *Inner City God*. London, Hodder & Stoughton.

Annan, N. (1990), *Our Age: Portrait of a Generation*. London, Weidenfeld & Nicolson.

Astley, J., and Pickering, W. (1986), 'Who cares about baptism?', *Theology* 89, pp. 264ff.

Badcock, C. R. (1980), *The Psychoanalysis of Culture*. Oxford, Blackwell.

Badham, P. (1980), 'Death-Bed Visions and the Christian Hope', *Theology* 83, pp. 269ff.

Badham, P. and L. (1982), *Immortality or Extinction?* London, Macmillan.

Baelz, P. R. (1968), *Prayer and Providence*. London, SCM Press.

Baelz, P. R. (1983), *An Integrating Theology*. London, ACCM/Church Information Office.

Bailey, E. (1986), 'Introduction' to *A Workbook in Popular Religion*. Dorchester, Partners.

Baker, T. G. A. (1983), 'Speech to the General Synod of the Church of England', in *The Report of the Proceedings of the General Synod* 13.3. London, Church Information Office.

Ballard, P. H. (1986), *The Foundations of Pastoral Studies and Practical Theology*. Cardiff, University College Cardiff.

Ballard, P. H. (1991), 'The Debate about Pastoral Theology', *British Journal of Theological Education* 4, pp. 1ff.

Barbour, I. (1974), *Myths, Models and Paradigms*. London, SCM Press.

Barker, D. (1978), 'A proper wedding', in M. Corbin, ed., *The Couple*. Harmondsworth, Pelican.

Barnes, G. G. (1984), *Working with Families*. London, Macmillan.

Bateson, G. (1972), *Steps to an Ecology of Mind*. London, Intertext.

Beattie, J. (1970), 'On understanding ritual', in B. Wilson, ed., *Rationality*. Oxford, Blackwell.

Bennis, W. G. (1964), 'Patterns and Vicissitudes in T-Group Development', in J. R. Bradford, J. R. Gibb and K. D. Benne, (eds), *T-Group Theory and Laboratory Method*. New York, John Wiley & Sons.

Berger, P. L. (1980), *The Heretical Imperative: Contemporary Possibilities of Religious Affirmation*. London, Collins.

Berger, P. L. and Luckmann, T. (1966), *The Social Construction of Reality: A Treatise in the Sociology of Knowledge*. New York, Doubleday.

Bettelheim, B. (1979), *Surviving and Other Essays*. London, Thames & Hudson.

Bion, W. R. (1961), *Experiences in Groups and Other Papers*. London, Tavistock Publications.

Bonhoeffer, D. (1967), *Letters and Papers from Prison*.[2] New York, Macmillan.

Bourdieu, P. (1977), *Outline of a Theory of Practice*. Cambridge, Cambridge University Press.

Bowden, J., ed., (1993), *Thirty Years of Honesty*. Honest to God *Then and Now*. London, SCM Press.

Bowering, M., ed., *Priesthood Here and Now*. Newcastle, Diocese of Newcastle.

Bowker, J. (1973), *The Sense of God: Sociological, Anthropological and Psychological Approaches to the Origin of the Sense of God*. Oxford, Clarendon Press.

Bowker, J. (1978), *The Religious Imagination and the Sense of God*. Oxford, Oxford University Press.

Bowker, J. (1991), *A Year to Live: A Cycle of Meditations on the Transforming Power of the Christian Story*. London, SPCK.

Box, S., Copley, B., Magagna, J. and Moustaki, E., eds, (1981), *Psychotherapy with Families: An Analytic Approach*. London, Routledge & Kegan Paul.

Brown, L. B. (1987), *The Psychology of Religious Belief*. London, Academic Press.

Browning, D. S. (1976), *The Moral Context of Pastoral Care*. Philadelphia, Westminster.

Browning, D. S., ed., (1983), *Practical Theology: The Emerging Field in Theology, Church and World*. San Francisco, Harper & Row.

Browning, D. S. (1991), *Fundamental Practical Theology*. Philadelphia, Fortress Press.

Bruce, S., ed., (1992), *Religion and Modernization: Sociologists and Historians Debate the Secularization Thesis*. Oxford, Clarendon Press.

Brümmer, V. (1984), *What Are We Doing When We Pray?* London, SCM Press.

Buttrick, D. (1987), *Homiletic: Moves and Structures*. London, SCM Press.

Campbell, A. V. (1972), 'Is practical theology possible?', *The Scottish Journal of Theology* 25, pp. 217-27.

Campbell, A. V. (1985), *Paid to Care? The Limits of Professionalism in Pastoral Care*. London, SPCK.

Carr, A. W. (1985), *The Priestlike Task*. London, SPCK.

Carr, A. W. (1989), *The Pastor As Theologian: The Integration of Pastoral Ministry, Theology and Discipleship*. London, SPCK.

Carr, A. W. (1990), *Ministry and the Media*. London, SPCK.

Carr, A. W. (1991), *Manifold Wisdom. The Churches' Ministry in the New Age*. London, SPCK.

Carr, A. W., ed., (1992), *Say One for Me: The Church of England in the Next Decade*. London, SPCK.

Carr, A. W. (1993), *Tested by the Cross*. London, HarperCollins.

Carr, A. W. (1994), *Brief Encounters. Pastoral Ministry through Baptisms, Weddings and Funerals*.[3] London, SPCK.

Chadwick, O. (1975), *The Secularization of the European Mind in the Nineteenth Century*. Cambridge, Cambridge University Press.

Clark, S. R. L. (1986), *The Mysteries of Religion*. Oxford, Blackwell.

Clayton, J. P., ed., (1976), *Ernst Troeltsch and the Future of Theology*. Cambridge, Cambridge University Press.

Clebsch, W. A. and Jaekle, C. R. (1975), *Pastoral Care in Historical Perspective*. New York, Aronson.

Collins, J. N. (1990), *DIAKONIA: Re-interpreting the Ancient Sources*. New York, Oxford University Press.

Cooke, B. (1976), *Ministry to Word and Sacraments: History and Theology*. Philadelphia, Fortress Press.

Cooper, C., ed., (1977), *Organizational Development in the UK and USA: A Joint Evaluation*. London, Macmillan.

Cranfield, C. E. B. (1976), *A Critical and Exegetical Commentary on the Epistle to the Romans, I*. Edinburgh, T. & T. Clark.

Crenshaw, J. L., ed., (1975), *Studies in Ancient Israelite Wisdom*. New York, Ktav.

Davie, G. (1994), *Religion in Britain since 1945: Believing without Belonging*. Oxford, Blackwell.

de Maré, P. B. (1972), *Perspectives in Group Psychotherapy: A Theoretical Background*. London, George Allen & Unwin.

Douglas, M. (1970), *Natural Symbols. Explorations in Cosmology*. London, Cresset Press.

Duffy. E. (1993), *The Stripping of the Altars: Traditional Religion in England 1400-1580*. New Haven, Yale University Press.

Dulles, A. (1976), *Models of the Church. A Critical Assessment of the Church in all its Aspects*. Dublin, Gill & Macmillan.

Durkheim, E. (1952), ET *Suicide: A Study in Sociology*. London, Routledge & Kegan Paul. Original 1897.

Durkheim, E. (1954), ET *The Elementary Forms of the Religious Life*. London, George Allen & Unwin. Original 1912.

Durston, D. (1989), 'Theological Reflection: Definitions, Criteria', *British Journal of Theological Education* (1989), pp. 32ff.

Dyson, A. O. (1987), 'Pastoral Theology', in A. V. Campbell, ed., *A Dictionary of Pastoral Care*. London, SPCK.

Ecclestone, G., ed., (1988), *The Parish Church?* Oxford, Mowbrays.

Edwards, D. L. (1987), *The Futures of Christianity: An Analysis of Historical, Contemporary and Future Trends within the Worldwide Church*. London, Hodder & Stoughton.

Eliade, M. (1957), *The Sacred and the Profane*. New York, Harcourt, Brace & World.

Eliot, T. S. (1944), *What is a Classic?* London, Faber & Faber.

Erikson, E. (1958), *Young Man Luther: A Study in Psychoanalysis and History*. New York, Norton.

Erikson, E. (1980), *Identity and the Life Cycle*. New York, Norton.

Evans, C. F. (1977), *Explorations in Theology 2*. London, SCM Press.

Faith in the City (1985). *The Report of the Archbishop of Canterbury's Commission on Urban Priority Areas*. London, Church House Publishing.

Farley, E. (1983), *Theologia: The Fragmentation and Unity of Theological Education*. Philadelphia, Fortress Press.

Farley, E. (1988), *The Fragility of Knowledge: Theological Education in the Church and the University*. Philadelphia, Fortress Press.

Farrell, B. A. (1981), *The Standing of Psychoanalysis*. Oxford, Oxford University Press.

Ferguson, M. (1981), *The Aquarian Conspiracy: Personal and Social Transformation in the 1980s*. London, Routledge & Kegan Paul.

Fierro, A. (1977), *The Militant Gospel: An Analysis of Contemporary Political Theologies*. ET London, SCM Press.

Fowler, J. W. (1981), *Stages of Faith*. San Francisco, Harper & Row.

Frazer, J. G. (1911-15), *The Golden Bough*. 12 vols. London, Macmillan.

Freud, S. (1900), *The Interpretation of Dreams*, in *Standard Edition of the Complete Psychological Works 4 & 5*. London, Hogarth.

Freud, S. (1907), 'Obsessive actions and religious practices', in *Standard Edition of the Complete Psychological Works 9*. London, Hogarth.

Freud, S. (1908), 'The relation of the poet to daydreaming', in *Collected Papers IV*. London, Hogarth.

Freud, S. (1925), *An Autobiographical Study*, in *Standard Edition of the Complete Psychological Works 20*. London, Hogarth.

Freud, S. (1927), *The Future of an Illusion*, in *Standard Edition of the Complete Psychological Works 21*. London, Hogarth.

Freud, S. (1930), *Civilisation and its Discontents*, in *Standard Edition of the Complete Psychological Works 21*. London, Hogarth.

Freud, S. (1939), *Moses and Monotheism*, in *Standard Edition of the Complete Psychological Works 23*. London, Hogarth.

Freud, S., and Jung, C. G. (1974), *The Freud/Jung Letters*. ET ed. W. McGuire, New Haven, Princeton University Press.

Freud, S., and Pfister, O. (1963), *Psychoanalysis and Faith: The Letters of Sigmund Freud and Oskar Pfister*. ET New York, Basic Books.

Fromm, E. (1950), *Psychoanalysis and Religion*. New Haven, Yale University Press.

Gill, R. (1975), *The Social Context of Theology*. London, Mowbrays.

Gill, R. (1977), *The Social Structure of Theology*. London, Mowbrays.

Gill, R. (1993), *The Myth of the Empty Church*. London, SPCK.

Goldman, R. (1964), *Religious Thinking from Childhood to Adolescence*. London, Routledge & Kegan Paul.

Gordon, R. L., ed., (1981), *Myth, Religion and Society*. Cambridge, Cambridge University Press.

Graham, E., and Halsey, M., eds, (1993), *Life Cycles: Women and Pastoral Care*. London, SPCK.

Greenwood, R. (1994), *Transforming Priesthood: A New Theology of Mission and Ministry*. London, SPCK.

Gunton, C. E. (1992), 'Knowledge and culture: towards an epistemology of the concrete', in Montefiore (1992), pp. 84ff.

Gunton, C. E. (1993), *The One, The Three and The Many. God, Creation and the Culture of Modernity*. Cambridge, Cambridge University Press.

Guntrip, H. (1971), *Psychology for Ministers and Social Workers*.[3] London, George Allen & Unwin.

Hardy, A. C. (1979), *The Spiritual Nature of Man*. Oxford, Clarendon Press.

Hay, D. (1987), *Exploring Inner Space*.[2] Oxford, Mowbrays.

Hay, D. (1990), *Religious Experience Today: Studying the Facts*. Oxford, Mowbrays.

Hebblethwaite, P. (1978), *The Year of the Three Popes*. London, Collins.

Hick, J. (1967), *Faith and Knowledge*.[2] London, Macmillan.

Hill, M. (1973), *A Sociology of Religion*. London, Heinemann.

Hinton, M. (1994), *The Anglican Parochial Clergy: A Celebration*. London, SCM Press.

Hirschorn, L. and Gilmore, T. (1992), 'The new boundaries of the "boundaryless" company', *Harvard Business Review* (May/June), pp. 40ff.

Hornsby-Smith, M. (1992), 'Believing without belonging? The case of Roman Catholics in England', in B. Wilson, ed., *Religion: Contemporary Issues*. London, Bellew Publishing.

Hudson, L. (1972), *The Cult of the Fact*. London, Jonathan Cape.

Hudson, W. S. (1965), *Religion in America. An Historical Account of the Development of American Religious Life*. New York, Charles Scribner's Sons.

Jackson, M. (1992–), Various notes in *Numinis, The Journal of the Alister Hardy Centre*. Manchester College, Oxford.

Jacobs, M. (1993), *Still Small Voice: An Introduction to Pastoral Counselling.*[2] London, SPCK.

James, W. (1902), *The Varieties of Religious Experience*. New York, Collier.

Jaques, E. (1955), 'Social System as a Defence against Persecutory and Depressive Anxiety', in M. Klein, P. Heiman, and R. Money-Kyrle, eds, *New Directions in Psychoanalysis*. London, Tavistock Publications.

Jaques, E. (1989), *Requisite Organisation*. Arlington, Cason Hall & Co.

Jaques, E. (1991), *Executive Leadership: A Practical Guide to Managing Complexity*. Arlington, Cason Hall & Co.

Jaques, E. (1995), 'Why the Psychoanalytical Approach to Understanding Organizations is Dysfunctional', *Human Relations* 1995, pp. 343ff (with a response by and discussion with G. Amado).

Jeremias, J. (1963), *The Parables of Jesus*. ET London, SCM Press.

Jung, C. G. (1921), *Psychological Types*, in *Collected Works 6*. London, Routledge & Kegan Paul.

Katz, R. L. (1984), *Pastoral Care in the Jewish Tradition*. Philadelphia, Fortress Press.

Kavanagh. A. (1979), 'Life-cycle events, civic ritual and the Christian', *Concilium* 112, 144ff.

Kelly, J. N. D. (1972), *Early Christian Creeds.*[3] London, Longman.

Khaleelee, O., and Miller, E. J. (1985), 'Beyond the small group: society as an intelligible field of study', in M. Pines, ed., *Bion and Group Psychotherapy*. London, Routledge & Kegan Paul.

Kirk, M., and Leary, T. (1994), *Holy Matrimony? An Exploration of Marriage and Ministry*. Oxford, Lynx Communications.

Klein, D. B. (1981), *Jewish Origins of the Psychoanalytic Movement*. New York, Praeger.

Klein, M. (1932), *The Psychoanalysis of Children*. London, Heinemann.

Kris, E. (1952), *Psychoanalytic Explorations in Art*. New York, International Universities Press.

Küng, H. (1993), *The Apostles' Creed Explained Today*. ET London, SCM Press.

Lake, F. (1966), *Clinical Theology*. London, Darton, Longman & Todd.

Lambourne, R. A. (1963), *Church, Community and Healing*. London, Darton, Longman & Todd.

Lampe, G. W. H. (1967), *The Seal of the Spirit: A Study in the Doctrine of Baptism and Confirmation in the New Testament and the Fathers*.[2] London, SPCK.

Laplanche, J., and Pontalis, J.-B. (1973), *The Language of Psychoanalysis*. ET London, Hogarth.

Lawrence, W. G., ed., (1979), *Exploring Individual and Organizational Boundaries: A Tavistock Open Systems Approach*. Chichester, John Wiley & Sons.

Lecky, W. E. H. (1865), *A History of the Rise and Influence of the Spirit of Rationalism in Europe*. New York, Braziller (1955).

Lewis, C. A. (1995), 'Cathedrals: Restricting and Liberating Space', *Theology* 98, pp. 179ff.

Lohse, E. (1971), *Colossians and Philemon*. ET Philadelphia, Fortress Press.

Luckmann, T. (1967), *The Invisible Religion*. New York, Macmillan.

Macquarrie, J. (1982), *In Search of Humanity: A Theological and Philosophical Approach*. London, SCM Press.

McIntyre, A. (1988), *Whose Justice, Which Rationality?* London, Duckworth.

McKnight, E. (1988), *Post-Modern Use of the Bible: The Emergence of Reader-Oriented Criticism*. Nashville, Abingdon Press.

Martin, D. (1978), *A General Theory of Secularization*. Oxford, Blackwell.

Meissner, W. W. (1984), *Psychoanalysis and Religious Experience*. New Haven, Yale University Press.

Melinsky, H. (1992), *The Shape of the Ministry*. Norwich, Canterbury Press.

Menzies, I. E. P. (1967), 'A Case-Study in the Functioning of Social Systems as a Defense against Anxiety', in A. D. Colman and W. H. Bexton, eds, *Group Relations Reader 1*. Washington, A. K. Rice Institute.

Metz, J.-B. (1981), *The Emergent Church: The Future of Christianity in a Post-Bourgeois World*. ET London, SCM Press.

Miller, E. J., ed., (1976), *Task and Organization*. London, John Wiley & Sons.

Miller, E. J. (1977), 'Organizational Development and Industrial Democracy: A Current Case-study', in C. L. Cooper, ed., *Organizational Development in the UK and USA: A Joint Evaluation.* London, Macmillan.

Miller, E. J. (1989), *The 'Leicester' Model: Experiential Study of Group and Organisational Processes. Occasional Paper 10.* London, The Tavistock Institute of Human Relations.

Miller, E. J. (1993), *From Dependency to Autonomy: Studies in Organization and Change.* London, Free Association Press.

Miller, E. J., and Gwynne, G. V. (1972), *A Life Apart. A Pilot Study of Residential Institutions for the Physically Disabled and the Young Chronic Sick.* London, Tavistock Publications.

Miller, E. J., and Rice, A. K. (1967), *Systems of Organization.* London, Tavistock Publications.

Miskotte, K. H. (1967), *When the Gods are Silent.* New York, Harper & Row.

Montefiore, H. W., ed., (1992), *The Gospel and Contemporary Culture.* London, Mowbrays.

Moody, C. (1988), 'Pastors or Counsellors', *Theology* 91, pp. 387ff.

Moody, C. (1992), *Eccentric Ministry: Pastoral Care and Leadership in the Parish.* London, Darton, Longman & Todd.

Moses, J. H. (1995), *A Broad and Living Way: Church and State, a Continuing Establishment.* Norwich, Canterbury Press.

Mueller-Vollmer, K., ed., (1986), *The Hermeneutics Reader: Texts of the German Tradition from the Enlightenment to the Present.* Oxford, Blackwell.

Myers, I. B. and P. (1980), *Gifts Differing.* New York, Consulting Psychologist Press.

Newbigin, L. (1988), *The Gospel in a Pluralist Society.* London, SPCK.

Newbigin, L. (1991), *Truth to Tell: The Gospel as Public Truth.* London, SPCK.

Newman, J. H. (1845), *Essay on the Development of Christian Doctrine.* London, J. M. Dent & Sons.

North, M. (1972), *The Secular Priests.* London, Allen & Unwin.

Obholzer, A., and Roberts, V. Z. (1994), *The Unconscious at Work. Individual and Organizational Stress in the Human Services.* London, Routledge.

Oden, T. C. (1984), *Care of Souls in the Classic Tradition.* Philadelphia, Fortress Press.

Parsons, T. (1951), *The Social System.* Glencoe, Illinois, Free Press.

Pattison, S. (1988), *A Critique of Pastoral Care.* London, SCM Press.

Pattison, S. (1994), *Pastoral Care and Liberation Theology.* Cambridge, Cambridge University Press.

Perry, M. (1992), *Gods Within. A Critical Guide to the New Age.* London, SPCK.

Peters, J. (1989), *Frank Lake: The Man and his Work.* London, Darton, Longman & Todd.

Peterson, E. H. (1993), *The Contemplative Pastor.* Grand Rapids, Eerdmans.

Pfister, O. (1928), 'Die Illusion einer Zukunft', *Imago* 14 (1928). ET H. Meng and E. L. Freud, eds, *Psychoanalysis and Faith: The Letters of Sigmund Freud and Oskar Pfister.* New York, Basic Books, 1963.

Pfister, O. (1928), 'The Illusion of the Future', ET of a shorter version with an introductory note by Paul Roazen in *The International Journal of Psycho-Analysis* 74 (1993), pp. 557ff.

Pines, M., ed., (1985), *Bion and Group Psychotherapy.* London, Routledge & Kegan Paul.

Polanyi, M. (1958), *Personal Knowledge.* London, Routledge & Kegan Paul.

Polya, G. (1971), *How to Solve It.*[2] Princeton, Yale University Press.

Ramshaw, E. (1987), *Ritual and Pastoral Care.* Philadelphia, Fortress Press.

Reader, J. (1994), *Local Theology. Church and Community in Dialogue.* London, SPCK.

Redfern, A. L. J., ed., (1994), *Styles of Ministry and Priesthood.* Birmingham, The Aston Training Scheme.

Reed, B. D. (1978), *The Dynamics of Religion: Process and Movement in Christian Churches.* London, Darton, Longman & Todd.

Reiss, R. P. (1994), 'Ordained Ministry – Contemporary Expectations', in A. L. J. Redfern, ed., *Styles of Ministry and Priesthood.* Birmingham, The Aston Training Scheme.

Rice, A. K. (1963), *The Enterprise and its Environment: A Systems Theory of Management Organization.* London, Tavistock Publications.

Rice, A. K. (1965), *Learning for Leadership: Interpersonal and Intergroup Relations.* London, Tavistock Publications.

Rizzuto, A.-M. (1979), *The Birth of the Living God.* Chicago, Chicago University Press.

Rogers, C. R. (1951), *Client-Centered Therapy.* London, Constable.

Rogers, C. R. (1974), *On Becoming a Person.* London, Constable.

Roszak, T. (1970), *The Making of a Counter Culture.* London, Faber & Faber.

Russell, A. (1984), *The Clerical Profession.* London, SPCK.

Rycroft, C. (1985), *Psychoanalysis and Beyond.* London, Hogarth.

Samuels, A. (1985), *Jung and the Post-Jungians.* London, Routledge & Kegan Paul.

Sangster, W. E. (1954), *The Craft of the Sermon*. London, Epworth.

Schafer, R. (1976), *A New Language for Psychoanalysis*. New York, Basic Books.

Schafer, R. (1978), *Language and Insight*. New Haven, Yale University Press.

Scharf, B. (1970), *The Sociological Study of Religion*. London, Hutchinson.

Schillebeeckx, E. (1980), *Ministry: A Case for Change*. ET London, SCM Press.

Schuster, H. (1969), 'Pastoral Theology', in K. Rahner et al., eds, *Sacramentum Mundi*. London, Burns & Oates, 4, pp. 365ff.

Schweizer, E. (1975), *The Good News according to Matthew*. ET London, SPCK.

Selby, P. (1983), *Liberating God: Private Care and Public Struggle*. London, SPCK.

Selby, P. (1991), *Belonging: Challenge to a Tribal Church*. London, SPCK.

Semrad, E. (1969), *Teaching Psychotherapy of Psychotic Patients*. New York, Griune & Stratton.

Shapiro, E. R. (1982), 'On curiosity: Intrapsychic and interpersonal boundary formation in family life', *International Journal of Family Psychiatry* 3, pp. 69ff.

Shapiro, E. R., and Carr, A. W. (1987), 'Disguised Countertransference in Institutions', *Psychiatry* 50.1, pp. 72ff.

Shapiro, E. R., and Carr, A. W. (1991), *Lost in Familiar Places: Making New Connections between the Individual and Society*. New Haven and London, Yale University Press.

Shiner, L. (1967), 'The concept of secularization in empirical research', *The Journal for the Scientific Study of Religion* 6, pp. 207-20.

Silverman, D. (1970), *The Theory of Organisations: A Sociological Approach*. London, Heinemann.

Skinner, J. (1922), *Prophecy and Religion. Studies in the Life of Jeremiah*. Cambridge, Cambridge University Press.

Smith, J. E. (1968), *Experience and God*. Oxford, Oxford University Press.

Sofer, C. (1961), *The Organization from Within*. London, Tavistock Publications.

Starbuck, E. D. (1899), *The Psychology of Religion: An Empirical Study of the Growth of Religious Consciousness*. London, W. Scott.

Stone, H. W. (1995), *Crisis Counselling*. London, SPCK.

Sykes, S. W. (1995), *Unashamed Anglicanism*. London, Darton, Longman & Todd.

Symington, N. (1994), *Emotion and Spirit. Questioning the Claims of Psychoanalysis and Religion.* London, Cassell.

Taylor, J. V. (1972), *The Go-Between God.* London, SCM Press.

Taylor, J. V. (1988), 'Conversion to the World', in G. Ecclestone, ed., *The Parish Church?* London, Mowbrays.

Thelen, H. A. (1985), 'Research with Bion's Concepts', in M. Pines, ed., *Bion and Group Psychotherapy.* London, Routledge & Kegan Paul, pp. 114ff.

Thiselton, A. C. (1980), *The Two Horizons.* Exeter, Paternoster.

Thornton, L. (1954), *Confirmation: Its Place in the Baptismal Mystery.* Westminster, Dacre Press.

Tilby, A. (1992), 'Alternative Images', in A. W. Carr, ed., *Say One for Me.* London, SPCK.

Tracy, D. (1981), *The Analogical Imagination: Christian Theology and the Culture of Pluralism.* London, SCM Press.

Tracy, D. (1987), *Plurality and Ambiguity.* London, SCM Press.

Turquet, P. M. (1975), 'Threats to identity in the large group', in L. Kreeger, ed., *The Large Group.* London, Constable.

Vitz, P. C. (1988), *Sigmund Freud's Christian Unconscious.* Grand Rapids, Eerdmans.

von Rad, G. (1962), *Old Testament Theology II.* ET London, SCM Press.

von Rad, G. (1964), 'Eirene', in G. Kittel, ed., *A Theological Dictionary of the New Testament.* ET Grand Rapids, Eerdmans, 2, pp. 404ff.

Wainwright, G. (1980), *Doxology. The Praise of God in Worship, Doctrine and Life.* London, Epworth.

Walrond Skinner, S. (1988), *Family Matters: The Pastoral Care of Personal Relationships.* London, SPCK.

Walter, J. A. (1989), 'Secular Funerals', *Theology* 93, pp. 249ff.

Walter, J. A. (1990), *Funerals and How to Improve Them.* London, Hodder & Stoughton.

Walter, J. A. (1994), *The Revival of Death.* London, Routledge.

Weber, M. (1952), *The Protestant Ethic and the Spirit of Capitalism.* London, Allen & Unwin. Original 1904/5.

Wessels, A. (1994), *Europe: Was It Ever Really Christian?* ET London, SCM Press.

Wicks, R. J., Parsons, R. D., and Capps, D., eds, (1993), *A Clinical Handbook of Pastoral Counselling.* 2 vols, revised edition. New York, Integration Books, Paulist Press. Capps was not an editor of vol. 2.

Williams, H. A. (1969), *The True Wilderness.* London, Mitchell Beazley.

Williams, H. A. (1972), *True Resurrection*. London, Mitchell Beazley.

Wilson, B. (1966), *Religion in Secular Society*. Harmondsworth, Pelican.

Winnicott, D. W. (1951), 'Transitional objects and transitional phenomena', in *Through Paediatrics to Psychoanalysis*. New York, Basic Books.

Winnicott, D. W. (1965), *Maturational Processes and the Facilitating Environment*. London, Hogarth.

Wittgenstein, L. (1953), *Philosophical Investigations*. Oxford, Blackwell.

Worsley, P. et al. (1970), *Introducing Sociology*. Harmondsworth, Penguin.

Wright, F. (1980), *The Pastoral Nature of the Ministry*. London, SCM Press.

Zizioulas, J. D. (1985), *Being as Communion. Studies in Personhood and the Church*. London, Darton, Longman & Todd.

Index of Names

Index of Subjects

A. K. Rice Institute 83, 249
Anglican Church 21-2
apologetic theology 102
applied theology 18, 102-3, 105, 107
art 255
atonement 109
authority 66, 67-8, 84: of Church
172, 176; of counsellors 17,
233-4; of pastors 188-9, 205-6,
218-19, 234; in Scripture 171-2
availability 213-14

baptism 163, 164, 192, 211, 212, 215,
221-2
behavioural sciences: influence
12-14, 37-8; *see also* psychology;
sociology
Bible *see* Scripture
body of Christ 138, 174-5, 177,
196-9

Calvinism 67
capitalism 66, 67
Church: body of Christ 138, 174-5,
177, 196-9; building 160; as herald 166-9, 176, 186-7; images
158-9; institution 159-62,
199-204; negotiated concept
160-6; pastor as representative
140; as sacrament 172-4, 176-7,
190-6; as servant 169-72, 176,
187-90
Clinical Theology 14, 46-7
common religion 207-23: process
218-21
communion of saints 28-9
community of faith 97-8, 99
confirmation 222

countertransference 55, 146, 148
crisis: of faith 115-16; of theological
understanding 115-16
cultural change 116-17
cure of souls 229
customary religion 209

dependence 88, 89, 185: and
common religion 213; and
religion 253-65
diaconate 170, 188
dreams 50-1

ecclesiology 157-78: and common
religion 211
emotions 52-4, 86
empathy 144-5
ethics 142
Eucharist 30, 173-4, 192
experience, personal 96, 99, 101,
116, 118-19, 126-8: as analogy
243-8; and reflection 143-51; and
theology 127-8

Faith in the City 76
folk religion 208
Freudian slips 48
fundamental theology 102, 105-6
funerals 150, 212, 261

Gestalt psychology 39, 85
group behaviour 42-3, 81-9:
T-groups 83
group relations training 83-4
group dynamics 84-9

hermeneutic circle 23-4
Holy Trinity 145, 232-3